LONGHORNS, SILVER AND LIQUID GOLD

The Irvin Family's Pioneer Ranching, Mining and Wildcatting in Texas and New Mexico

Tom Scanlan

To Rosemarie, who believed in me enough to leave her home and family of twenty-one years and cross the United States with me to an uncertain future. She raised our children far more than I did and so much of what they've become, they owe to her. She was my love and best friend for nearly sixty years and that has made me a better person than I could ever have been without her.

To my daughters Karen and Alison, their husbands Mark and Blaine, their wonderful children Shelby, Alex, Charlotte and Thomas, and to my sister, Pat, all of whose lives have enriched my own. They are a constant reminder to me of the value of family and that life is a series of adventures.

And to my parents, who gave me much more than they knew.

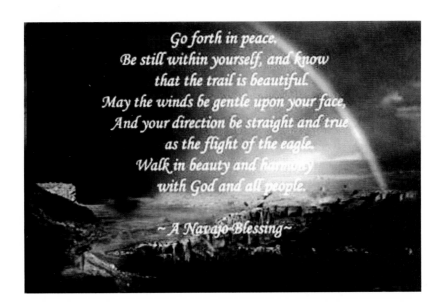

Go forth in peace,
Be still within yourself, and know
that the trail is beautiful.
May the winds be gentle upon your face,
And your direction be straight and true
as the flight of the eagle.
Walk in beauty and harmony
with God and all people.

~ A Navajo Blessing ~

Ron,

You'll find more
than a few 'close shaves'
in this story.

Table of Contents:

Preface 7
Acknowledgements 11
Introduction 13
   1. The Irvins Arrive in Texas 27
   2. Powhatan and Son Begin Cattle Ranching 35
   3. Nathanial Marries Levina 42
   4. Westward to New Mexico Territory 46
   5. Mining Boomtowns 56
   6. Apache Raids 60
   7. Silver, the Road to Riches 76
   8. Was Nat Irvin a Cattle Rustler? 86
   9. Return to Texas 93
   10. Ranching in Irion County, Texas 104
   11. Ranching in Fisher County, Texas 120
   12. Tom Irvin Marries 126
   13. Better Prospects in Farmington, NM 131
   14. Life in Early Farmington 140
   15. New Mexico Becomes a State 161
   16. U.S. Enters World War I 174
   17. The Post-War Years 178
   18. Nat Irvin's Firstborn, Tom 197
   19. World War II 205
   20. The Post-WWII Years 211
Epilogue 227
Tom Irvin's Ancestral Family Tree 229
Nathanial and Levina Irvin's Family 230
Working Map of Irvins' Travel Routes 231
Notes 232
Bibliography 241
Index 243

Preface

This work is a fact-based narrative about a young Texas rancher and his family trying to eke out a living at a time, and in places, where circumstances often conspired against them. This rancher was my maternal great grandfather, Nathanial Hunt Irvin. For most of my life, I knew nothing about this man and his remarkable history. I only began to learn about his adventurous and fascinating life after I'd retired from almost thirty years of college teaching.

One of my first post-retirement projects was to put together a family history. I wanted to learn more my ancestors, to whom I owed my very existence. This seemed like a simple enough task. Contact a few relatives, which I did, and put together a family tree. This tree would be something that I could pass on to my children, who might someday find it interesting and appreciate its significance.

I soon discovered that one of my relatives, a first cousin on my father's side, had already put together a decent family tree which included most of my father's living relatives and extended a few generations back into his Irish ancestry. Records from rural Ireland are scarce and not easily available. So, I focused on the maternal side of my family, the Irvins, many of whom I'd met and some of whom I'd lived with.

Most of my mother's closest surviving relatives live in or near two small towns in northwestern New Mexico, Farmington and Bloomfield. My wife, Rosemarie, and I made several trips to New Mexico and met with relatives I had known as a child. With the help of an aunt and a first cousin and some of their family, we put together an initial Irvin family tree.

I was surprised at how many of the Irvins I did not know about. Even though I'd lived with my mother's parents for extended periods several times during my childhood, I never knew that my grandfather and namesake had nine brothers and sisters. I didn't know that he was the oldest. I didn't know that his three children, including my mother, were born in Texas.

I was also surprised at how little my relatives knew about their ancestry. Many of the names we came up with were incomplete. Some were misspelled. Dates and places were sometimes just an educated guess, or a consensus of opinion. In order to complete even this initial Irvin family tree, I still needed to fill in a significant amount of missing or uncertain information, especially birth dates and places, as well as weddings and deaths.

My earliest attempts to research this missing information involved trips to the library and to the local LDS (Latter Day Saints) microfilm repository, one of the most complete resources available anywhere in the world. This was a slow and inefficient process because the local facilities had only a limited number of references and microfilms and microfilm readers.

Fortunately, a genealogical software program titled *Family Tree Maker* became available at about the same time that I started my family tree project in the early1990's. I purchased one of the earlier versions, available on 3.5-inch and 5.25-inch floppy disks. Shortly after that, I subscribed to Ancestry.com. That program and my Ancestry membership greatly simplified and speeded up my research, providing an easy way to store and organize my family history information, and provided an easier way to access the primary LDS repository. It also provided a way to contact other users researching some of the same people.

In the decades since I worked on that first Irvin family tree, genealogical research has improved enormously. In more recent years, many other documents, such as early newspapers, books, photographs, municipal and tax records have been digitized and made available online, often free. These additional sources opened the door to an enormous amount of information about my Irvin ancestors.

I put together a 'working map' of west central Texas and New Mexico (see pg. 231). After marking locations where the Irvin ancestors had settled, a pattern of their travels began to emerge. This visual approach helped make sense of why they settled where they did. They were always moving westward, always to less populated regions, always settling near a river. The map also showed the nearest large towns where there might be newspapers available to search.

Even so, I eventually needed to travel to certain remote locations in southern New Mexico and west Texas to discover much of what I've learned. An unexpected benefit of those trips was the amount of history that I learned while meeting with some of the long-time residents and local historians of those small towns where my relatives once lived. To that end, I joined local historical societies in northwest New Mexico and west Texas, as well as the state historical societies. I attended some of their conferences, heard some very informative lectures, and met some fascinating people. I also visited local museums and libraries where I met directors and docents who took an interest in my research and were generous with their time, providing information and advice that furthered my research. Some became friends that I stay in contact with to this day.

In the final years of my research, the best sources of information were archived local newspapers. Most archived newspapers are now digitized and available online. Some are available through the publisher and genealogical websites and some from the Library of Congress, but the sources that I found most useful were dedicated websites such as newspapers.com and newspaperarchives.com. All of these websites are easy to search with nothing more than a last name, a location, and an approximate date.

I was amazed at how thoroughly journalists covered the news over a century ago, even in towns where the population numbered only in the hundreds. Those newspapers, mostly four-page weeklies, weren't just about stories of national and international interest. There were colorful and folksy accounts of local doings. There were obituaries, of course, as well as birth and wedding announcements. Those articles were often accompanied with brief biographies and lists of attendees. These local stories fleshed out the lives of my ancestors, made them come alive. And, those old newspapers were often great fun to read. The ads were sometimes as informative as the articles. What were people buying a century or more ago? How much did those items cost? How did this change over the years?

As I continued researching, each new fact increased my enthusiasm to learn even more. New information not only answered existing questions, it sometimes posed new questions, leading me in a different direction. My family research became more and more like detective work. I loved the challenge of solving a problem, resolving a discrepancy. Sometimes there was the thrill of an unanticipated discovery. At times my research was very much like completing a jigsaw puzzle, where one discovery provided a clue to the next, and eventually a coherent picture would begin to show itself.

The picture that emerged was surprising and fascinating. Nathanial and Levina Irvin and their children had migrated westward to Texas and then New Mexico at a critical time in the history of both of those states. These were all newly settled places. Life then could be extraordinarily difficult and often dangerous. I realized that an account of their lives would be incomplete without an account of the history of those times and places. This would require additional research and writing but it was absolutely essential to understanding how they chose to live and where they chose to live. So, much of their story will include brief histories of the time and places where they live.

One of my most surprising discoveries was that my great grandfather Nathanial Irvin was an only child. The fact that he was an only child in those times was rare enough; the fact that all ten of his children survived to maturity against sometimes incredible odds is truly extraordinary. However, his being an only child did enable me to limit my research to a much smaller number of descendants. Otherwise, I might still be working on this project!

The woman Nathanial Irvin married was equally extraordinary, perhaps more so than her husband. She had to raise those ten kids! And she outlived her husband by twenty-five years. Her maiden name was Levina Ricketson, whose family lineage goes back to Massachusetts in the mid 1600's. Nathanial Irvin died a few years before I was born, but I had the pleasure and good fortune to spend time with Levina during some of my childhood years. And, I saw her again briefly, less than a year before her death, when I returned to New Mexico in 1955 to enroll at New Mexico Tech.

Neither Nathanial nor Levina Irvin nor anyone in their immediate family became nationally famous nor particularly wealthy. What makes their story so appealing is that they were ordinary people living in extraordinary times. What follows is an honest and documented account of their journeys and adventures in Texas and New Mexico back when our nation's southwest was still young and untamed.

Acknowledgements

I'd like to thank the following individuals for their help and/or encouragement while I was working on this book:

Harley Shaw, local historian, author, and editor of Hillsboro Historical Society's newsletter, for showing me around Hillsboro, New Mexico and their foundling museum and pointing out an article in their newsletter that provided important direction and inspiration to my research.

Mike Maddox, local historian and author from Farmington, New Mexico, for his informative and inspirational posts on San Juan County Historical Society's website.

Bart Wilsey, director of the Farmington Museum in Farmington, New Mexico, for his help and advice concerning local literature related to my research and the excellent historical museum which he oversees.

Suzanne Campbell, head of the West Texas Collection at Angelo State University in San Angelo, Texas, for her invaluable assistance in accessing microfilm records, and to her assistants, especially graduate student Jessica Tharp.

Mike and Darlene Hamilton, a ranching family in Mertzon, Texas, for their warm hospitality and for showing me around the area where my ancestors ranched, as well as sharing their friends and town and way of life with me during my stay with them in 2018.

Joyce Gray, local historian at the Irion County Office in Mertzon, Texas, who spent hours with me at the County office showing me documents about the history of the area and allowing me to photograph sections of some of the books.

Evelyn Lemmons, historian and archivist at Fort Concho in San Angelo, Texas, who met with me and briefed me on the history of Tom Green and Irion Counties.

And finally, thanks to those numerous amateur family history sleuths whose public genealogical postings helped supplement my findings while guiding my own investigations, especially those who were generous in sharing additional information by email.

Introduction

My clearest memories of my Irvin ancestors date back to the years of World War II. I was eight years old when the bombing of Pearl Harbor on December 7, 1941 changed so many of our lives. My father was in the Navy, stationed in the Atlantic on the battleship, *USS Texas*. When war broke out, my mother, my sister Pat, and I were living in Naval housing called Anchorage, near Providence, Rhode Island.

The following year, Dad was assigned temporarily to the Navy Department, so we moved to southern Maryland, just north of Washington, DC. He would soon be going off to sea again, but we made Maryland our home for most of the war years. However, during dad's long absences at sea, or whenever we had to cross the country to live near his new duty station, we stopped in New Mexico and stayed with my mother's family. Her parents and most of her relatives lived in northwestern New Mexico, some near the very small town of Bloomfield, others in the nearest larger town, Farmington. Both were located in the fertile valleys of the three converging rivers in San Juan County. Consequently, they were agrarian communities; small farms, fruit orchards and ranches, as their names suggest. Over time, oil and gas exploration became a bigger draw, but there are still many farms and ranches there today.

My mother didn't drive, and flying to New Mexico wasn't simple during wartime, so we always traveled by train. We'd pack our bags and take the Santa Fe Chief to Gallup, New Mexico. From the train depot in Gallup, we'd climb aboard a dusty Trailways bus and travel north 110 miles to Farmington on a two-lane road. The three-hour drive took us through a mostly uninhabited landscape of sage-covered mesas and striated yellow and red sandstone buttes. We'd see an occasional lone Navajo walking along the road, hoping to hitch a ride. Sometimes we'd spot an isolated Navajo home, or hogan, a half mile or so off the main road. Occasionally we'd see a family on horseback and maybe a small flock of sheep. Not much else.

Near the end of that drive, in the small town of Shiprock, the bus turned east and followed a narrower two-lane road that paralleled the San Juan River and passed through a number of smaller towns. These were little more than settlements located on the wider parts of the river valley. They had colorful names like Waterflow and Fruitland. Finally, we'd roll into downtown Farmington, the largest town in the area, although only a few thousand people. It was adjacent to the northeastern edge of Navajo country, which includes our nation's largest Indian reservation and a checkerboard of Navajo lands that extended further east and south.

Mom's sister, Ruth, would always meet us at the bus station. From there we'd drive about fifteen miles east on an even narrower two-lane road to the smaller town of Bloomfield, whose population was only in the hundreds at that time. We'd usually stop there at Pearls, the town's only general store, and have a cold soft-drink. These trips were in the summer, and even at an altitude of nearly 6000 ft. and not far south of the Rocky Mountains, it could still be quite warm. Ruth's aging Dodge sedan had no air conditioner. In those days, no one carried their own little bottles of water so we were all pretty thirsty after the long bus ride.

The last leg of our journey, the part I liked best, was south across the San Juan River over an old iron truss bridge and then left onto a one-lane dirt road that climbed precariously up a steep cliff onto a high mesa covered with sagebrush and small pinon pines. Once atop the mesa, we followed barely visible tire ruts another five miles south over rolling hills, dipping down and crossing dry arroyos until we finally reached the small cluster of simple wooden structures where mom's parents and her sister's family lived. We called these homes the 'camp'.

Some of my happiest childhood memories are those of our visits to the camp. I loved the primitive conditions and the beautiful isolation. I awoke each day to the pungent smell of sage and went to sleep each night with the smell of sage. The memory is so powerful that whenever I return to that part of the country, I always stop the car and walk through the sagebrush. I will break off a sprig and hold it to my nose. After a few deep whiffs, all of those childhood memories come back in a rush. The smell of sage is one of my "Proustian cakes". The dusty and metallic smell of the air after a thunderstorm on that high mesa is another.

Memories of my summer stays at the camp have bonded me forever to New Mexico. I remember the sound of wind—and nothing else—along with the deep blue of the sky, broken only by far off thunderheads, usually in the direction of the San Juan Mountains and the Rocky Mountains to the north, both ranges easily visible from the camp. There were only two small towns, Bloomfield and Aztec, separating our camp from the Colorado border, just twenty-five miles north.

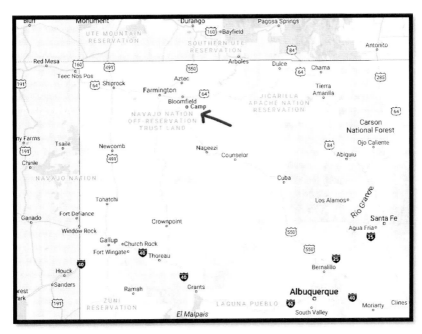

Northwest New Mexico, showing location of the 'camp'

My grandparent's home was a two-room cabin built of rough one-inch plank walls and roof, covered with tarpaper to keep out the wind and rain. The plank floors had tin can lids nailed over the knotholes to keep out the rattlesnakes. There was no indoor plumbing, no well, no telephone and no electricity. Their black, cast-iron stove burned wood, mostly sage and pinon pine, which grew locally. Grandma's stove had four burner lids and a small side tank to heat water. There was an enamel washbasin for washing your hands and dishes, and a galvanized tub for washing your body and clothing. The kitchen and dining area filled one room; the other room was their bedroom. There was a one-seat outhouse a hundred feet east of their kitchen door.

A few hundred feet south, a similar but larger structure housed my mother's sister, Ruth and her husband Nick, and their daughter Iris, whom everyone called Midge. Midge was just two years older than my sister, Pat, so this house was where mom and my sister stayed when we visited the camp. There was a large room with a wooden benched picnic table, a woodstove, a small icebox, and a small oilcloth covered table with a washbasin next to the door entering the room. We cooked and ate all of our meals there and also used it as the family living room.

This room was separated from a similar sized room by a garage area whose roof connected the rooms. That other room was divided into two bedrooms. Like my grandparent's home, all the structures were tarpaper covered plank, with bare plank floors, except the garage floor, which was dirt.

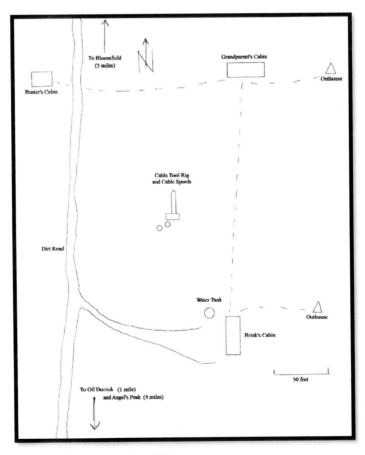

Sketch of Camp

16

Just west of the entrance to this cabin was a large, round 1500-gallon metal water tank. Because it was our only source of water, we rationed it carefully, bathing only once a week in a galvanized tub. Although a dipper hung from the top edge of the water tank (which was covered, to keep out bugs and windblown sand), we usually drank from a canvas water bag that hung from a nail in the open but covered garage that connected the kitchen-dining area to the two bedrooms. It was shady there and the open, west-facing front of the garage let the breeze blow through, keeping the water in that bag refreshingly cool.

I still have that same brand of water bag hanging in my garage today. 'Minnequa Imported Flax Water Bag. Made by the Pueblo Tent and Awning Company in Pueblo Colorado'. Under a prominent red drawing of an Indian in full headdress are the directions, 'soak in water before using'. It's a flat, rectangular bag, wider than it is deep, small enough to drink from easily by removing the small round metal cap and tipping the far end. These bags cooled water quite efficiently by evaporation. They are still widely used throughout the Southwest, where the high temperatures, low humidity and constant winds are ideal for evaporative cooling.

During our visits, I stayed with Nick and Ruth's son, Paul, whom everyone called Buster, in a one-room structure a few hundred feet west of my grandparent's house. Our cabin had two small beds, really just iron cots. There was also a chair, a small wooden table, and a kerosene lamp. Buster and I used our grandparent's outhouse, which always seemed a rather long walk, especially at nighttime, when the coyotes were yipping close by and you never knew where a rattlesnake might be slithering around, hunting by night as pit vipers do. It was no place to go barefoot; even in the middle of the night, cowboy boots and denims were essential.

There were no kids my age to play with because there were no other families nearby. The closest homes were in Bloomfield, over five miles north. I palled around with my cousin Buster when he had the time, but he was five years older than me and often had chores and other interests. Most of the time I was on my own, so my primary activity was exploring.

*Buster at his cabin
1936*

*Author's mother Iris, on left, with
sister, Ruth and brother, Tom (Buster's
cabin in background) 1946*

That country was very different from most places I'd lived. The mesa where the camp was located was crisscrossed with canyons and arroyos, the horizon broken only by occasional sandstone formations to the south, and distant mountain ranges to the north and east. The vegetation was primarily sage brush and pinion pines and sparse clumps of grass. My favorite destinations were south of the camp, where the canyons were larger and deeper. I often explored those canyons and used a prominent sandstone formation, Angel Peak, as the primary landmark to find my way back home. You didn't want to get lost in that canyon country because no one lived there and there were no roads nearby. And all of this was long before cell phones.

I usually explored by myself, day after day, hours at a time, carrying no water, and only a walking stick that I used mostly to probe for rattlesnakes before I stepped through dense brush or climbed cliffs whose ledges weren't visible from below. There were a few places near the bottom of the deeper canyon walls where cool, potable water trickled to the surface, even in midsummer. I explored miles of those canyonlands. The canyon deepened as you walked south and then branched off into numerous other canyons. Deep in the canyons, there was no way to see Angel Peak or other familiar landmarks. The wonder is that I never got lost, though I do remember times when I had to backtrack to get my bearings.

Author's family at canyons south of camp, Angel's Peak in background, left 1973

Other days I'd just hang around camp. I'd occasionally see a coyote or a jackrabbit, more often a horn-tailed lizard (horny toads) and inch long black beetles that elevated their hind-end if disturbed (stink bugs). There were quail and doves and hawks but few songbirds. When you woke up in the morning, you would usually hear the mournful sound of the doves. Sometimes the dead quiet of a windless afternoon would be interrupted briefly by the shrill cry of a hawk gliding lazily in the updraft, hundreds of feet overhead. That was it. No people, no cars, no airplanes. No wonder I still relish quiet places.

Whenever the opportunity arose, one of my favorite activities was to go for rides with my cousin, Buster in the Model A into Bloomfield to Pearl's General Store. We always had a cold bottle of pop from her ice-filled cooler, cream soda being my favorite. After chatting with Pearl and any customers that happened to be there, we stocked up on a few minor supplies and picked up a 50-pound block of ice that needed to be wrapped double in burlap for the drive back to camp. That ice would only last a week or so in the camp's only icebox at the Brink cabin.

It was an even bigger adventure to drive into Farmington with Buster, usually in the old Dodge sedan. Farmington was a *real* town. I remember that there was a bank, and a hotel and a drug store-- and a Piggly Wiggly supermarket! Lots of other buildings, too. Even sidewalks! But it was thirty miles farther, round trip, than Bloomfield so he and I visited there less often. The best part of that trip was a chocolate milk shake at the drugstore. It was so thick you had to stir it first in order to drink it, and there was always a full second glassful in the frosty stainless-steel mixer cup.

Less often, about once a month, Buster and I would drive the Model A into Bloomfield to rent a water tanker truck. He'd drive it over to the large irrigation ditch just north of town, where we'd enjoy a swim while the pump filled the tanker. Because the water was runoff from mountain ranges to the north, it was quite cool and that swim was a great way to beat the heat. When it had filled, we drove the tanker out to the camp and pumped the water into the storage tank that sat just outside the Brink house. After that, we'd need to drive the truck back to Bloomfield and pick up our car, so filling the water tank made for a full day's adventure.

Buster and I shared a few adventures that were a bit riskier but much more exciting. He functioned as the older brother that I'd never had. He pushed me and taught me to do stuff I might never have otherwise attempted. Best of all, he taught me to drive their Model A, a 1932 red coupe! I was only twelve at that time and he was barely legal then, at sixteen, but he and his sister had been driving for years. It was their only way to get to school from the camp.

It wasn't as simple back in those days to start a car. I had to advance the spark, pull out the choke, then back off on both once the four-cylinder engine sounded like it intended to keep chugging. I was small so I could barely reach the pedals. Fortunately, I could pull out the throttle instead of using the floor pedal, and if I had to, I could stop the car with the hand brake. It was even harder for me to steer the car because I could barely see in front of the car from behind the wheel. Fortunately, it was usually not a problem if you went off the road because the road was just two sets of tracks (muddy ruts in wet weather) through the sage and arroyos. There were a few drop-offs where it required a bit more care, especially going down the cliffs just before crossing the San Juan River into Bloomfield. Buster always handled that part of the trip, besides which he didn't want me driving in town. Nor did I. Nor, I'm sure, did the local sheriff. We never told anyone about my driving because our parents would have skinned us both for putting their trusty little Ford at risk.

Author and Model A, 1941   *Author atop grandfather's cable tool rig, Buster's cabin in background left   1946*

As risky as my driving might have seemed, our riskiest adventures together were those times that Buster took me to some of the old Indian ruins and sweathouses along the mesa south of the San Juan River, a mile or so west of the Bloomfield bridge. There were no roads leading into the ruins, so we had to drive into Bloomfield and then park on the north side of the river. From there, we would strip to our undershorts and then wade across holding our clothes and boots above the water.

The river was sometimes muddy after a recent rain so I couldn't see the potholes and areas of quicksand that made the crossing treacherous. It was also deeper and swifter after a rain. Wading across was easy enough for teen-age Buster, but it was difficult and dangerous for a young kid like me. I knew how to swim but the idea was to keep my clothes dry and stay on my feet so the current wouldn't carry me off. To me, making that crossing while fighting the current and feeling blindly for firm footing, was truly terrifying. I would never have attempted it for

21

anyone but my cousin. Many years later, I published a short story, "Crossing the San Juan" based on persisting memories of those precarious crossings.

San Juan River near Bloomfield, New Mexico

Even after crossing the river, there were dangers. The cliffs rising upwards from the river's south bank were only scalable by narrow foot trails which were seldom used anymore and were gradually crumbling away. Buster could step or easily jump across parts of the trail that had caved away, but for some of those places, I needed to make a running jump and he'd catch me on the other side. If he didn't catch me, I would have fallen thirty or forty feet onto hard sandstone bordering the river.

I had to surmount each of those perils again, of course, on our return trip to the car. My hiking trips with the boy scouts back in Maryland always seemed pretty tame compared to our hikes to those old Indian ruins.

Evenings at the camp often included an after-dinner walk a mile or so south up a gradual rise to the old abandoned oil derrick. The air was cool in the evenings and we'd often see quail. There were spectacular sunsets, the whole sky filled with crimson streaked clouds, which gradually darkened on our return trip to the camp. Then we might go into the kitchen and fire up the Coleman, a gasoline pump lantern that provided a bright white light you could read by, or more likely, play poker. Or we might sit outside in the Dodge and listen to country-western music from the powerful radio stations in Clint or Del

Rio, Texas. The grown-ups often enjoyed an evening smoke. Uncle Nick and Grandpa both 'rolled their own', in spite of the availability of 'ready-mades'. They always carried a small cotton sack of Bull Durham tobacco and a small packet of cigarette paper. Because there were no electric lights, we usually retired early. We always woke and got up the following morning at sunrise.

I remember quite fondly the occasional dinners over at Grandma's cabin. Her biscuits were legendary, light and buttery, still hot and floury from the oven. Chicken was fried, sizzling and popping, in a huge black iron skillet, after which water and flour were added and stirred into gravy that was meant to smother biscuits. I still occasionally enjoy biscuits and gravy, if just for the memories. It's often a popular breakfast item at many restaurants in the southwest.

Author's grandparents, Tom and Irene Irvin c.1930

Grandpa sometimes took my sister and I on walks, educating us on local minerals, plants and insects. One of these walks was especially memorable. We were walking through an area of densely clustered sagebrush when, quite suddenly, grandpa cautioned my sister and me not to move. While we both stood as still as possible, probably holding our breath, he clubbed a rattlesnake that my sister had nearly stepped on. She still has the rattles.

There were a number of other Irvin relatives living in the area, but most often we visited my great grandmother Levina Irvin, whom we all called Mammy, and her oldest daughter, my great aunt Daisy Graham. They each had a home a mile or so east of downtown Farmington, just off the Farmington to Bloomfield road, so we usually visited them whenever we shopped in Farmington. Pearl's little general store in Bloomfield didn't stock a wide variety of food, and there were nine hungry mouths to feed out at the camp. Not counting a dog named Stupid and a couple of overweight, white Persian cats that somehow managed to evade the coyotes.

Levina, the family matriarch, was in her eighties. She had been widowed and living alone since 1931, but still took in her sons, PB and NH, both in their late forties if they were between jobs or when they were ailing. Those two sons went by their initials because neither cared much for their given names, Powhatan Bolen and Nathanial Hawthorne. I'd have done the same.

Levina sometimes looked after a granddaughter, my cousin Natalie, the child of one of her widowed sons, PB. Mostly, though, Natalie was raised by my great aunt Daisy and her husband, John Graham, who had no children of their own. Natalie was often at Mammy's, however, because there she'd get away with lots more than John and Daisy would ever allow.

My cousin Natalie was a pretty brunette with flapper-style bangs like those of a Chinese toddler, that framed her mischievous little face. She was not quite two years older than me, and there were no other kids nearby, so she was my playmate during those visits. In fact, Natalie was the main reason I looked forward to our trips to Mammy and Daisy's.

Mammy's place was memorable. Her front yard was separated from the dirt road down to Daisy's farm by a two-foot-wide irrigation ditch that flowed from the Animas River less than a mile north of their property down to the San Juan River, less than a mile south. There was a third, smaller river, La Plata, just west of town. The water inside Levina's home came from a well. Her kitchen faucet was a fire-engine red cast iron hand pump. The water it pumped out had only one temperature-icy cold. A handmade copper mug hung close by for anyone to use when they were thirsty. It only required a few strokes of that long cast-iron handle to fill that mug full of cold, clear water, even in mid-summer. In spite of, or maybe because of, a very slight metallic taste, nothing I've ever drank, before or since, was ever more refreshing after coming inside from the heat of a summer day.

I recall most vividly one very special afternoon when Natalie and I were at Mammy's home. It was an exceptionally warm day, so we were playing in the kitchen instead of outside. Levina was trying to fix dinner. In order to shoo us out from underfoot, she told the two of us to go take a nap. We were no sooner in the bedroom than Natalie suggested that we practice kissing! Well, that afternoon's activity left quite an impression. She was a bit more proficient in the art of kissing than her younger, naive cousin from back east. To this day, I find a flapper haircut of close-cut bangs especially attractive on brunette women. Talk about the persistence of memory!

When Mammy wasn't chasing Natalie and me out of her kitchen, she'd sometimes give us a tour of her huge garden in the back yard, where we always enjoyed a few of her ripening, dark purple Muscat grapes. On rare occasions, she even let us follow her down rickety wooden stairs into her root cellar in the back yard, where she had shelves lined with Mason jars full of home-canned vegetables, fruit, and jams. Farmington was famous for their produce. It was the orchards and fertile farmland that originally drew Levina and her husband to this small community, back in the first decade of the 1900's. It must have seemed like paradise to Mammy after her many years of living on the drier and much more barren rolling prairies of west Texas.

We could walk from Mammy's house along a narrow dirt road through cornfields and fruit orchards down to the riverside home of my great-aunt Daisy. Their house was built within a huge grove of trees that shaded their house and yard and completely hid it from view until you were almost there. It seemed a world apart from the scrub pines and sagebrush of the mesa just a few miles away. Daisy's place still defines the term, oasis, for me. They had several dogs and there were swings hanging from the trees and a huge, screened back porch where you could sit on a glider and avoid the insects that typically buzz around river basins full of fruit trees. Daisy's biscuits ran a close second to Grandma's, but her peach and apple pies were second to none. Her home was a marvelous place to while away a lazy Saturday afternoon, so Natalie and I played together there whenever we weren't up bothering Mammy.

So, these were the times and places and relatives that I knew best and remember most fondly. I always thought of these relatives as part of an extended family, even though we only lived with them occasionally. The memories of those relatives and places have faded, but sometimes an old black-and-white photograph remind me of those simpler and happier childhood days. I did not really appreciate until many years later just how much my childhood stays in New Mexico had shaped my life.

Now, many years later, while working on this book, I have come to appreciate just how difficult and dangerous a journey had brought them to this place. That journey, and the journey of their ancestors, was probably much like other ranchers who settled in west Texas and New Mexico in those times. It's an amazing story that requires no embellishment. That story begins over a century and a half ago, in the mid-1800's.

Author's last year at the camp, 1946

1. The Irvins Arrive in Texas

My great-great-great grandfather Absalom Irvin's family, were the first Irvin family on my mother's side to migrate to Texas. That was sometime after 1837 and before 1840. Records show that Absalom was born sometime around 1788 in North Carolina. I have found no U.S. records for either of his parents. They may have arrived in America as indentured servants from the British Isles.

Indentured servitude was common in those years. It provided paid passage and living expenses for those willing to work off their debt to their sponsor after arriving in America. Typically, this involved a previously contracted agreement to provide four to seven years of farm labor, after which the indentured was free to stay on, usually at a better wage, or could move on and try to make a living on their own.

It's best to begin Absalom Irvin's story with that of his brother-in-law, Nathaniel Hunt Greer, because Absalom's life and Nathaniel's were closely entwined. Also, there are more and better records available for the more eminent Nathaniel Greer.

Nathaniel Hunt Greer, legislator and patriarch of an extensive pioneering family, was born to John D. Greer and Sarah Hunt in what is presently Hancock County, Georgia, on October 26, 1802. He grew up in Jasper County, Georgia, and married Nancy Ann Terry Roberts in October 1821. They eventually had fourteen children, nine of whom survived childhood.[1]

Nathanial had a sister, Sarah Hunt Greer, born January 10, 1794 in Hancock, Georgia. She married Absalom Irvin in Georgia sometime around 1812. I have no idea how they met, nor what their circumstances were at the time, but these two were my great-great-great-grandparents. Their fate, as you will see, was tied closely to Sarah's brother, Nathanial. This snippet of family history also explains where Levina's husband, Nathanial Hunt Irvin, got his first and middle name.

It was common practice in those days to use ancestral names as well as Biblical names when naming a child. This practice was still somewhat common in my generation; my own first name is that of both my grandfather and uncle, and my middle name is that of my father. Later generations have moved away from this practice and it's not uncommon today to name a child after a popular entertainer or athlete, a practice that will likely prove frustrating to future generations working on their family histories.

Absalom's brother-in-law Nathaniel Greer was quite a mover and a shaker. He became justice of the peace of DeKalb County, Georgia, on January 30, 1825, where he also worked as a real estate agent. Later, moving west with the frontier, he established a trading post in the portion of Creek territory that became Chambers County, Alabama. He was a founding elder of the First Presbyterian Church of Lafayette and served as the county's first sheriff, its first state representative, and as a U.S. Senate commissioner to investigate land fraud.

After helping suppress the Creek (Indian) uprising of 1836, Nathaniel set out with a party of twenty to Texas, landing at the port of Velasco (about 30 miles west of Galveston) on March 4, 1837. This was the time of westward expansion but there were no extensive railroads yet in the southeast, so travel westward was by horse, wagon or sail. If one could afford it, travel by sail was the preferred choice, being considerably faster and less dangerous than the months long trip by horse and wagon. Assuming, that is, the captain and crew are capable, the ship is sound, and the weather and sea are cooperative.

It's likely that Greer and his party boarded their vessel in the port city of Mobile, Alabama, the second largest of the port cities on the Gulf of Mexico at that time, and a much shorter and easier journey overland than to the larger port of New Orleans. There were few steamships at this time, so their ship was probably a three or four-masted schooner. These ships sailed at speeds averaging five to ten knots, and could travel at night, weather permitting. Even at minimum speeds, that's over 120 miles a day, ten times faster than wagon travel.

Just a few years earlier, the port city of Velasco had played a crucial role in this very turbulent period of Texas history.[2] Velasco, named after a Mexican general, was originally located on the Gulf Coast on the east side of the mouth of the Brazos River, where present-day Surfside is located. Back in

1821, the schooner *Lively* had landed there with thirty-eight men, the first of Stephen Austin's colonists. At that time, even though Texas was part of Mexico, Austin obtained permission to bring American settlers into the area, settling originally in what is now southern Brazoria County. Velasco consisted of just a single house until 1831, when Mexico set up a customs port there and dispatched troops to help the customs collector. More than 25,000 settlers eventually entered through this port.

A year after Velasco became a customs port, a battle was fought between Texas colonists, known as Texians, and Mexico. The Mexican commander, Domingo de Ugartechea, tried to stop the Texians from transporting a cannon up the Brazos River to attack the city of Anahuac. The Texians were led by Brazoria Alcade, John Austin, and the schoolteacher and farmer Henry Smith. The Texian militia eventually defeated the greatly outnumbered Mexicans. Ugartechea surrendered to the Texans after a three-day battle, once he realized there would be no reinforcements and his soldiers had run out of ammunition. This was known as the Battle of Velasco. It was a predecessor to the actual Texas Revolution.

Relationships between the colonist Texians and the Mexicans continued to deteriorate. The next battle, one of the most publicized and pivotal in the history of Texas, was the Battle of the Alamo. It was fought on February 23 to March 6, 1836. About one hundred Texians were garrisoned at the Alamo Mission, a former Spanish religious outpost near San Antonio de Béxar (modern-day San Antonio, Texas). The Texian force grew slightly larger with the arrival of reinforcements led by James Bowie and William B. Travis, the co-commanders of the battle that would follow . The Texians were surrounded by approximately 1500 Mexican troops under President General Antonio López de Santa Anna, who were determined to retake Texas. For ten days, the two armies engaged in several skirmishes with minimal casualties. Aware that his garrison could not withstand an attack by such a large force, Travis wrote multiple letters pleading for more men and supplies. The letters were smuggled out at night, at great risk to the courier. To no avail; the besieged Texians received fewer than one-hundred reinforcements.

In the early morning hours of March 6, the Mexican Army advanced on the Alamo. After repelling two attacks, the

Texians were unable to fend off a third attack. As Mexican soldiers scaled the walls, most of the Texian soldiers withdrew into interior buildings. Defenders unable to reach these points were slain by the Mexican cavalry as they attempted to escape. Those Texians inside the fort were either killed or captured. Those Texian defenders who were captured, instead of being held prisoner, were soon afterwards slaughtered.

Santa Anna's widely reported cruelty during this battle helped inspire Texas settlers and adventurers from the other states to join the Texian Army. Led by General Sam Houston, the Texas Army engaged the Mexican army in the Battle of San Jacinto, fought on April 21, 1836, in present-day Harris County, Texas. This was the decisive battle of the Texas Revolution. Santa Ana's Mexican army was caught off guard and defeated. That fight lasted just 18 minutes.

After the Battle of San Jacinto, Velasco was made the temporary capital of the Republic of Texas (a provisional capital had been located upriver at Washington on the Brazos). The capital was then moved to Columbia, then to Huston, and finally to Austin.

The Texas Revolution officially ended when General Santa Anna signed the Treaties of Velasco on May 14, 1836, acknowledging Texas independence from Mexico. Even though this involved only a small area of the extreme northern edge of Mexico, it was a bitter defeat for the Mexicans, who had won their own battle for independence from Spain just fifteen years earlier.

So, Absalom's brother-in-law Nathaniel Greer landed in Texas less than a year after Texan independence, when there was still considerable turmoil and danger. There were continuing uncertainties about who owned what land and where. And there were still the Comanche's and the Kiowa to deal with, for whom it didn't matter if the settlers were Texans or Mexicans.

Following their Velasco landing, Nathaniel Greer and his party of twenty migrated northwest up the Brazos River about 100 miles to Washington County, settling there along the East Fork of Mill Creek.

Shortly thereafter, three of Nathaniel's married siblings in Alabama followed him to Texas: James Alexander Greer, Sarah Hunt Greer, and Nancy Reddick Greer. His brother James was slain by Indians in Montgomery County in 1840 and his widow took her children back to Alabama. Nancy Greer and her husband Willis Johnson settled in Dewitt's Colony (later named Gonzalez), but only for a brief time. Dewitt's Colony was experiencing a number of Indian raids, including the Comanche's. Sometime prior to independence from Mexico, but after the outbreak of the Texas Revolution, Willis moved his family back to Alabama for safety. Willis returned later to fight for Texas and subsequently resettled his family in Washington County in 1838.

Nathaniel Greer's sister Sarah and her husband Absalom Irvin also migrated to Texas, along with three of their four children. Their four children were: Fany Irvin, born in1814 in Georgia; Hannah N. Irvin, born in Alabama in 1832; Powhatan B. Irvin, born in Georgia on July 12, 1835, and Absolom D. Irvin, who was born in Georgia around December,1836. That last birthdate makes it likely that Absalom and Sarah did not leave Georgia for Texas before 1937. It's not clear from available records exactly when Absalom Irvin's family arrived in Texas. They are not listed in the 1840 census for Hancock County, Georgia, where their last child was born, so they must have left Georgia before 1840. Their names first appear in the US Census report of 1850 for Washington, Texas--though they likely arrived there at least a year or so before 1840. This roundabout way of calculating when Irvins arrived in Texas is necessary, because there is no US census for 1840 Texas. Texas was not yet a state. It was merely a settlement outside the United States, which had won its independence from Mexico.

Although the rebellion had pretty much subsided by this time, these early settlers were still being attacked by Indians. In order to protect these new colonies and to drive Indians out of areas that favored settling, the Texas Rangers were officially formed in 1835. They were fully involved in this difficult and dangerous task at the time the Irvins arrived in Texas.

At that time, an Indian on horseback with bow and arrows could shoot numerous arrows in the time it took a Ranger to reload a single shot pistol or rifle, which were mostly percussion cap at that time. There were even a few older and less reliable flintlocks still in use. Initial efforts to fight off the Indians were not very successful. After the Rangers were equipped with the new five-shot Colt Paterson revolver in the 1840's, they became far more effective against the Indians. Even though this was still a cap and ball weapon, requiring a time-consuming task of inserting new powder, ball and cap, it was far better than the previous single shot weapons. And the practice of the day was to carry spare cylinders, loaded and capped for fast reloading. The effectiveness of this new weapon against the Commanche was demonstrated in 1844, when fifteen Rangers led by Captain Jack Hays used the newly issued Colt Paterson to defeat a band of 80 Comanches at the battle of Walker Creek northwest of San Antonio. However, larger number of Commanche were killed off by a small pox epidemic in 1849, which had been brought west by settlers heading to California to make their fortune finding gold.

In spite of the danger and uncertainties, Absalom was the first of the Irvin's in my direct family lineage to settle in Texas— at a time when it was a newly formed independent republic, free of Mexico, but not yet a state. Absalom Irvin and his wife Sarah made their first home in Washington County, also known as Washington-on-the-Brazos, or simply, Washington.

Washington-on-the-Brazos was sometimes called "the birthplace of Texas" because that was where Texas delegates had first met to formally announce Texas' intention to separate from Mexico and to draft a constitution for the new Republic of Texas, organizing an interim government until an officially elected government could be put in place. Washington-on-the-Brazos became the county seat, and immigration into the area increased significantly soon after Texas independence.

An independent republic bordered by two powerful nations was a fragile and somewhat perilous situation. Many of the settlers favored statehood, but others, especially the Hispanics, feared they would lose their autonomy. Texas was not granted statehood until almost a decade after their independence, knowing that this would displease Mexico. Statehood occurred on December 28, 1845. As expected, just a few months later this annexation led to a large-scale war with Mexico, on Apr 25, 1846. That war ended with Mexico's defeat on Feb 2, 1848.

Absalom Irvin and his family stayed put through all of this turmoil, and for a while, so did his brother-in-law, Nathaniel

Greer. Absalom's ever-ambitious brother-in-law was granted 1,280 acres of land in what is now Hill County in September 1838. He became a justice of the peace and in 1839 represented Washington County in the Fourth Congress of the Republic of Texas.

As a respected and influential member of his community, it would seem he'd found a place to call home. Later, however, Nathaniel Greer's entire family converted to Mormonism, and in 1855 they and many others embarked for Utah. During the trek, on June 24, 1855, Nathaniel died of cholera. His unmarked grave is on a hill in Kansas a half-mile east of the Nemaha River. Sarah Irvin had lost her beloved, and very ambitious younger brother.

Sarah and Absalom's oldest son, Powhatan B. Irvin, who was to become my great-great-grandfather, seemed to have inherited some of his uncle Nathaniel Greer's ambition. He wasted no time in establishing himself in Texas. The Federal Census of 1850 for this area describes him as a farmer. The Montgomery, Texas Agricultural survey conducted in Oct 15, 1850 described Powhatan Irvin's holdings as: 4 acres improved, 70 acres unimproved land; value $150, value of machinery $10, 1 horse, 2 milk cows, 5 other cattle, 20 swine, value of livestock $150, and 120 bushels of Indian corn. Not bad for a sixteen-year-old!

I wasn't able to locate land records but his farm was probably adjacent to his parent's land, possibly a parcel of their original holdings. Families stayed close for a variety of reasons, especially because the Comanche's were still raiding farms at this time.

Powhatan Irvin was given that unusual first name by his mother Sarah, because it was believed that Sarah's mother was descended from Pocahontas, the daughter of the powerful and famous Chief Powhatan. He was the ruler of the Powhatan tribal nation, which included as many as 30 Algonquian communities located in the Tidewater region of Virginia. The chief's daughter Pocahontas famously saved the life of English colonist John Smith in Jamestown, Virginia in the early 1600's. The story goes that when her father was about to slay John Smith, whom his tribe had captured, Pocahontas covered Smith's head with her body and his life was spared.

Powhatan was only a young boy during the Mexican-American war, and most of that war was fought in Mexico with only a few battles along the border of Mexico and Texas. However, the outcome of that battle was certainly going to affect his life even though he wasn't a participant. After Mexico's defeat, huge portions of land were ceded to the United States with the Treaty of Guadalupe Hidalgo. Those lands included California, parts of Arizona, New Mexico, Nevada, Utah, Colorado, Texas, Oklahoma, Kansas and Wyoming. Just a year after this treaty was signed, in 1849, discoveries of rich deposits of gold in California led to massive migration westward, the 'great California gold rush'. Those early prospectors became known as the 'forty-niners', a term immortalized in many ways, including the lyrics of "Oh, My Darling Clementine", a well-known folksong.

As it turned out, most settlers in that foundling state of Texas were not that easily tempted by the lure of gold. That chancy venture required a long and difficult travel much farther west. These earliest settlers had invested their time and money, and in some cases, their blood, in their Texas ranch lands. Like most of his neighbors, Absalom Irvin's family elected to remain. There was plenty of opportunity and adventure to be found in their new home state of Texas.

Absalom's young son Powhatan, most often called PB, had learned how to use the land to harvest food and to raise stock by working alongside his father and his siblings. Now he had his own land. It was time for him to start his own family.

2. Powhatan and Son Begin Cattle Ranching

Powhatan Irvin, now age 21 and a successful farmer and stockman, married 20-year-old Mary Francis Williamson on November 6, 1856, in Washington County, Texas. Mary's parents, like Powhatan's, were also from the southeast and had migrated to Texas before its statehood. She was the oldest daughter among the Williamson's family of seven children.

Powhatan and Mary's first child, my great grandfather, was born on May 30, 1859. They named their firstborn Nathanial Hunt Irvin. Powhatan and his son Nathanial often shortened their names to just their initials, PB and NH., a relatively common practice with long first names. Nathanial sometimes also went by 'Nat'.

Shortly after Nathanial's birth, they also had a daughter but she died as an infant. Nathanial was to be their only child. He was the first of this line of my Irvin ancestry to be born in Texas. This first Texas-born Irvin, this solitary son of some of the earliest Texas pioneers, would soon grow up to lead a life that would be filled with opportunity and adventure.

PB and Mary Irvin were listed in the July 9,1860 Bee County, Texas census, and their son, Nathanial, was listed as one year old, so they must have traveled there from Washington County when Nat was just an infant. Interestingly, a Sarah Irvin, age 17, was also listed at their residence. That didn't make sense to me at first. There were no such siblings and obviously they didn't have a child that old! I later discovered that Sarah was the wife of PB's younger brother Absalom Jr..

Absalom Jr. had married Sarah in Brenham, Washington County, TX in January of 1860. However, the July 31, 1860 Washington County census listed both Absalom Jr. and his wife Sarah as staying at Sarah's parent's home, the McFadden's, and he is listed as a farm laborer. He may have met Sarah while working on her father's ranch and after marrying, he and Sarah stayed with her family. Sarah, however, evidently accompanied Powhatan and Mary during their move to Bee County, possibly to help care for young Nat, and possibly because Absalom was helping drive his brother's herd to their new homesite. Later records from Bee County list neither Sarah nor her husband Absalom D. Irvin, Jr., so they probably remained in Washington County.

But Powhatan and Mary had definitely pulled up stakes and moved from Washington County to Bee County. They most likely decided to leave the more settled area of Washington County and move to the less populated and newly settled Bee County because at this time raising cattle was becoming more lucrative than farming. Many settlers who came to Texas primarily as farmers began to raise cattle during this time in Texas history. There was more open land and plenty of rain for good pasturing in Bee County. Free-ranging longhorn cattle were abundant, and could be rounded up, raised, and sold to beef markets.

The county seat of their new home in Bee County was the small town of Beeville, located on Poesta Creek. Beeville was about 150 miles southwest of Brenham, Washington County. The Bee in these names wasn't a reference to an abundance of bees in the area, however. They were named for Col. Barnard E. Bee, who had served as Secretary of State and Secretary of War of the Republic of Texas. The town was settled originally back in the 1830s. Several Beeville settlers were killed by Indians during those early years. By the time the Irvins arrived, the town had an Inn, a store, a post office and a brand-new courthouse. Even as late as 1880, a few years after the Irvin's had left that area, Beeville was still quite small, with only an estimated 300 inhabitants, two general stores, two hotels, a gin and gristmill, and a blacksmith shop.[3]

Less than two years after Nathanial's birth, our Nation became embroiled in a Civil War. Texas was heavily involved from the outset. It was one of the original four states that formed the Confederate States of America on February 4, 1861. Even before fighting broke out, about one-quarter of the U.S. Army, the entire garrison in Texas, was surrendered in February 1861 to state forces by its commanding general. He then joined the Confederacy. Fighting began on the east coast with the bombardment of the Union's Fort Sumter in Charleston, South Carolina on April 12, 1861 but the war spread quickly. As the

36

war expanded, the Confederacy passed several conscription acts, although most of the army was made up of volunteers.

In its early years, the Texas army's main function had been to provide protection for the settlers, which mostly meant fighting the Comanche's and sometimes the occasional bandits and horse thieves who preyed on the new settlers. Without resources for a standing army, Texas had created small ranger companies mounted on fast horses to pursue and fight the Comanche. Now the army was fighting both the Comanche and against its own countrymen in the Union army.

By this time, Spencer repeating rifles were starting to replace muzzle loading rifles and fighting became deadlier. Although Smith and Wesson had invented a cartridge revolver in 1856, it wasn't widely available at the time and cartridge ammunition was hard to come by. More important, rifles had a much longer range than handguns and were far more accurate, so the rifle became the weapon of choice in the infantry. The other primary army weapon was the canon, which the artillerymen often used early in a battle to destroy fortifications. Finally, a man on horseback had the advantage of speed and distance. Consequently, armies became organized into specialized groups. There were foot soldiers, the infantry; smaller numbers of mounted soldiers, the cavalry; and a still smaller group of men and canons, the artillery.

The small community of Beeville contributed a full company of men to the Confederate Army. Records show that Powhatan enlisted as a private in the Texas Confederate Army, 8th Infantry, in 1862 when his son Nathanial was about three years old. So, Mary was often alone with young Nat during this time, though soldiers were granted leave from time to time, depending on the local war situation.

The 8th Infantry Regiment, which Powhatan had joined, consisted of the 8th Texas Infantry Battalion and Shea's Texas Artillery Battalion. It contained one cavalry, four infantry, and five artillery companies. They were deployed in the southern and eastern borders of Texas, along the Mississippi River. As a battalion, this force was stationed along the Texas gulf coast. They prevented a Union invasion at Corpus Christi in August 1862, and in September they captured J. W. Kittridge, an officer of the Union fleet. In 1863 the Eighth maintained outposts at several coastal islands. After December 1863 the Eighth was transferred to East Texas, but many entered Waul's Legion instead. Some fought against Union soldiers as late as February 1864. Others fought in the Red River campaign or continued to defend the Texas coast. The regiment was mustered out of service on May 22, 1865.[4]

Powhatan had served as a Texas Army scout, according to the Civil War Enrollment list of 1864 in Bee County, Texas. The registry described his occupation as 'stock raising'. Another record I found listed him as being returned to the 8th regiment on January, 10, 1864, after being AWOL. Had he decided to return home to check on his young family or had he joined friends to take a short 'leave' into the nearest town in order to escape the rigors of military life? The record doesn't offer any explanation for his absence, only that he was returned to regiment.

Powhatan's brother Absalom had also chosen to join the army. The Texas Confederate Army Muster records show that an A.D. Irvin enlisted on August 6, 1863 for six months, at age 30. The age is off a few years but the name and initials are the same. He was assigned to Company B, 23rd Battalion, Cavalry volunteer, under Captain James L. Dallas.

Raising cattle and driving cattle had become a major occupation in Texas by this time, even though it dated back well before the Civil War. Those earlier cattle ranches and drives were primarily from eastern Texas to the port in New Orleans. During the Civil War, when ranchers were joining the Army and markets to the east were cut off, the wild longhorns proliferated. Following the Civil War, an ambitious settler could easily round up a sizable herd of longhorn if there were a good market for it. However, prices for beef in Texas were very low at this time, cattle being so plentiful. Cattle could not be sold for more than $2 a head in Texas. By 1866 an estimated 200,000 to 260,000 surplus cattle were available. Prospects for cattle ranchers looked pretty grim.

Fortunately, there was a huge demand for beef back east. After the Civil War ended, an enterprising Phillip Armour opened a meat packing plant in Chicago, and with the expansion of the meat packing industry, demand for beef increased significantly. By 1866, cattle could be sold to northern markets for as much as $40 per head, making it profitable for cattle to be herded long distances to market. Consequently, long cattle

38

drives became a major economic activity, particularly between 1866 and 1886, when 20 million cattle were herded from Texas to railheads in Kansas, for shipments to stockyards in Chicago and points east.

By 1867, a major cattle shipping facility had opened in Abilene, Kansas. The town became a center of cattle shipping, loading over 36,000 head of cattle in its first year. This route from Texas to Abilene became known as the Chisholm Trail, named for Jesse Chisholm who marked out the route. It ran through Oklahoma, originally called Indian Territory. There were surprisingly few conflicts with Native Americans, who usually allowed cattle herds to pass through for a toll of ten cents a head. Later cattle drives forked off to railheads at Dodge City and Wichita, Kansas. By 1877, the largest of the cattle-shipping boom towns, Dodge City, Kansas, shipped out 500,000 head of cattle. [5]

Cattle drives to these railheads involved thousands of cattle and dozens of cowboys. Some drives were made up of small ranches who banded together. Because most ranchers couldn't leave their families for these long drives, many small ranchers commissioned larger ranches to herd their cattle and were paid for their cattle after the drive was completed and the drivers returned. This was probably how Powhatan and his brother Absalom made their living during their early years as small ranchers. In later years, the building of additional railways south into Texas enabled rail shipments to replace most of those long cattle drives.

But the ranchers still had other problems to contend with. Comanche raids. Many ranchers had been away from home, serving in the Army, and the Army was involved with fighting Union soldiers, not Indians. The Indians took advantage of this to step up their raids on the families that were left behind with less firepower to defend themselves.

Although many settlers were discouraged by Indian attacks and the harsh conditions of west Texas, there was also a major incentive for settlers to stay on, and even for new settlers to continue arriving. That incentive was the passage of the Homestead Act which had been signed into law by President Lincoln on May 20, 1862. This law, the first of several homesteading acts, provided 160-acre parcels of government land west of the Mississippi to settlers who chose to stay and live on that land. This was a sizeable tract of land, equal to one-quarter of a section or one-quarter square mile, large enough for sustainable farming or stock raising if water was available. The Irvin's chose to stay on. According to the US Census of 1870, Powhatan, Mary and Nathanial Irvin continued ranching in Beeville County, Texas until sometime in the 1870's.

The Irvins, like other settlers in this part of Texas, were gradually continuing their transition from farmers to cattlemen. Powhatan was a long way from prosperous during his first years in Bee County. The 1861 tax records for Bee County show that he had a string of seven horses and only a small herd of 25 cattle. He had no sheep nor is there any listing for real estate holdings. It's possible that he was working for a larger ranch at that time.

However, two years later, land tax records show that PB Irvin owned 45 acres. By 1868, his estate had grown to 75 acres, he had 20 horses and 200 cattle. He stated that he had no cash on hand when the tax census was taken, but most of the others listed on the same page also claimed to have no cash on hand. No surprise that individuals were reluctant to publicize their private savings, particularly if it meant they'd be taxed more for doing so. The following year, 1869, PB's string of horses had increased to 25 and his miscellaneous property (farm implements, wagons, buckboards, and the like) was valued at $290, better than most others listed on that same page. Powhatan was finally beginning to prosper as a rancher and cattleman.

By this time, Powhatan's son, Nathanial would have been able to help with most of the farming and stock raising chores. The 1870 Census showed that Nathanial, now eleven years old is in school. Interestingly, there is now a fifteen-year-old James Brown living with the Irvins, also in school. Was he a war orphan taken in by PB to help out on the ranch? He's not listed with PB's family in the 1880 New Mexico census, so he did not stay with the family.

Young Nathanial spent his boyhood years on his parents' ranch in Beeville learning to farm and raise stock. He was old enough to remember the Civil War and he may even have remembered Indian raids, which were especially fierce and numerous during the Civil War. The Comanche, especially, continued to harass small ranches where there was little protection available. With his father away in the army, even though he was just a young boy, Nat probably learned to use a rifle and may have helped defend his family against such raids.

In order to put an end to Indian attacks, which were discouraging ranchers from settling in the area, a military campaign referred to as the 'Red River War' was launched by the United States Army in 1874. This was a campaign to remove the Comanche, Kiowa, Southern Cheyenne, and Arapaho Indian tribes from the Southern Plains and to relocate them to reservations in Indian Territory (now Oklahoma). In the span of a few months, army columns crisscrossed the Texas Panhandle, locating, harassing, and capturing the highly mobile Indian bands. Most encounters involved only small skirmishes in which neither side suffered many casualties. By the final months of 1874, fewer and fewer Indian bands had the strength and supplies to continue fighting. Though the last significantly sized group of Indians did not surrender until mid-1875, this war marked the end of free-roaming Indian populations on the southern Great Plains.[6]

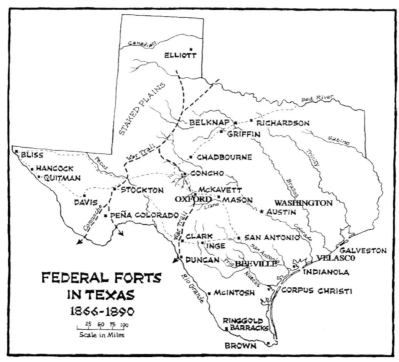

Texas Federal Forts 1866-1890, including towns where the Irvins had settled (P-C Library Map Collection, U. of Texas)

41

3. Nathanial Marries Levina

However disappointed Powhatan and Mary might have been because they had only one child, their son Nathanial made sure that the Irvin name would continue. On March 12, 1879 he married Levina Ricketson in what is now known as Oxford, in Llano County, Texas. (Originally, I was unable to determine the exact date of their marriage. The Llano County Courthouse and records were destroyed by fire in October 1880, and it's almost certain that their marriage record was lost in that fire. The newspaper that carried Nat's obituary many years later was also missing and Levina's obituary did not mention it. With the help of the San Juan County Historical Society, I finally obtained a copy of Nat's obituary after I'd finished writing this book but shortly before publication.)

I don't know how or when Nat and Levina met. It almost certain that this happened after the Irvin's had left their Bee county ranch and were driving their herd of cattle north and west toward New Mexico Territory. This would have been in the late 1870's, at a time when there was a great deal of publicity about rich silver strikes in southern New Mexico. This could be a bonanza for someone with a sizeable herd of cattle. Boom towns pay high prices for beef. The Irvins would have stopped at Oxford, one of the few towns on their route, in order to replenish supplies and to rest and graze their cattle before heading west into the drier and less populated country they still had to cross before reaching El Paso. I don't know exactly when the Irvins left Bee County nor how long they stayed in Llano County, but it was long enough for Nat to meet Levina. Maybe while buying supplies at the local store, or perhaps at the local weekend barn dance. I never thought to ask Levina when I talked to her in 1955, and no one else among my relatives seems to know. One can only imagine.

Although I have no knowledge of how they met, there is much I can tell you about Nathanial's young bride, Levina. Levina Ricketson's ancestors on both sides have been traced all the way back to England. They were among the earliest settlers of New England. Her ancestry in America spans nearly ten generations and they fought in several wars, including the Revolutionary War and the Civil War.

The first Ricketson in her ancestry to arrive in America was William Ricketson, who was born in Portsmouth, Hampshire, England in 1640 and died in Dartmouth, Bristol, Massachusetts on March 1, 1690. He is my 8th great grandfather. He married Elizabeth Mott, who was born in Portsmouth, Newport, Rhode Island on August 6, 1659. Her parents were both born in England though they married in Portsmouth, Newport, Rhode Island.

William Ricketson is believed to be the first, and probably the only, Ricketson to immigrate from England to America at that time, arriving in Portsmouth, Rhode Island sometime prior to 1679 when he married Elizabeth. Unfortunately, little is recorded about William except that he was a Quaker and a skilled carpenter. William Ricketson owned nearly 500 acres bounded on the west by the Noquophoko River. The land overlooked Buzzard's Bay. This area is now known as Ricketson Point.

His great grandson, Timothy Ricketson Jr., is listed in the Revolutionary War DAR Patriot Index as giving patriotic service in Georgia, where he died in 1786.

Hiram Ricketson, Levina's father and my 2nd great grandfather was an only child. He married Amelia Wright in Coffee County, Georgia in 1855. They had eleven children. Their second child was Levina Ricketson, my great grandmother, and the oldest ancestor of mine that I knew personally. Levina Ricketson was born in Georgia on July 14, 1861. Her father Hiram had served in the Confederate Army in the 1st Battalion of Georgia Sharpshooters.

Levina's father Hiram & mother Amelia Wright

Levina's uncle Aaron and her brother Abner

Hiram and his family moved from Coffee County GA (formerly Ware County) to Llano County, Texas, sometime around 1867-1868, based on the birthdates and birth places of his children. They were living in Burnet, TX in the 1870 Precinct listing. This is about 25 miles east of the town of Llano. Hiram Ricketson died in Llano County, Texas on April 20, 1914. Levina's mother Amelia died four years later. They are both buried at the Oxford Cemetery, which is just outside of Oxford, Texas.

Llano County was about 160 miles northwest of Beeville, Texas. The small village that was later named Oxford was first settled there in the mid-1850s. It received its name from Confederate veteran A. J. Johnson, who arrived in 1880, helped plan the town, and named it after his hometown of Oxford, Mississippi. Johnson captained the Packsaddle Mountain fight, an 1873 battle that drove raiding Indians out of Llano County.

In the 1870s, the village was still little more than a frontier trading center with a few log buildings housing business establishments, a post office, and some homes. It wasn't until 1879, that the first bank was founded.[7]

However, by this time, Nathanial and his young bride Levina, along with his parents, were already moving their herd northward and westward on their way to New Mexico Territory. As I mentioned earlier, several very rich silver deposits had been discovered in southern New Mexico Territory. Miners and merchants were flooding into the area. This created a huge demand for food supplies. Beef was selling there at a much higher price than in Llano.

Still, the drive to New Mexico was going to be a long and difficult journey. Why didn't the Irvins settle in Oxford? Levina's parents and family were living there, and there was plenty of land and good grazing available. However, Nat and his father, PB, were evidently always eager to move on to the next place, looking for something better.

It's a good thing that they did move on. The village of Oxford didn't pan out too well in the long run. A few decades after the Irvins left, ranching in this area took a downward turn. The town continued to grow a bit during the 1880's, acquiring a number of new enterprises that served the county's residents, mostly farmers and ranchers. It eventually even became a local trade center for cattle and cotton. But Oxford declined in the early 1900s and lost its post office by 1924. In 1968 its population was reported as thirty-three, and it continued to be reported at that level well into the 1980s. By the early 1990's, there were no longer population figures available for the town where Nathanial married the love of his life. Oxford (previously Llano) is now listed as a ghost town.

4. Westward to New Mexico Territory

I had always been told that my grandfather and great aunt were born in Silver City, New Mexico. However, I could find no evidence of the Irvins in Silver City for that period of time. US Census reports only provided the state of birth, and not the city. When I contacted the proper New Mexico state authorities in order to obtain their birth documents, no such records were located for Silver City.

When I located my grandfather Tom Irvin's obituary, it mentioned that he was born in Lake Valley, New Mexico. Even though his birth date was off by six years, I did a search for Irvin in Lake Valley in that time period. I eventually found online a single page from an 1880 Census for Hillsborough Precinct in Dona Ana County, New Mexico. Irvin was misspelled as Irving, and it required looking at other information on that page, such as birthplace of parents and his spouse's name to determine that this was, in fact, Nathanial Irvin. That was all the information I had on Irvins in Lake Valley until I visited Hillsboro and met Harley Shaw. What I learned in Hillsboro from Harley was a game changer that set me on an entirely new course of investigation.

Harley Shaw is a resident of the tiny but historically famous town of Hillsboro, New Mexico. He's the editor of the town's local historical society's newsletter and a bit of a historian, himself. Until I met him, I had almost no knowledge of the Irvin's adventures in this part of New Mexico. Harley unknowingly provided the key to a treasure trove of additional information for this story.

Harley Shaw at front gate of his home in Hillsboro, New Mexico Apr. 2018

I drove to Hillsboro, New Mexico, in June of 2016. I'd been visiting a friend in Socorro, New Mexico, and attending a retirement party there for the president of New Mexico Tech, one of my alma maters. Hillsboro was less than two hours south west of Socorro. I contacted Harley by email and he provided directions to his home. Cell phones wouldn't work there--too remote. I drove south from Socorro and turned off the highway near the town of Truth or Consequences. From there I proceeded west some twenty miles on a winding, hilly, two-lane road to the tiny but historic mining town of Hillsboro. The town is nested in a region of rolling foothills alongside a stream just south of the Black Range mountains. There was no service station and only a few commercial buildings, including a small café. After first driving too far (the town ends after a couple of blocks), I doubled back and found the narrow dirt road that led to Harley's home.

Harley, with his full gray beard and weathered blue jeans seemed to fit right in with this small isolated village and its aging homes. He welcomed me warmly and then showed me around his home and extensive library. After that we walked into town and he unlocked a very old building that had once been a Chinese restaurant and then a bordello. The town folk were in the process of renovating and converting it to a museum. Entering that old building was like stepping back in time. It was filled with hundreds of artifacts from the days when Hillsboro

47

was a booming mining town. There was everything from the restaurant's old iron cook stove to the bordello's rinky-tink piano. Each of the separate rooms was filled with various old tools and tack made it easy to imagine what life might have been like there a hundred or more years ago.

The most exciting and productive part of my visit, however, was something Harley showed me shortly after I met him. It was a very recent article in the Hillsboro Historical Society's journal that mentioned a family of Irvins in Lake Valley. That journal article, which I'll tell you more about shortly, provided several important clues that eventually led to the discovery of much more information about my ancestors' life in Lake Valley.

Based on census records and marriage dates, the Irvins made their move to Lake Valley, New Mexico Territory, sometime in 1879. It was just a tiny mining camp at the time, and a long way from the Irvin's Texas ranch. How did they travel to Lake Valley? It's very unlikely that Nathanial and his family traveled to Lake Valley by rail. Steam locomotives were just beginning to travel that southern route, at least part of the way, from the area of Texas they lived in to the southern towns of New Mexico territory, such as Deming. From 1873 to 1881 the Texas and Pacific laid almost a thousand miles of track even though they encountered numerous delays and legal challenges along the way. However, most travel at that time was still done by horse and wagon, especially if there were stock to be driven. That is how the Irvins likely traveled.

Because the Irvin's were described in that 1880 Hillsboro census as stockmen, they must have brought at least a small herd of cattle and possibly other livestock. The best records that I had for PB Irvin's stock holdings at that time showed that he owned 25 horses and mules and 200 cattle. PB and Nat, with some help from Levina and Mary, might have been able to drive a herd of that size but could have hired an extra hand or two for the journey. Likely they also transported chickens in crates, at least a few swine and maybe goats or sheep. They would have carried seed and basic farming tools. They would also need tools to maintain the wagon and to build a home. After all, this was previously unsettled territory. And, given the terrain they had to cross, they'd also have needed a large supply of water for parts of this trip.

The distance from their ranch in Bee County in west Texas was about 650 miles. A wagon trip would have taken them at least six to eight weeks because a horse drawn wagon could only travel ten to twenty miles a day. What was it like to travel by wagon? I've excerpted some of the following from several articles about wagon travel along the Oregon Trail during that time.[8] Travel across the plains of west Texas and southern New Mexico Territory would have been similar.

Family with Covered Wagon During the Great Western Migration, 1886 NA 518267

The covered wagons used to cross the western plains were a smaller, lighter version of the big Conestoga wagon used further north. Those bigger wagons were called "prairie schooners". The cloth top that protected people and possessions from extreme weather conditions would billow in the wind and a caravan of Conestoga's resembled a fleet of ships sailing over the plains. A frame of hickory bows supported the wagon top. The top could be rolled back for ventilation. Waterproofed with paint or linseed oil, the top was of heavy-duty canvas, often made from hemp.

For most of Irvin's trip, there were a few well-established dirt roads used by stage coaches. Big wheels helped the wagon roll easily over bumps and dips in the road, and wide rims helped keep the wagon from sinking into soft ground. The rear wheels were about five or six feet in diameter, the front ones four feet or a bit less. The front wheels had to be smaller to permit sharp turns and because too big a wheel would jam, when turned, against the wagon body.

The wagon's 10 by 3.5-foot body could haul a load of a ton and a half, but most advised keeping the weight below this limit. The lighter the wagon, the less likely it was to bog down in muddy streambanks or prairie sloughs, and in the Southwest, sandy terrain. A lighter wagon was also less likely to tire the long-suffering teams pulling it. Massive axles supported the weight of the wagon body and load. A broken axle would be disastrous, so prudent wagoners usually took along a spare. In addition, every wagon would be provided with certain essential spare parts used to hitch the animals to the wagon.

There was a toolbox on one side of the wagon's and a brake lever and water bucket on the other. Hanging from the rear axle would be a grease bucket, filled with a mixture of animal fat and tar to keep the hubs of the wheels greased.

There would be spare lariats for every horse and mule because some generally wore out before reaching the end of a long journey. The lariats were also useful when crossing deep streams, and for letting wagons down steep hills and mountains, and also for repairing broken wagons.

The main body of the wagon was packed to keep the center of gravity low and to avoid puncturing the canvas cover. Heavy supplies--a plow, bedstead, chest of drawers, stove, spinning wheel and bags of seed--go on the bottom, carefully wrapped to avoid jostling in the springless vehicle. Then come lighter goods--kitchen utensils and clothes--wrapped and strapped down. On top are stored necessaries for the trip: flour and salt, a water keg, cooking pot, rifle, ax, blankets, and even folding campstools.

By the time the necessities were packed and the prized possessions were loaded there was little room remaining. In decent weather most people cooked, ate, and slept outside. In bad weather the family slept in tents, under the wagon or inside, atop the load. As the trip got harder and the teams started to tire, some items might be abandoned alongside the trail. Passengers often walked much of the time or rode along on separate horses or mules.

What animals were used to haul the wagons? There were pros and cons to all the choices. Horses were thought to be faster but required additional grain to keep them fit for the arduous journey. That meant that valuable space in the wagon had to be used to store their provisions. The stamina of the horse was not equal to the mule or the oxen and they were more likely to stray or be stolen by marauding Indians.

Mules tended to have more stamina than the horses. Mules could travel about 20 miles a day. They also were more surefooted in treacherous climbs due to the fact that, unlike a horse, they are able to see where they are placing their hind feet. Although known as "easy keepers" they still required a certain amount of grain to keep them fit when working under severe conditions. Randolph B. Marcy, a captain in the US Army, stated in his guide book, "Upon good firm roads, in a populated country, where grain can be procured, I should unquestionably give the preference to mules, as they travel faster, and endure the heat of summer much better than oxen; and if the journey be not over 1000 miles, and the grass abundant, even without grain, I think mules would be preferable. But when the march is to extend 1500 or 2000 miles, or over a rough sandy or muddy road, I believe young oxen will endure better than mules."

Oxen was the choice of a majority of the emigrants to Oregon, decades earlier. They were a little slower, traveling only 15 miles per day on average. However, oxen were dependable, less likely to run off, less likely to be stolen by the Indians, better able to withstand the fatigue of the journey and were more likely to survive on available vegetation.

Grass and water were normally abundant in the eastern portions of the route. Farther west there were long stretches where grass and water were scarce, and it required animals in good condition to endure the fatigues and hard labor associated with the passage of these deserts. In the summer, the best mileage could be made by starting at dawn and then stopping midday near grass and water during the heat of the day. When it cooled, the animals could be hitched to the wagons again and the journey continued in the afternoon. Sixteen or eighteen miles a day could be made this way without injury to the animals.

Although I didn't know initially whether the Irvins traveled with a larger group in a wagon train or with just a wagon or two of their own, the conditions of their travel would have been similar to what has just been described, most likely a wagon drawn by mules.

After something like six or more weeks of mostly dry, dusty and difficult travel, absent major breakdowns or other catastrophes, the Irvins would have reached the small but burgeoning silver mining camp. At that time, based on the census, it was likely no more than a clutter of tents and hastily erected shacks. PB and Nat would have picked out a piece of land nearby to graze their stock and build a home. Typically, this would be a house or cabin, some sort of shelter for tools, tack and seed and a minimal stable/corral for horses and perhaps other domesticated animals such as pigs, sheep, chickens, milk cows and goats.

Based on the census of that area, Nat's parents lived in a separate dwelling just a short distance from Nat and Levina's cabin. Homes in this area were usually built of log and adobe. An account which follows of an Apache raid by Sarah Gibbons mentions that the Irvin ranch was a relatively good refuge because it was made of small pickets. This would be like a log cabin except the logs were smaller in diameter and were stood vertical instead of being laid horizontal. Building such a shelter would require additional weeks, during which the family would continue living in their covered wagons.

So, they had to haul all of their possessions, along with water and food, for nearly two months under very primitive and uncomfortable conditions, and then they still had to build a house before they could finally settle in. And before building that new home, something pioneering settlers had to do every time they moved, they also had to find a spot that was sheltered from the weather, close to clear water and easy to defend. It's difficult to imagine such a life in our own age of moving vans and planned communities and eager realtors. What a way to start out a new life, especially for the newlywed Nat and Levina Irvin. Furthermore, Levina was pregnant at the time!

Nat and Levina Irvin and their infant son were among just ten individuals listed on the sixth page of the August 21, 1880 census for Hillsborough Precinct, Dona Ana County, New Mexico Territory. The first three names were NH Irving [sic], age 21, stockman; Levina, age 18, wife; and Thomas, age 7/12 (7 months old) born January, son. Birthplaces were Texas for both Nat and Levina, and New Mexico Territory for infant Thomas. All in good health. If you do the math, Nat and Levina had wasted no time in starting their family.

The other seven individuals listed ranged in age from 28 to 58, all single, including two brothers and a widower. Their birthplaces included Tennessee, Scotland, Canada, Maine, Pennsylvania, New York and Maryland. They were all described as miners. All in good health. Because they were all listed on the same page, they would have lived relatively close to each other. These were Irvin's neighbors.

The nearest town to this small mining settlement was Hillsboro. That little town, which is still inhabited today, had its beginning at about the same time the Irvins arrived. Local historians described the area and its early settlers as follows:

Starting in 1877 and ending in 1939, Hillsboro was the center of a lively commercial complex that could have been the source for every dime western novel and Hollywood western ever made. The town received its name when Joe Yankie tossed his name into a hat, along with other names submitted by the various founders. Yankie's name was drawn and he got to name the town. The original spelling was Hillsborough, the name of Yankie's hometown in Ohio. It was shortened to Hillsboro in 1884. Within Sierra County, of which Hillsboro was the seat, lived Apache warriors, Navajo hunters and traders, Mexican farmers and ranchers, Scots-Irish cowmen, wandering rustlers and gunslingers, gentle goat and sheep herders, grizzled prospectors, expectant mining speculators, adventurous scientists, novelists, circuit preachers, lawyers, engineers, and amidst it all, shopkeepers seeking stable livelihoods. Surrounding three vital and booming towns—Lake Valley, Hillsboro, and Kingston—was rugged and nearly impenetrable wilderness inhabited by wolves, grizzly bears, black bears, and mountain lions. Mule deer, tiny Coues white-tailed deer, and wild turkey helped feed the rare individual who wandered the timber-covered mountains.[9]

Nat and Levina Irvin had travelled to New Mexico with Nat's parents, though I did not realize this at first. However, later accounts of an Apache raid implied there were two adult male Irvins in Lake Valley. This required a closer look at the 1880 Hillsborough census. After a bit more searching, I was able to locate the rest of the nine pages of that census online. I discovered an individual listed as Peter B Irving on the previous page from where I had found N H Irving. Could this be Nat's father, Powhatan B Irvin?

Peter B Irving's last name was spelled the same as NH Irving's, so the spelling is consistent, even if incorrect. Also, the age listed for Peter B Irving is the same as P B (Powhatan) Irvin, as is his birthplace, Georgia. In addition, the wife's name is listed as Mary, the same as Powhatan's, and she was listed as being from Alabama, the same state as PB's wife. The wife's age seemed too young by 5 or more years but I've discovered, particularly with wives or older daughters, that their age is sometimes understated on various census records. One of my great aunts appears to have been born a couple of years later each time the next census was taken. I should add that this occurred mostly before she was married.

Census takers often made small errors based on what they thought they heard when questioning residents. On other documents, I noticed that Powhatan rarely gave his first name but instead used his initial, P (or PB), which could have sounded like Pete. Also, both Nat and Peter Irving listed their vocation as stockman, whereas the majority of names on this census were miners, merchants and soldiers. Finally, because Peter and Mary Irving were the next to last names listed on page five of the census, and Nat's family were the very first names listed on page six, they must have lived close to each other, but in separate dwellings. There was little doubt that this Peter B and Mary Irving was actually PB Irvin's parents. *I had almost overlooked this important information when I had earlier dismissed the name as wrong spelling and wrong first name.*

So, the entire census of Lake Valley at this time in 1880 consisted of only nine partially filled pages, a total of just 170 persons. Most were single men, usually miners or soldiers, but there were a number of families, as well. Many of those were in professions, trades or business. They included a metallurgist, a blacksmith (whose name, aptly, was Smith), a butcher, a brickman, five general merchants, ten laborers, six stockmen, a store clerk, a physician, a hotel keeper, a cobbler, a millwright, two carpenters, a druggist, a washerwoman, a teamster, a prospector, and an attorney, Edward E. Furman, who had signed each the census pages. There was also a detachment of fourteen US soldiers from Companies M and C of the 9th Cavalry. They were all identified as Black (early censuses always included that information). These soldiers were sometimes referred to as 'buffalo soldiers', presumably because their hair resembled buffalo fur. They were mostly in their twenties, and only two identified themselves by rank, a sergeant and a corporal. They were the highest-ranking soldiers listed. No commissioned officers were listed. The sergeant would have been in charge of this small detachment. These fourteen soldiers were the primary bulwark between the settlers and the Apaches.

There were fewer soldiers in this part of the country than in the state of Texas. Forts were few and far between. Travel was slower and much more difficult. New Mexico, unlike Texas, was not a state. The federal government was reluctant to expend much time or money where the residents had no votes. They rarely provided assistance until situations became quite desperate. Settlers pretty much had to fend for themselves. Partly for this reason, New Mexico and Arizona were now among the most dangerous places in our country. It was only the promise of great riches and a better life that drew settlers to this part of our country. This had always been so, but much of our country had by now been settled and civilized. But not here. This part of our country was still the frontier.

5. Mining Boomtowns

The final decades of the nineteenth century saw the emergence of a number of mining boomtowns in the southwest. Some, like Tombstone, Arizona, remain famous to this day. Tombstone is best remembered for the famous shootout behind the OK corral in 1881, when Doc Holiday and the Earp brothers had a showdown with a notorious band of outlaw cowboys.

Silver boomtowns in southern New Mexico Territory actually began with major discoveries in Silver City, which was founded shortly after rich silver strikes in 1870. Because of the richness of the strike, the town attracted all types and soon became a mecca of lawlessness. In the late 1800's, Butch Cassidy and the Wild Bunch were familiar with every saloon and "soiled dove" in Silver City. Between robberies, they worked as cowhands at a nearby ranch. Billy the Kid spent his early years in Silver City and was arrested at least twice by the town sheriff. This area had also been a favorite camping area of the Apache, and copper had been mined in the area long before the discovery of silver.

Lake Valley, New Mexico, 1880 (LV schoolhouse/museum)

The place where the Irvins settled, about 40 miles east of Silver City, was just beginning to become a boom town at the time they arrived. Silver was discovered in Lake Valley sometime around 1876 and the word had spread rapidly. Lake Valley, named after a small lake in that area (no longer there) got its start as a small mining tent camp. The most accurate account of that discovery is probably the one provided by the American Institute of Mining Engineering:

> The history of the camp of Lake Valley need not be here narrated, except so far as to correct some erroneous statements of long standing, and to connect the names of several distinguished mining men and scientists with the various enterprises. The discovery of silver in the district was made in 1876 by Mr. McEverts, a cattle-man, who located several claims, which afterwards yielded some of the richest ores. Two years later, while stopping at the McEverts ranch, Mr. George W. Lufkin, a civil engineer from New Jersey, saw specimens of the high-grade silver ores, and immediately acquired a half-interest in the property. From this time on the development of the camp was rapid. Among the eminent names connected with the various enterprises of the district, at one time or another, may be mentioned those of George Lufkin, George D. Perkins and Whitaker Wright, of Philadelphia; Dr. F M Endlich and Prof. E. D. Cope, scientists of the Hayden governmental surveys; Ellis Clark (who has left us the only succinct account of the mine operations), E. W. Hadley, and S. A. Miller and Frank Springer, who first determined the exact geological age of the country-rocks.
>
> The fickleness of fortune is exemplified in the case of Lufkin, who, after sinking a shallow shaft, sold out his interests for a song. Before his successors had pushed the work in the shaft 2 ft. deeper, they struck the "Bridal Chamber," a small pocket of very high-grade ore, which yielded more than $1,000,000.[10]

As a consequence of digging a few feet deeper, the Bridal Chamber was discovered in August of 1881. A blacksmith turned prospector, John Leavitt, discovered a fabulous silver lode just 40 feet beneath the surface. There was a mass of horn silver 4 feet thick. Ore from this mass assayed at an incredible 15,900 ounces of silver to the ton. One of the richest silver deposits in the world, this mine eventually produced more than 2.5 million ounces of silver. It was named the Bridal Chamber for the sparkling light reflected by cerargyrite crystals lining the cavern. Much of the ore was so pure that it was shipped directly to the U.S. Mint. The ore was so pure that in some sections of the claim miners cut silver from the walls with handsaws. One especially large piece weighed over five tons and had to be removed in pieces.[11]

Bridal Veil Mine c1900 (New Mexico Bureau of Geology and Mineral Resources)

It turns out that George Lufkin was a neighbor of Nat's. He is listed on the same page of the 1880 census as Nat Irvin's family, one of just seven others on that page, implying just a few residences away from Nat. It's likely that the Irvins knew George Lufkin well and may have been inspired to try their hand at silver prospecting, based on his claims.

Shortly after Lufkin and McEverts, many others had begun to file mining claims in the area. Those listed in the 1880 census of this area were seeking to make their fortune in this rapidly growing silver mining town, especially those who listed their occupation as miners. At about this same time, in 1877, placer gold and gold quartz veins were discovered about twenty miles north in the hills around Percha Creek, a mining camp that became the town of Hillsboro. Less than ten miles west of Hillsboro, another mining camp was growing into the town of Kingston. All three of these mining towns grew up together, though not at the same pace.

The Irvin's were all ranchers--cattlemen. Did they make this difficult trip from southwest Texas to try their hand at gold or silver prospecting or mining? Or had they brought a herd of cattle and probably sheep and horses to sell to the miners? The 1880 census tell us that they earned their living as stockmen. There was as small lake in the area, and plenty of land suitable for grazing. Miners and the town that would grow up around the mines would need beef. This must surely have seemed the right place and the right time for PB and Mary Irvin, along with their young and newly married son and daughter-in-law to start their new life. There was opportunity aplenty to make good money, certainly lots more money than they would have made if they had stayed in Llano County, Texas.

And, as it would soon turn out, they would certainly find this area a great deal more exciting than the isolated plains of west Texas.

The prospect of sudden riches attracted every type of person, not just ambitious miners, ranchers and merchants. There were gamblers and prostitutes, bank robbers and horse thieves, claim jumpers and murderers. And, this area soon became accessible from anywhere in the country. In March 1881, the ATSF from Santa Fe and the Southern Pacific lines from San Diego were connected at Deming, New Mexico, just south of Silver City, forming a second national transcontinental rail route. Deming was only about 35 miles south of Lake Valley. This little town in Lake Valley was ready to boom.

6. Apache Raids

In spite of all this, there was the constant threat of Apache raids. Whereas Commanche raids in west Texas had decreased by this time, there were still occasional Apache raids. These were primarily Mescalero Apache, but sometimes they were Chiricahua Apache. Such raids were much more commonplace in southern New Mexico territory. Also, by this time, the Apache's weapon of choice while on horseback was much more likely to be a repeating rifle than a bow and arrow, spear or tomahawk.

There were a series of Apache raids going on when the Irvin's arrived in Lake Valley. An especially violent and widely reported raid took place just a few miles northwest of where they settled. Here's one account of that raid from the *Phoenix Herald* as relayed from Santa Fe, NM:

INDIAN TROUBLES. Women and Children Horribly Mutilated. The Marauders are Southern Chiricahua Indians. Latest from the scene of hostilities. (Special to the Herald.) Santa Fe, New Mexico, September 24th, 1879. On the 11th instant, ten Mexican men, women and children were murdered in the Jaralosa Cieniga, some three miles west of McEvers ranch. The women and children were horribly and disgustingly mutilated. Their heads and faces were battered in, iron bars being used for the purpose.

Beside those killed there were over twenty-five women and children badly wounded. In the fight that took place at the cornfield at McEver's ranch, over thirty horses were killed.

The Indians belong to the Southern Chiricahua tribe, and are old Cahise's bands. They are well mounted on horses from Hooker's command that was defeated some time since. They are all well-armed and equipped for a long campaign. They have been reinforced by Loco and Victorio's band, and number about 80.

Capt. Beyer, with a command of 45 men aided by Joe Yankie, in command of fifteen frontiersmen left here recently and are now on the trail.[12]

Such a raid would have been quite frightening, if not completely discouraging, to recently arrived settlers. Especially to those as young as Nat Irvin and his wife Levina, who was pregnant with their first child, my grandfather, during that time.

The Irvins had a number of encounters with the Apache, but this was the first one that I discovered, thanks to some help from a local historian. I was shown a fascinating article in the February 2016 edition of the Hillsboro Historical Society's newsletter by Harley Shaw, a Hillsboro resident and editor of that newsletter. This was the article that I mentioned earlier, an article which inspired me to conduct a much more thorough research into the Irvins' activities in Lake Valley.

That article is Sarah Gibson's eyewitness account of that same Apache raid described above. Sarah's account was written in 1917, many years after the raid. The raid took place at the McEver's ranch south of Hillsboro in the northern part of Lake Valley (I should note here that there is disagreement among historians about how McEver is spelled, so it is sometimes written as McEverett.). Gibson's ranch was just south of McEver's, and Irvin's ranch was just south of Gibson's ranch. In Sarah's own words, the Irvins were smack in the middle of that raid! Here is part of her account:

A man in Hillsboro offered Bill Gibson a place of cows and ranch on a lake about twelve miles below town, where they moved and began to work. All this time, Bill was regaining his health. There were only two families beside themselves; one was the McEveretts, wife and daughter who lived on the upper part of the swamp. Irvins, his wife, son and his wife lived below and the Gibson's had the middle ranch. All was peace and contentment for at least two or three months. One day while the father was gone hunting, the mother and oldest boy, Johnnie, was outside when suddenly he called to his mother to come and look. On doing so, what did she see? Some distance away was now and then something black popping up and down behind some rocks, which looked very much like Indian heads.

After a consultation with her boy, Johnnie, they decided to go on down to the (Irvins) ranch and see what it really was. But when they reached his place, Mr. Irvins took Johnnie and went to see what the trouble was. He was a stubborn old fellow, and when he came back, told her she was scared for nothing, as there was nothing there. It must have been crows she saw jumping around on the rocks. But after they started back home, Johnnie said there were moccasin tracks all around there where they were. So, this made her more uneasy and when they reached home, they could see the upper ranch and heard some shooting and could see enough to know there was trouble up there. He (Bill) was there from hunting and while she was getting dinner and they were talking about the incident when John came running in and said he heard shooting at McEveretts and believed they were shooting at somebody. On investigating, they could see there was trouble. Bill sent John after the horse, where he was tied in the swamp and by the time he got back, young Irvins was there, for they had heard the shooting too.

The men with John took their guns and went up there. Irvins and the two women came later so the mother and children went on up with them. Before they got there, they could see the shooting and the men taking part in it. Mrs. Gibson could see Bill taking aim at an Indian who wore a very large hat and he made the remark to Irvins "Here, hold my horse (as he dismounted and handed him the bridle), I want that hat". He fired and the red man fell off his horse with a loud yell, but his comrade caught him and carried him away in his arms. So, Bill missed getting his hat. In the fighting, one white man was wounded. A bullet hit him in his arm, tearing the flesh from it and went through his breast to the other arm. But fortunately, he got all right. The Indians were after the horses and the men were shooting at the Indians to make them leave the horses alone. Everybody stayed at McEverett's all night, almost afraid to look out. The next day, the men ventured out to see what the Indians had done.

This was not all the mischief they did this time, for they heard afterward that on their way out from town, the Indians stopped at a Mexican family's and made them all undress and then left them, laughing at them and what they thought fun. After they left, one boy wanted them all to leave and hide, telling them they would be back and kill them, but the family only laughed and said "no, they won't be back". But the boy left and went to a cave he knew about and stayed there. That night, after the Indians had had a fight with the white men from town, killing seven white men in battle, they came back to the Mexican's house and killed the whole family of nine except the boy who was hiding. When they went out the next day to see what was done there, everything was quiet. After that, the government sent some men there to build a sort of fort of adobe. They built it in eight or nine days and left 500 rounds of shells and two kegs of powder and thought that was good protection.

But on the tenth day after the last excitement, Mr. McEverett and a hired man was out in the field with a wagon and horses hauling corn fodder, which was piled in shocks. They felt uneasy still, for they carried their guns with them and set them down by the wagon. Everything looked nice and peaceful, but they were suddenly surprised by about fifteen shots by some more men nearby and several red men jumped from beneath the shocks of fodder from all over the field. The men jumped from the wagon just as the bullets passed over their heads. When they (the Indians) started shooting at them, they run for shelter in the tall sunflowers, which grew all around them. The women from the house started outside and could see someone from the Gibson ranch and waved. The man, who was wounded before, was going to Gibson's and heard the shooting. Also, the children. Bill was not home, having gone with the team several hours before to Irvins to go out on the prairie to haul hay. Mrs. Gibson sent the man when he got there at top most speed to stop them if possible. The women from Gibson's waived for him to come on down there, they

63

thought it better for them to run from danger than face it, so they waived them (McEverett's) to come on down there, which they did. The girl, about 17 years old, tried to ride her pony away which she thought a great deal of, but it was the pony the Indians wanted and they began shooting at her until she had to leave her pony and fly, which she did, never looking back or stopping for water, but just kept ahead until she reached Irvins. Some of the boys from Gibson's come running in crying, "here they come, Ma". This excited them all so they began getting the little ones together for a run to the lower ranch where all the men were. John run to the top of the hill and shouted, "here they are". The mother took one of the twins and a box of cartridges. Mollie, the oldest daughter, took the other twin and Polly, the other girl, took a small youngster named Lane. They started on a run when John said, "here they are". Imagine the excitement.

The mother started to exchange loads with Polly as Lane was too heavy for her small arms, to run, and on doing so she dropped the box of cartridges in the dirt and had to stop to pick them up. She thought of the quickest way of doing it, as one will in a tight place, by scooping them up dirt and all in Lane's hat. By this time, Mrs. McEverett caught up with them and picked Annie, another one that couldn't run, up across her shoulder and away they went. By the time they was well around the point of the hill, here come Bill and the men with the hay wagon. They were very glad of this for the Indians were getting pretty close. While they were all piling in the wagon, one of the men started after a horse, which was tied in the pasture, but the Indians began shooting at him over the heads of the others in the wagon. They wanted the horse. (The man, Coffee, got to Irvins just as the men were getting on the wagon to leave for the hay). They all found shelter in Irvins house which was made of small pickets.

Here they stayed until the next day before anyone ventured out. While there, everything seemed quiet and they didn't think there were any Indians anywhere. So, they were all brave enough to get out and look around.

64

Bill was one of them who was always there when any fighting or excitement was going on. They could not see or hear any Indians, so Bill and Mr. Irvins were standing by the wagon with a post between them facing each other and talking it over, when Whiz, Buzz, a bullet hit the post which was sticking up just between them and another one hit the ground between young Irvins' legs. This caused a scatterment for shelter again where they remained until someone come from town.

How did they get word? Listen! You remember Mr. McEverett and his hired man run into the sunflowers to hide at the beginning? Neither knew where the other one was all this time. The hired man found his way out during the night and away to town, where he gave the alarm. Mr. McEverett ventured out from hiding about nine o'clock at night and went to his home, or where his house was that day, for the Indians had blown the house up with powder that was in the house, first removing the bedding, trunks and clothing. The beds they put in one pile and burned. The clothes they took from the trunks and others and hung them across some poles, which were in the yard used as tying places, and set fire to them. In one of the trunks was a packet where the girl had put a ten-dollar bill. This they had not found.

From here, Mr. McEverett made his way to the Gibson place, but it was deserted. So, he went cautiously to the Irvins place, hiding and listening several hours to be sure the occupants were white before he made his appearance and presence known at the house. No doubt he expected to find some or maybe most all of them murdered but no, not one even hurt, except from fright. When he found they were white he hollered and you may be sure there were some proud people there. They all thought sure he was killed. But it was sad to see their home all tore up. But they built again and stayed there.[13]

Sarah's account states that several raids took place before the Gibson family finally gave up and left for Arizona in June, 1880. Consequently, Gibson's are not listed in the 1880 census for this area, because the census was taken in August, 1880. McEvers sold his ranch and mining interests in 1880, evidently also before the August 1880 census, because he's not listed either. Of those three ranch families, only the Irvins stayed on.

There are several other accounts of those Apache raids on McEver's ranch. Craig Springer, a member of the Hillsboro Historical Society, has summarized some of these raids.[14] Based on his article, the raid Sarah Gibson described was probably in September, 1879, led by Apache chief Victorio. Springer's article mentions, "On Sept. 11, 1879, a posse of armed citizens from Hillsboro — led by town pioneers Joe Yankie and Nicholas Galles — confronted Apaches at H.D. McEver's ranch 15 miles south of Hillsboro. McEver's ranch would shortly become the first townsite of Lake Valley (not the current site), following a significant silver strike." Nicholas Galles is listed in the 1880 Hillsborough census, though not Joe Yankie. This attack is sometimes called the 'Hillsboro massacre' because of its proximity to that small town and the fact that as many as fifteen men may have been killed during the skirmishes.

Springer describes another attack on McEver's ranch a week or so later, this time involving the Ninth Cavalry (among those famed as 'buffalo soldiers'), a number of whom were stationed in Lake Valley according to the 1880 Census. Army reports indicated that as many as 100 Apaches were involved in these attacks.

Following is a military account of that McEver ranch raid, as reported by several Army field communications:

Santa Fe, New Mexico, Sept. 18, 1879. To Assistant Adjt.-Gen. Fort Leavenworth. Kan.: The commanding officer at Fort Bayard reports by telegraph as follows:

Just received the following from McEvers, near Hillsboro: "We had a five-hours' fight with all of 100 Indians. We have 10 killed and several wounded. All our stock is gone." I have sent every available soldier out with Damson and Day; I hear Beyer, Hugo, and Lieut. Wright are all in the vicinity, and should be able shortly to overtake Victoria. *Morrow, Officer commanding.*

The commanding officer at Fort Bayard has been instructed to use every endeavor and all possible means available to punish 'these Indians. *Loud, A. A. G.*

It is believed that there are enough troops at Bayard to deal with these Indians, and they are all out after them. *John Pope, Brevet Major-General commanding.*

The Ordnance Department this morning telegraphed to the commandant of the arsenal at Fort Union, New Mexico, to issue arms and ammunition to Gov. Wallace, not to exceed 300 rifles and 1,000,000 cartridges.[15]

Chiricahua Apache Chief Victorio
(from Wikipedia, Public Domain)

As mentioned earlier, my great grandmother Levina Ricketson Irvin was pregnant with their first child during these first raids. My grandfather, Thomas Hiram Irvin was born on January 8, 1880. You might wonder why the Irvins did not leave this dangerous environment after these bloody raids, as the Gibson's and some other families had. But they stayed on, maybe hoping that this would be the end of it. A second transcontinental railroad, uniting the ATSF and Southern Pacific railroads was nearing completion. A railroad would make it easier and faster to move troops into the area if they were needed. And, as a result of these raids, the Army now maintained several small forts in the proximity of McEver's ranch. Surely the Apache raids wouldn't continue under those circumstances.

However, as I continued researching the Irvin family's experiences in Lake Valley, I discovered that the Apache raids did not end at this time. And in one of the next raids, a third Irvin family was involved! An article by Lee Silva describes another widely publicized Apache attack in Lake Valley, sometimes referred to as Nana's Raid, which was led by Apache chief Nana on August 18, 1881. Nana and Victorio had very close ties; Nana was married to Victorio' sister. Following is part of Silva's article:

> The warrior Nana may have been an octogenarian, but his unrestrained presence in southwestern New Mexico Territory in the summer of 1881 filled white folks with old fears as quickly as a flash flood fills an arroyo. By mid-August, a combined military and civilian party had taken the field to stop or at least contain the Warm Springs Apache leader and his marauders. Nana, believed to be about 80 and afflicted with arthritis, had launched a spectacular raid that June in response to wrongs that he had suffered. Most of Nana's resentment stemmed from a mid-October 1880 Mexican militia ambush at Tres Castillos in Old Mexico. The great Mimbres Chief Victorio and close to 80 other Apaches had been massacred there, though Nana and his followers had been able to evade the ambushers and escape into the Sierra Madre. If, 10 months later, the makeshift American posse hoped to achieve another "Tres Castillos," Nana had other ideas. He planned to turn the tables on them and remind them that Apaches knew a thing or two about carrying out an ambush.
>
> Nana's raid began when he and his wide-ranging warriors (less than 40) attacked a surveying crew in northern Chihuahua, Mexico, in late June 1881. They then fought their way north through the Sacramento, San Andreas, San Mateo and Black Range mountains. By August 17, the ancient warrior was in the vicinity of Hillsboro, New Mexico Territory. On the 18th, the Apaches shot their way through the small mining community of Gold Dust without injuring anyone. The

raiders then half-heartedly struck the Trujillo Ranch, about five miles south of Hillsboro. The half-blood owner was suspected of supplying the Apaches with arms and ammunition. Nobody was injured there either, but the Indians continued south to attack Perry Ousley's ranch; they burned his place and killed him.

Next, the raiders moved past Tierra Blanca Creek to Absolom D. Irwin's ranch, about three miles north of Lake Valley. (The present-day ghost town of Lake Valley is at a different site.) Absolom was away on business, but his wife, Sally, and their five children made a run for it. Some of them got away, but Sally was severely beaten and a baby was snatched from her arms. Although Absolom arrived in time to put out the ranch house fire, his family was gone. Believing them captured, he rode to Lake Valley to give the alarm.

In response to the recent atrocities, a posse formed at Hillsboro and arrived at Lake Valley by the night of the 18th. When someone reported seeing Indians seven miles away on Berrenda Creek, the Lake Valley Mining Company superintendent, George Daly, took charge of the posse. Support was solicited from Lieutenant George Washington Smith at a nearby military encampment. Smith had been dispatched with elements of Companies B and H of the 9th Cavalry, with orders to block the Apaches' passage south. Somewhat reluctantly, Smith and the black troopers joined up with Daly's civilian posse, some of whose members were full of bravado by the time they left William Cotton's saloon shortly after midnight. Accounts vary as to the number in the party, but a fair estimate would be 16 to 20 so-called buffalo soldiers and 20 civilians.

The force followed Berrenda Creek and then a creek known today as Pollock Creek, which dipped into Dry Gavilan Canyon. That canyon in turn ran into Gavilan Canyon, which is where, at 10:30 a.m. on August 19, Nana ambushed the Americans. Accounts vary as to exactly what happened, but it is certain that Lieutenant Smith and Daly, the leaders, were killed in the opening salvos. Apparently, Smith was unhorsed in the first volley, but he was helped back on his mount, only to be mortally shot. Bullets struck several other soldiers and civilians as well, causing some of the men — including Sergeant William Baker of Company H — to flee. Sergeant Brent Woods of Company B rallied what men he could and even advanced before calling for an orderly retreat. The wounded were also evacuated. Under Woods' direction, the ambushed party threw up rock barricades and fought the Apaches for about six hours.[16]

Silva goes on to describe numerous other casualties and atrocities before the fighting ended, and added that Sergeant Wood was later awarded the Medal of Honor for his action. The arrival of additional troops from Lake Valley under General Hatch was all that saved the lives of the men hidden among the rocks. Warned by their Scouts of the approaching troops, the Apaches split into small bands and fled across the border. They took with them all of the horses of the Lake Valley posse. Nana was later captured and returned to the reservation but then later escaped at about the same time that Geronimo fled the reservation.

Apache chief, Nana, 1886 (NA 43-0741a)

Now, just who was this Absolom D Irwin, whose ranch described as located north of Lake Valley, had been attacked by Apaches? That name looked awfully familiar. I'd seen more than a few misspellings during my family history research, and Irvin was often misspelled as Irwin (the handwritten script 'v' is easily misread as 'w'). My very first thought was that Silva was referring to Powhatan Irvin's brother. But some of the facts didn't fit. For one, Absolom Irwin's wife was named Sarah, not Sally.

I checked local newspapers and census reports from that period and came up with an Absalom Irvin family that somewhat fit the description in Silva's article. The June 19, 1880 Census of the Nogal Mining District, Lincoln County, NM (on the other side of the Rio Grande, some hundred miles or so northeast of Lake Valley) listed an Absalom Irvin (not Irwin) and his family. There were seven, not five, children listed, the youngest being age 2. The wife's name was listed as Sarah, not Sally. But the Absolom Irvin family described in the Nogal 1880 Census was otherwise a very close match to the family described in this Apache attack. That family was almost certainly Powhatan's brother's family! Later evidence proved it so.

So, there were three Irvin families in Lake Valley by 1882. There was Nat and Levina Irvin's family, Nat's parents PB and Mary living just to the south, and his uncle Absalom and his family living on a ranch a few miles north. Probably these Irvins had all traveled to New Mexico Territory at the same time in their own small wagon train, driving their cattle herds along with them. They would have turned north when they reached the Rio Grande river and followed the river up to the Nogal mining district. Absolom must have found an area he believed would be a good ranch land and decided to stay there with his herd. Powhatan and Nat decided to push on west to Lake Valley.

Shortly thereafter, Powhatan, after setting up a homestead in Lake Valley, probably informed Absalom that there were fortunes to be made in Lake Valley, be it the high prices that beef was bringing or a lucky find of silver or gold. Absalom evidently moved his herd and family west to Lake Valley shortly after the 1880 census was taken. His timing couldn't have been worse. His family narrowly escaped being massacred within a year of their arrival!

I expect that this attack was a bit harrowing for Nat and Levina Irvin, as well. My family history records show that at the time of Nana's attack on Absolom Irvin's ranch, Nat's wife, Levina, would have been pregnant with their second child, Daisy! Census reports have her birth listed as January of 1882 in Silver City, New Mexico though she was probably born at their ranch in Lake Valley.

So, the Irvin's had a number of encounters with the Apache during their several years in Lake Valley. Sometimes these encounters were friendly, unlikely as that might seem. One such encounter was related to me back in 1955 by Levina Irvin herself (who died the following year, just a few months shy of age 95) and repeated by other relatives. As she told it, her family had several contacts with Chiricahua Apache chief Geronimo during the last years before his surrender to the Army in 1886. She purportedly knew Geronimo and sometimes fed him and watered his horses when he stopped by their home while traveling through Lake Valley. She said that on one such visit, she even let Geronimo hold her infant son, and that he'd complimented her on the child's appearance. This probably happened sometime between 1880, the year her son Tom was born, and 1882 the year her second child Daisy was born. I say this because she did not mention Daisy in that story.

Did this really happen? After all, Geronimo eventually became quite famous, especially after he was captured and eventually relocated to Indian Territory (now Oklahoma). It was not uncommon for persons who lived in that part of the country to claim that they knew Geronimo, or that they remembered some chance encounter with him back before he was captured. Was Levina, like so many others, just basking in Geronimo's fame?

I don't think so. In addition to similar stories from my close relatives, there are at least two other independent corroborating accounts. Another Ancestry member, someone I don't know and have never met. whose family tree includes Levina Irvin, relates a story that Levina and her husband Nat once hid Geronimo under hay in one of their stables to help him elude Army soldiers searching for him. Another source, the daughter-in-law of Fred Carson (married to Elsa Irvin), Thelma

Carson, left a number of Family history notes which were posted online by her grandson. One note, referring to Nat and Levina Irvin, stated, "They had known Geronimo before he was captured and were instrumental in securing his eventual release."[17] Furthermore, as you will soon discover, Levina Ricketson Irvin was a tough and practical woman and had experienced enough in her lifetime that she didn't need to make up such a story. So, when she says that Geronimo held my infant grandfather in his arms, I believe her.

The Apache raids in that area continued on and off for several more years, according to a Hillsboro Historical Society publication, *Around Hillsboro*:

> The environs around Hillsboro were raided by the few Apaches who rejected reservation life with a vengeance that exacted the toll of life, property, and public treasury. African American buffalo soldiers of the ninth cavalry were stationed at Camp French at Hillsboro in 1880. Five years later, the eighth cavalry and the 25th infantry would spend a year at Camp Hillsboro/camp Boyd. Apache scouts were detailed to Hillsboro, and army supplies stations were set up at McEver's ranch.
>
> The Burt Lancaster movie Ulzana's Raid was rooted in a kernel of truth. Only a mere mile or so from Hillsboro, the Apache Ulzana and his band tested the horse soldiers in 1885. The cavalry, manned with the likes of Tom Horn, chased the marauders, who ably melded into the mountains. In a few weeks, 38 people would be killed by Ulzana's raids.[18]

The raids in this area were just the last of many Apache wars. Battles with the Apaches had been waged for many decades. Long before the discovery of silver and gold in this part of New Mexico, there had been a series of battles between the Apaches and each other, between the Apaches and the Mexicans, and between the Apaches and Americans. Following is a brief description of just one such battle that took place back during the Civil War:

It was July 15, 1862, and Union Captain Thomas Roberts led a column of volunteers into Apache Pass in southeast Arizona. They were headed to New Mexico to fight Confederates. They were in for a surprise. Some 500 Apache warriors, led by Mangas Coloradas and Cochise ambushed them. Over the next two days, the fighting was fierce and there were casualties on both sides.

The army final drove off the Indians by opening up with artillery. But it was just one fight; the war lasted about 10 years before Cochise signed a peace treaty.[19]

Why were there so many Apache raids at this particular time and place? Most Apaches had been peacefully settled in various reservations by this time, some in Arizona, some in New Mexico. When silver, and later, gold, were found in this part of New Mexico, it was not then occupied by Apaches. So, these later raids weren't a simple situation where the Apaches were fighting to defend their lands. In fact, each of the raids described earlier had different origins.

Some raids were driven simply by the need for food, horses, and ammunition, mostly used to evade, and if necessary, fight the soldiers and villagers who pursued them. Often these were renegade bands of Apache's, such as Victorio's and Geronimo's, that had fled the reservation because of poor conditions or because the reservations were not located in their favored homelands. Old chief Nana's raid, one of the deadliest in these times, was apparently inspired by the dance of an Apache 'medicine man' called the dreamer, and was meant to revenge the death of Nana's friend, chief Victorio, who had recently died at the hands of the Federales in northern Mexico. I can't begin to do justice to the story of all of these battles, but others have. I would recommend that a good place to start is an excellent and recent book on the subject, Apache Wars, (Paul Hutton, 2016). Much more detailed accounts can be found in the recent trilogy of books about the Victorio Campaign and Nana's war by Robert Watt (Robert Watt, 2017, 2019).

Although most earlier battles ended with the eventual defeat of the Apaches by either the Mexican military or the American military, these later raids often raged on for long periods of time before the defeat, capture or surrender and resettlement of the Apaches that were involved. Civilians often suffered the brunt of these battles. My ancestors, the Irvins, had unknowingly migrated to a 'hornet's nest' where the last part of this history of Apache wars was still playing out. The Apache raids didn't actually end until 1886, when Geronimo and his small band of warriors finally surrendered.

Yanosha, Geronimo's son, "Chappo", Geronimo's half-brother, Fun, and Geronimo, just before their surrender on March 27, 1886 (photo by CS Fly   Lib. of Congress)

However, despite experiencing these continued Apache raids, the Irvins did not leave Lake Valley at this time. Why not? Fellow ranchers and miners were getting killed. Their own families narrowly escaped being massacred on several occasions.

7. Silver, the Road to Riches

Well, the Irvin families weren't just busy raising their young children and beef cattle and fending off Apache raids. They were witnessing the many silver strikes in Lake Valley and the sudden fortunes this bestowed upon those who found and mined the precious metal. So, as you might expect, the Irvins tried their hand at silver prospecting. Powhatan and his brother Absolom partnered in their own silver mining venture. Their silver mines, near Hillsboro, were described in a June, 1882 issue of a Las Cruces newspaper as follows:

> Since the immense richness of the mines at Sierra City is fully demonstrated by the production of silver bricks from the new mill, I wish to call the attention of the public to Irvin's Camp, four or five miles north and a little west of Daly (Silver Camp on the headwaters of Hijerlosa [ed. note-probably Jaralosa] creek, and about one mile above Watts Brothers' cow ranch. There is a large body of ore there, which, in many respects, is the exact counterpart of that of Silver Camp. The formation is lime and iron; the leads appear to be blankets, and the ores—iron, carbonates, black, red and yellow—are found on the surface and embodied in talc and lime formation.
>
> The Friendship, Austin and Texas mines are owned by A. D. Irvin & Brother, of Lake Valley. Considerable development has been done on them— sufficient to show a large amount of ore, assaying from $14 to $93 per ton; in fact, on the Friendship, a piece of float [ed note: loose rock from the ore vein] running as high as $800 was found and tested.[20]

These assays represent considerable value for those times. So, Nat's father and his uncle, in addition to their cattle, evidently owned some valuable mining interests in Lake Valley. They likely sold their silver mines for a handsome profit before leaving New Mexico. And they weren't the only ones getting rich in that area.

Sometime in late summer of 1882, a new location for the town of Lake Valley was erected a few miles north of the original. This was the Lake Valley generally referred to as a 'boomtown'. These were complete cities unto themselves, which sprung up almost overnight to accommodate the rapid influx of population spurred on by glowing news accounts of one new silver find after another.

Downtown corner of Lake Valley, 1890 (Lake Valley Museum)

The best description I've found of Lake Valley's sudden growth from a ramshackle mining camp of tents and wagons to a fully operating town was an account published in a Las Vegas, New Mexico newspaper. The reporter brings Lake Valley to life with his folksy and detailed account of his visit to that town:

> The great excitement engendered throughout the territory by the rich strikes in the Lake Valley and Kingston District, prompted a Gazette reporter to turn his attention in that direction; consequently, he gathered his grip and blankets a few days ago, and started for the country where the Wheel of Fortune in its fickle turning has made men rich in an hour.

The ride from Las Vegas south is a pleasant one this season of the year, as old sol does not send his rays so vertical as he did a few months ago. In the morning, just at sunrise, the train filled with passengers on their way to the silver fields pulled into Nutt station, the nearest railroad station to Lake Valley. At present it is not a very inviting place, but few houses as yet having been erected, but a bright future is beginning to cast its light before and Nutt station may yet make itself felt as a good point.

Ed Moore is running an excellent restaurant there, and Dan Herrigan, an old Las Vegan, is keeping the only hotel in the place. He keeps a well-arranged house and sets a good table.

R. B. Boone keeps a well-ordered saloon and is doing a thriving business, toning up the appetite of those destined for the mines.

Mr. J W gray has also commenced the erection of a large hotel at this point.

After a hastily dispatched breakfast fifteen or twenty wealth Seekers clambered into or on top of one of Cosgrove's six-horse Concord coaches, which had pulled up in front of the office, and started for Lake Valley. About as many more men took passage on an independent line.

The road is level and smooth, the entire distance and the scenery along the road is varied and beautiful. The twelve miles intervening between the station and the new city was soon passed over, and at 9 o'clock the anxious wayfarers were landed at their destination.

Lake Valley is a wonderful City, and the hustle and noise puts one in mind of the early days of east Las Vegas. The sound of the hammer and saw is the only noise to be heard. It is now only about five weeks old and yet it contains fifty or sixty business houses, and others are going up rapidly. The only trouble is to get lumber fast enough, but the enterprising lumber firm of Leavitt and Watson are doing heroic service in supplying this need. They have erected a large building for storing sash, doors, etc. and their stock of other lumber is the best to be found in the country. Lumber commands about $45

78

per thousand and is sold as fast as it can be laid on the ground.

The Sierra Hotel is a principal at present and is doing a splendid business. It is almost impossible for the genial proprietors to supply the demands of the transient customers.

Bradley and Turner have a well-ordered saloon. They are making money by doing a square business.

A.M. James, formerly of this city, has pitched his tent in the new field and has an extensive trade in the general merchandise business.

Smith Brothers also have a large two-story store.

Cotton and Duke were the first to get their saloon in ship shape and are consequently reaping the reward. Their billiard tables and back bar fixtures are as good as can be found in towns of much greater age.

The Cobweb Saloon keeps a large stock of liquors and boasts the first pool table in the town.

Jay McIntyre formerly of this city, is Marshall, and puts in his time keeping the boys straight. He makes a good, as well as good-looking officer

Southwick and Berela carry a large line of miners supplies and general merchandise. They are doing well.

McBride and Cloberg are just finishing a 25 by 60-foot billiard Hall. It will be furnished with three billiard tables and back bar fixtures and carry one of the largest lines of goods in the camp. They formally did business at the lake but the building of the new city necessitated a change of Base.

Will Hudgins, a genial saloonist of White Oaks, has erected a fine saloon in the new Eldorado and commands a good share of the trade, which, of course is not small.

R.D. Bennett is also driving a thriving liquor trade.

Colonel A. Woodall is building a large adobe hotel. It will soon be ready for occupancy.

E A Dorwart is following the wood-butcher business, and of course has more than he can attend to.

H P Alden, formerly with Fred Benitez, is putting up a handsome jewelry store. He will put in a full line of goods.

G.N. Rhodes, formerly with robins and Moody of this city, is going into business in Lake Valley.

RF Brownrigg is erecting a good-sized adobe hotel.

Mr. Clapp, the postmaster, is just completing a handsome adobe office and business house.

There are two blacksmith and wagon shops in the town, which have all the work they can do.

John F Kopp has secured a neat building and is putting in a full line of stationery and periodicals.

As a business point Lake Valley is a success. We have only been able to give an outline of the business which has sprung up in so short a time, and the town is moving so rapidly that a report made at one time would necessarily be imperfect as to the business a week later.

Charles W Green, formerly of the new Mexican, will issue the first number of the Lake Valley Herald on the 5th of October. He is meeting with the best of success in his new Enterprise.

The mines of Lake Valley and the Kingston district will be treated in a subsequent article.[21]

The very next day, as promised, the newspaper carried an article on the mines of Lake Valley by the same reporter:

LAKE VALLEY. Her mines and future prospects. As was indicated in a previous article, the mines of Lake Valley which have excited such wonder both at home and abroad, would be treated of at a proper time. After the Gazette man had looked upon the rapidly-growing young city of Lake Valley for a while, he leisurely strolled up to the north part of the town where the mill, sampling works and the mines are situated. The sampling works are kept busy only a portion of the time but is a great aid to the mines in the vicinity, as it enables prospectors to get an intelligent idea of what they are doing without any great expense. The machinery is of the best material of the latest improved kinds and thus far has given perfect satisfaction to the owners and to those who have had their ores treated there. Tabor and Wurzbach are the builders and the present owners and operators. The Sierra Grande and the Sierra Platte mining and smelting companies have been consolidated. This company owns the principal mines in the district. Mr. Gillette, formerly of the Canyon del Agua company of San Pedro, is the general manager.

The mill, superintended by Mr. E.D. Town, is a wonderful affair. A description of it is utterly out of question, as twenty stamps in full operation tend to confuse those not accustomed to such rackets, and furthermore it would take days of careful examination instead of only a few hours of casual looking.

The mill at present is running on Bridal Chamber ore, which is wonderfully rich in silver. During the month of August, the mill produced $200,000 in silver bullion, and about $212,000 during the month of September. The mill is capable of turning out double these amounts during any one month if run at its full capacity, but as yet the company has not wanted any larger amount. Charles Heiman is the assayer for the company, and when he gets through with a rock its exact richness is known. He uses both e wet and dry processes and has apparatus of the very best in use.

The next curiosity of ye reporter was to take a look at the great mines about which so much has been written of late and which created so much excitement at the Denver Exposition and turn the attention of Colorado capitalist in the direction of New Mexico. It was the ore from the Bridal Chamber mine which created such universal astonishment in mining circles and secured the presidency of the American Mining Association to New Mexico over the older Rivals of Utah, Colorado and Nevada.

On approaching the mines there is nothing special to excite the attention of the uninitiated. A low, Rocky Hill spreading out like a palm leaf from the mouth of the canyon, a number of dykes of reddish looking rock, a few drifts and shafts and that is all. A closer observation, however, reveals the worthless looking rock to contain silver in great quantities. It does not require an expert to determine the silver bearing rock. It is patent to the most casual observer. Hundreds of tons of this or is now on the dump awaiting treatment, and hundreds of tons are being lifted from the rich beds beneath.

William Skyrm, the gentlemanly foreman of the mines, was sought out and requested to show a party of sightseers through the mine. This he readily consented to do, and the party was told to follow on. Once in the mine, a stranger is perfectly lost. The tunnels, shafts and passageways of various kinds create so much confusion in the minds of those unacquainted with such places, that the first impulse is to retrace your steps and seek a more sunlit region. But a few candles and the friendly voice of the guide soon restores confidence and the intricate windings of the tunnel are gone through. At every step the great wealth of the mines is made more apparent. Shafts are descended and the thickness of the vein of ore is pointed out, the wall rocks shown and the dip explained. At some places the foreman would hold his candle up to a body of ore for a few minutes and the rock would show small buttons of silver. Thus, the interesting voyage went on till a depth of about sixty feet have been reached when the famous Bridal Chamber was entered. Here a scene is presented that is not readily forgotten. Great masses and ledges of ore is to be seen on all sides. At one place a large chunk of ore valued at $60,000 was to be seen, and above you for a distance of twenty or thirty ft a solid bed of rich silver bearing rock was revealed. To all appearances the mineral is almost inexhaustible. It has been struck on all parts of the property and as the work of development goes on the mineral appears to become more abundant. There are millions of dollars in site with no indications of it giving out. Several other companies own mines in the vicinity, but as yet no great amount of work has been done, though there are evidences that they too have secured bonanzas of no small importance.

These are the mines which have astonished the world, and form the backing for Lake Valley, and right here it is meet to say, that there are a few towns in the west which have been favored with such a solid foundation.

At present about one hundred and fifty men are at work in the mines.

The quarters of the officers are provided with every luxury, and visitors are treated with the greatest Hospitality.

The Kingston district will receive attention in tomorrow's issue.[22]

The following year, Lake Valley mines were still producing silver at a record levels. *The Black Range* newspaper, a local newspaper in Chloride, New Mexico "devoted to the mining interests of the Black Range Country", reported the following:

"The Sierra Nevada mine at Lake Valley is now producing daily 6,000 to 10,000 ounces of silver. The total output up to January 5, for six months, commencing July 21st, 1882, was $869,138.88. It is a grand record for a twenty-stamp mill."[23] [ed. note: Stamps used a series of cams to repetitively lift and drop heavy metal weights onto the ore, in order to pulverize it for further processing. They were powered by running water or steam engines. They date back to Roman times and were used to process metallic ores from their mines. A twenty-stamp mill would be able to crush thousands of tons per day.]

But, not all of the news was good news. Problems were also developing for silver mining in the area. Much of the money used to pay for mining and processing came from investors back east and even overseas. Some of this money was obtained fraudulently with inflated assay reports on claims with little or no promise. Local newspapers reported these problems, "In spite of all that has been said and published, and in spite of the undeniable richness of Sierra properties at Lake Valley, the stocks of the company continue to decline and on the 10th the Sierra Grande had fallen to $2.15. The public is getting cute and not as easily swindled by sharpers as it was a year or two ago."[24]

By late spring of that year, some operations were now being scaled back. The mill at Lake Valley was shut down.

Unscrupulous wheeling and dealing had begun to hurt mining in the area, as this news story relates:

> The mill at Lake Valley is again silent. Some stockjobbing scheme is on hand, evidently, for nobody for a moment supposes that there is any diminution of the rich ore supply. New Mexico's richest mines have so far been her greatest curse because they have fallen into unscrupulous hands that are used to working the capitalist instead of their properties. Lake Valley will never be a thriving town until either the Sierra properties change hands or other dependence is found. The Tabor sampling works will be taken to Kingston.[25]

Because mining was the major source of income in Lake Valley, its decline influenced other activities in the town. The *Lake Valley Herald*, the town's only local paper, also shut down, which that same May issue of *The Black Range* seemed to report with some satisfaction:

> The publication of the *Lake Valley Herald* has been discontinued and the office has been moved to Kingston. Mr. Greene has paid a few hundred dollars for the fun of publishing a big paper in a small town and can tell how he likes it. If his experience is of any value to him, he will reduce the size of the *Tribune* at Kingston a column or two to match the town and increase the price of subscription to the territorial standard. When the *Lake Valley Herald* started, the *Black Range* said that it would survive six months. It lasted eight months.[26]

Lake Valley did produce a lot of silver, however, before its decline. The Bridal Chamber alone yielded $2,775,000 in ore.[27] At that time, the Bridal Chamber ore body had never been equaled in richness by any silver mine in the world.[28] In spite of this, Sierra Grande shareholders lost money. There was little likelihood of new investment money flowing into this area's mines. Although many Sierra Grande investors lost money, the owner, J. Whitaker Wright, became a multi-millionaire by promoting mining stocks. However, justice prevailed. He was later convicted of stock fraud in a widely publicized trial in

London Court in 1902. Following his conviction, he committed suicide--in the courtroom!

There were other outcomes that did not end well. A primary investor and promoter of Sierra Grande mining, George Daly, had been killed by Apaches during the Nana raid and his body returned to Lake Valley on the very day that the Bridal Chamber lode was discovered. And, ironically, rancher George W. Lufkin, one of the first discoverers of silver in the area, died penniless and is buried in the now abandoned Lake Valley cemetery.

Shortly before this time, however, mining activity in Kingston, just few hours ride to the north, was starting to pick up. An Albuquerque newspaper reported, "This morning finds me in one of the liveliest camps I have struck for years. Town lots are selling as high as 15,000. One week ago, they could have been bought at $25. I am told the Las Vegas town company sold 100 lots yesterday. Three lots of surveyors are at work on lots. The mines are the richest I ever saw."[29]

Lake Valley might be faltering, but one had only to move north to Kingston. The Irvins chose not to. Why not?

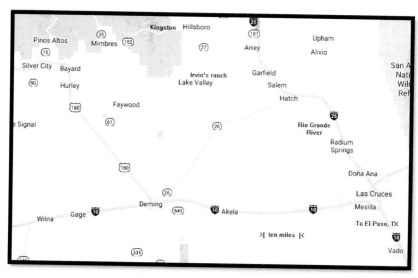

Southwestern New Mexico showing Irvin's ranch

8. Was Nat Irvin a Cattle Rustler?

My research indicates that the Irvins left Lake Valley sometime in 1883. Did the Irvin's leave Lake Valley at about this time because it was beginning to look like Lake Valley was a dying town? Or was it because of ongoing Apache raids? Or might there have been still another reason? The answer may well be, 'all of the above'.

Cattle rustling in southern New Mexico was becoming a major problem at this time. According to a Las Cruces newspaper:

> From every ranch in the county and along the Rio Grande, from just below Socorro to the county south of Mesilla, including Palomas, Colorado, Lake Valley, Leasburg, Dona Ana, and many other towns, comes intelligence of cattle in large numbers having been run off by rustlers during the past week. Great excitement prevails all along the line, and several armed bands of citizens are on the road after the villains. They have not yet returned. The whole town herd of Dona Ana city has been run off. Large shipments of fresh beef have recently been made from an obscure railroad station between here and Rincon to parties in El Paso. The hides, with the brands on, have been found at the depot and claimed by the rightful owners. Great indignation is felt against the station agents for their carelessness, and against the consignees at El Paso.[30]

Well, Nat must have found a way to make staying on in this wild part of New Mexico Territory worth his while. While his father and uncle tried their hand at prospecting and silver mining, was he still raising cattle for profit? In one way or another, he was still in the cattle business. A short article in a March, 1883 edition of *The Black Range* newspaper reports:

> Major Fountain and his militia have done good work in breaking up the gang of rustlers who have for so long a time engaged in robbing the stockmen of southern New Mexico. John Watts, Bice Bush and John Shannon

were shot and killed at Lake Valley while attempting to escape from the militia, while Nat Irvin and Mr. Gatz of Lake Valley, and John Colviller and five others of Kingston are in jail with Kinney at Las Cruces, and Burk, Brohman and several others are hiding in the mountains to escape arrest. Major Fountain deserves a tribute of praise from the territory more substantial than thanks for the efficient manner in which he discharged this arduous duty. [31]

My great grandfather Nat Irvin was a rustler? I knew this was a very lawless time in southern New Mexico, but the possibility that Nat Irvin was an outlaw just wasn't credible! Why would a young cowboy who was probably making good money and had a wife and two infant children turn to rustling cattle? Who was this Major Fountain that arrested him? And who was behind all this rustling?

None other than the notorious John Kinney was the head of this gang of rustlers. He was a big-time rustler in New Mexico who ran a very large and lucrative operation. One account of his rustling activities states:

His operations ranged from Socorro, New Mexico Territory, south to the Mexican state of Chihuahua, and from El Paso west toward Silver City and down into Sonora, Mexico. While other rustlers worked closely with cooperative butchers to quickly eliminate evidence of their crimes, Kinney was savvy and systematic enough to eliminate the middleman whenever he could. His ranch just south of Rincon, New Mexico Territory, locally dubbed "Kinneyville," included a slaughterhouse and dressing station. This gave Kinney the flexibility to ship either beeves or choice cuts by rail to wherever he could find buyers. With no middleman taking a cut of his profits, Kinney made the most of an operation that reportedly stole thousands of horses and cattle from honest ranchers. Eventually, people began to talk, and the press took notice. The Santa Fe *New Mexican* took to calling Kinney "King of the Rustlers.[32]

The article mentions that Kinney used threats and violence to intimidate lawmen who might try to curtail his activities. He apparently depended on some local ranchers in Lake Valley to help with his 'round-ups'. He may have coerced Nat into either working for him or else become a victim of his rustling—or worse. Or, maybe Nat was just in the wrong place at the wrong time when Major Fountain's local militia came charging into Lake Valley, intent on rounding up as many outlaws as possible. Historians of this period have reported that Fountain's militia, as well as others, were sometimes a bit too hasty   in   rounding   up   suspected   criminals.

Man standing is reputedly John Kinney

Major Albert Fountain

Whatever the case, rustling had become so rampant in this area that something had to be done. The article continues:

> As 1883 opened, reported thefts of livestock skyrocketed. The *New Mexican* claimed Kinney's men rustled an estimated 10,000 head in January alone. The number was doubtlessly exaggerated. When later arrested, Kinney henchman Margarito Sierra confessed to knowledge of 17 separate thefts of 171 horses, cattle and oxen over six months. At that rate Kinney's men would have had to carry out 1,000 thefts in January to meet the *New Mexican*'s estimate. No matter how

dubious the figures, however, other reports indicated Kinney's wife and brother were banking huge sums for him in El Paso.

Anger and frustration over mounting thefts of livestock convinced Territorial Governor Lionel A. Sheldon it was time to eradicate Kinney's operation. Short of a presidential finding of insurrection, the U.S. Army was forbidden by the 1878 *Posse Comitatus* Law from taking out such criminals. Fortunately, Sheldon had another force at hand: New Mexico's volunteer militia. On February 12, 1883, he ordered the militia's commander, Major Albert Jennings Fountain, to take the field and treat the rustlers as public enemies.[33]

Major Fountain and his posse eventually captured or killed most of Kinney's gang. The record is clear on what happened to John Kinney and some of his gang, following their arrest. A local newspaper reported:

> Major Fountain of Dona Ana county and Mason J. Bowman, sheriff of Lincoln county, have received appointments authorizing to convey to the Kansas penitentiary at Leavenworth, the lately convicted criminals mentioned as follows:
> From Dona Ana county: John Kinney, the rustler, for cattle stealing, five years; Anastacia Rivera, one of the Kinney gang, horse stealing, five years; Juan Bendal, another of the Kinney gang, cattle stealing, five years.[34]

But, even though there's a detailed listing of other Kinney's gang members and their sentences, I found no mention whatsoever of Nat Irvin being convicted or sentenced. Nor was there any mention of his trial in any Las Cruces newspaper from that time period. However, there was a brief article in the May 5, 1883 *Rio Grande Republican* (a Las Cruces newspaper) listing the names of 'those who arrived to stay at the Montezuma hotel today'. The list included N. H. Irvin of Lake Valley. The Montezuma was one of Las Cruces' finest hotels. Although it's very unlikely that Nat Irvin was convicted of rustling, he may have spent a few days or weeks in in town awaiting trial.

Maybe pre-trial investigations demonstrated that he was innocent. It's quite likely that he had neighbors and family vouch for him, and with no clear evidence against him, the case never even went to trial. My great grandmother Levina never mentioned that her husband had been convicted of rustling. Of course, she never mentioned his arrest, either, not to me, anyway.

Major Fountain and his militia continued in their quest to round up cattle rustlers in southern New Mexico and had numerous successes. But the man whose efforts led to Nat Irvin's arrest eventually succumbed to a fate that might well have been the consequence of arresting the wrong man for rustling. In the process of pursuing suspected rustlers, Fountain had arrested a cowboy, Oliver Lee, who happened to be a friend of Fountain's longtime political foe, Albert Hall. While traveling to court in 1896 to prosecute the case, Fountain was murdered and his young son disappeared. Oliver Lee was a key suspect and was eventually arrested for Fountain's murder. Lee was defended by Albert Hall in a famous trial that took place in Hillsboro three years after Fountain was found murdered. In a trial that only lasted eight minutes, Lee was acquitted. Fountain's murderer remains a mystery to this day. There is a fascinating account of this convoluted tale on *True West* magazine's website.[35]

I can't help but wonder just what the Irvin family must have thought when Major Fountain's murder was widely reported years after young Nat's arrest. I doubt there were many tears shed.

I can't be sure of the final disposition of Nat Irvin's arrest but it was quite clear that the Irvins left New Mexico later in 1883 or sometime early in 1884. A May, 1884 Las Cruces newspaper carried this notice:

NOTICE. U. S. Land Office, Las Cruces, N.M. May 17, 1884. Complaint having been entered at this office by Edward Snyder against Powhatan B. Irvin for abandoning his Homestead Entry No. 338, dated Dec. 26th, 1882, upon the n e 1/4 n w 1/4 and n 1/2 n e 1/4 section 34, township 17 s, range 7 w, in Dona Ana county, New Mexico, with a view to the cancellation of said entry; the said parties are hereby summoned to appear at this office on the 18th day of June, 1884, at 10 o'clock a. m. to respond and furnish testimony concerning said, alleged abandonment.[36]

The Irvin's had pulled up stakes and Mr. Snyder was looking to take over the property. As it turned out, he probably shouldn't have bothered. Lake Valley's days as a place to make your fortune were numbered.

Although I don't' know the full story about why Irvins left Lake Valley when they did, it's likely that Nat's wife Levina had experienced quite enough excitement. She may have laid down the law. I can almost hear her saying something like, "Nat, I'm not going to have another child and raise my family in a place where if the Apaches don't kill you, you get arrested for rustling cattle. We are leaving this godforsaken valley and going back to Texas!" It's also possible that Nat's father and uncle had made a handsome profit selling off their mining claims and were ready to move on.

Powhatan and his brother, Absalom, evidently parted ways at this time. There are no records suggesting that Absalom's family returned to Texas. Maybe they stayed on in the Lake Valley area for a few years before leaving, but it's more likely they would have left at about the same time as Powhatan and Nat Irvin's families. According to the 1900 US Census, Absalom and his wife Sarah and three of their youngest children (now in their early to mid-twenties) had moved to Graham County, Arizona. Absalom died in Cochise, Arizona in 1916. Sarah had predeceased him in 1908.

It's just as well that the Irvins left Lake Valley when they did. The little mining town continued to fall on hard times. Congress passed the Gold Standard Act in 1900. Up until this time, U.S. currency was based on both gold and silver. This act led to the collapse of the price of silver. Two years later most of the town burned. Eventually Lake Valley, former boom town and stage stop, with 12 saloons, three churches, two newspapers, a school, stores, hotels, stamp mills and smelters, gave up. The post office closed in 1954 and the last resident left town in 1994.[37]

Lake Valley today is a ghost town, maintained and protected by the Bureau of Land Management. The area is still somewhat popular to tourists, especially those interested in old mining towns. When I visited the site, it was impossible for me to imagine that this was once a town of thousands. It was a desolate and remote area of rolling hills with few remaining signs of previous habitation. There is no longer a lake nor even a recognizable lake bed. The few mines that I saw were boarded up and posted with warnings. Here and there were a few ramshackle buildings, crumbling and unfit for habitation. There is, however, a restored one room school house which tourists can visit. It houses an interesting collection of artifacts and photos from the town's boom period, along with newspapers from that time.

Lake Valley is now just a seldom visited ghost-town. April, 2018

Before leaving the area, I spotted a solitary abandoned and rusty automobile. It looked very much like the first car that I had owned back in 1949 when I was finally old enough to drive. I inquired later and found out that, sure enough, it was the same exact model, a 1935 Plymouth. What are the odds!

9. Return to Texas

Nat and Levina, along with their young children Tom and Daisy, and Nat's parents, Powhatan and Mary, probably headed back toward Llano, that part of Texas from which they'd originally left. Levina's family were all in that area. However, that's not where they settled. They ended up, instead, purchasing land near a recently settled town named Arden, some 120 miles northwest of Llano. Tax records and newspaper articles establish that they had settled in this area by early 1884. Census records reveal that Nathanial and Levina Irvin's third child, a daughter they named Willia, was born in Arden, Irion County, Texas on September 2, 1885.

Arden was located on Rocky Creek, a tributary of the Concho River, in what was then Tom Green County. The area was rich with history but was not yet heavily populated, even though the Butterfield Overland Stage carried travelers through this area as early as the 1850's. Most were headed for the California goldfields or were scouting out territory for rail lines, but few settled in the Concho River area at that time, partly because there were few towns and little protection from the Indians. The Apache leader, Victorio, the very same chief who led the attack in Lake Valley ranches described earlier by Sarah Gibson, was one of the major obstacles settlers faced in the late 1870's. His band of some 300 western Apache, Mescalero, and Chiricahua harassed and plundered the early ranchers in that area until driven out of the area by the 10th Cavalry from Fort Concho.[38] The railroad did not reach the nearest large town, San Angelo, until 1888.[39]

One of the earliest settlers of this area was R. F. Tankersley. While he was on a scouting expedition from Brown County, Texas in 1858, he visited the Concho River country that would later become Tom Green County in 1874 and later yet, be divided off as Irion County. He described flowers of all kinds, tall green grass, pecan trees growing along the river banks and many tributaries feeding into the river. Buffalo roamed the hills along with deer, antelope, coyotes, wolves, badgers, bears, panthers and wild turkeys. It was the most ideal ranch country he'd ever seen and a place where he'd like to live. He brought his family in ox-drawn wagons along with his cattle herd to this place in 1864, just twenty years before the Irvin's arrived.[40]

Irion County played an important role in Texas history and the Irvins were a part of that history. Following is an excerpt from a description of Irion County during those early years:

> The county embraces 1,051 square miles of rolling prairie, grass, mesquite, and, in some sections, exposed rock. From 1858 to 1861 coaches of the San Antonio-San Diego Mail and the Butterfield Overland Mail crossed the region but no settlements were established in what is now Irion County until the late 1870s, after the Indian threat had been eliminated. Cattle and sheep thrived on the well-watered range. John Arden brought the first flock of sheep from California in 1876, and in 1880 the 7D Ranch was established by Billy Childress with longhorn cattle from Atascosa County.
>
> Beginning in the 1880s a few pioneer farmers built small irrigation systems, and several ranchmen planted hay and grain. Underground water resources were tapped with windmill-driven pumps; the first cotton crop was planted in 1886 by W. H. White. In 1889 the Texas legislature formed Irion County from Tom Green County, and that same year the county was organized with Sherwood as county seat.[41]

Geographically, the altitude of this area ranges from two thousand to twenty-eight hundred feet; the average rainfall is twenty inches and the average annual temperature is sixty-five degrees. The terrain is hills and rolling plains, broken by big draws, which are in turn tributaries of the Concho River system. The county was once described as having more springs and running streams than any other county of its size in Texas[42].

It must have seemed a wonderful place to settle and to build their new ranch. But Cattle ranching was beginning to change by the time the Irvin's returned to Texas. In the old days of free range, when the cattle were mostly longhorn, the cattle roamed freely where the grazing was best, usually adjacent to rivers or streams. Their owner rode out among the cattle to keep track of where they were and how many there were. When it was time to round up the herd and brand the yearlings, neighbors pitched in and helped one another. Cattle with brands from other owners were separated out and returned to his herd. Sick cattle were treated or put down. Older cattle were selected for marketing, which often involved long cattle drives to locations with buyers and shipping locations, usually the closest rail head.

By the 1880's, the ranching population had increased considerably and unowned grazing land had become less abundant. Most of the land in Tom Green County was pretty well bought up in 1880.[43] With the introduction of barbed wire in the mid-1870's, more and more ranchers were beginning to fence their property. If there was no running water on the property, wells were drilled and windmills pumped water into surface tanks or cavities where the cattle could water. Also, at this time, some ranchers in the area were improving their stock by cross-breeding longhorn with shorthorn cattle, and then gradually changing to Herefords. Importantly, a railhead and main shipping point was established in the closest large town of San Angelo, only a one-to-two-day cattle drive from Arden.

I was able to locate the Irvin's ranch by using an old 1889 Irion County plat map and tax records posted online at the Texas General Land Office. Once I'd pinpointed their sections on the plat map, I could compare this to a geographic map that I'd sized to match it. I could then compare this to a satellite image to get some idea of topography, rivers and vegetation. Their ranch was located just west of Arden, and originally consisted of two contiguous 160-acre homestead plots bordering the middle branch of the Concho River. This was an ideal location, providing a reliable source of water, good pasture, and only a mile or so out of the town of Arden.

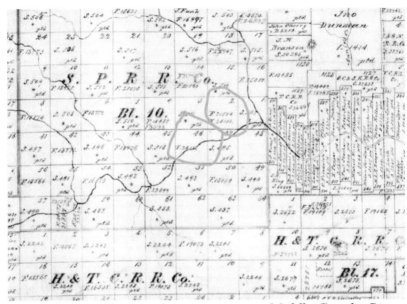

1889 Plat map showing Irvin sections on Middle Concho River.
They later purchased several more sections contiguous to these.

With the kind help of a local rancher, Mike Hamilton, I visited this site in April of 2018 while researching material for this history. The total population hadn't really changed much since the years when the Irvins lived there. The entire population of Irion County today is only 1599, according to the 2010 U.S. Census. But now, most of the population is in Mertzon. As for Arden, that same census records a population of just one person. Most of Irion County's population today are still cattle ranchers but considerable income, and in many cases, most of their income, is generated by gas and oil royalties.

Mike, a third-generation Irion County rancher himself, most generously put me up at his ranch home north of Mertzon, the county seat of Irion, during part of my stay in that area. His home was ideally located near the junction of the small road to Arden with the main road from Mertzon to San Angelo. Mike introduced me to a good percentage of that area's townsfolk the day we attended the Irion County annual ranch rodeo and barbecue in Mertzon. I couldn't have picked a better time to visit.

Mile Hamilton and his wife, Darlene, with grandson outside their home near Mertzon, Texas. (April, 2018)

The tiny town of Arden near the Irvin ranch had a most interesting history, according to an account put together by descendants of the first settlers:

> Arden, Texas was never a platted town or an official Town site, never more than a community center save for its post office in several different locations, never a large Commercial Business area, having at best no more than two stores at any one time, a school house in several different locations, a polling place, yet in its 50-year service it met the demands of a shifting population and played an important part in the lives of countless people and its history is a definite part of the history of two counties - Tom Green and Irion. Although all of its former institutions are abandoned save that of a polling place to preserve Precinct lines and governments, many of its former residents look backward with Nostalgia and happy memories to the years when they lived in the Arden area. Descendants of former residents join with those who once lived there, and who are still mobile, return each Labor Day in September in a pilgrimage to The Grove on the banks of Rocky Creek to picnic, meet old friends, make new ones, visit the cemetery, meet new arrivals in the 6th and 7th

generations, and share reminiscences both happy and sad, of old Arden.

In the totality of time its years of organized existence as a community cover only a small part of time, yet it was once a vital link in the state, national and transcontinental events, chiefly in the area of exploration and transportation. Roughly, its area and sphere of influence covered the Northeast quarter of present Irion County but prior to actual settlement was a part of Bexar territory, then Tom Green County, and finally an active part of Irion county. In area it was some 20 x 20 mi in scope, was almost completely bisected by Rocky Creek from Southwest to Southeast, and its extreme Southern limits contain some 20 mi of the meandering course of middle Concho River.

It's geography and archaeology are as old as the hills and artifacts and other signs are more testimony to the presence of Indians at one time. Such local history as is available, first from the Spaniards, and later from United States and Texas history, tell us that the area was crossed by many Explorations, both Commercial and Military. Although evidence is not conclusive, the middle Concho River could be the Lost River of the Coronado Expedition, and there was positive proof that the area was crossed by Spanish explorations as early as that of Mendoza in 1654. The Goodnight Loving Cattle Trail ran through the area at a point less than 1 mile from the northeast corner of the county, followed the Southward course of east Rocky Creek to its confluence with Middle Country River, and then turned Westward along that stream toward Horsehead Crossing on the Pecos River. This Trail followed almost exactly the route established by the Butterfield Overland mail route from Fort Chadbourne to the Pecos River. The Emigrant Trail to California as well as the northern route of the San Antonio - San Diego Mail Route follow the course of the middle Concho River and Traverse the area from east to west. The only significant battle with Indians, that of the battle of Dove Creek occurred in 1865 and was staged only a few miles south of the area. Countless graves and unmarked headstones along the course of middle Concho

98

River are mute testimony to those who gave their lives to push civilization Westward.

The first permanent settler of note and the one to give his name to the area was one John Arden who moved extensive herds of sheep estimated at 20,000 head, into the area in 1876, making his headquarters on east Rocky Creek on the land now owned by Bill Tullos. His holdings were along this creek and although sheep men met with disfavor by cattleman his right to free grazing was not challenged. Following his tragic death his widow operated these holdings for a time adding some land, but later leased out to others and eventually sold her interest. Ranching was, and still continues to be, the chief occupation and source of income of the area.[44]

The town of Arden had a post office by 1890 as well as one of the first rural schools in the county. Roads in the county were primitive, often just the tracks left by horse and buggy or horse drawn wagons on regularly traveled routes. Directions were usually given it terms of miles between well-known ranches or landmarks and were sometimes marked by signs or stone monuments. Road travel in those times was as much as 30 miles a day with a good team of horses drawing a hack or buggy. Consequently, the largest town and most important town in that vicinity, San Angelo, could be reached easily in a day's time.

Author at Texas Historical Commission's sign at Arden, Texas, April 2018.

View toward Irvin ranch site near Arden, Texas (April 2018)

Because San Angelo was the only large town in the area, and the main shipping center for cattle, the Irvins made numerous visits there while living in Irion County. Whereas Arden was a settlement, San Angelo was a real town. Following is a description of San Angelo based on the handbook of the Texas State Historical Society and on *Early San Angelo*, by Virginia Noelke.[45]

The town of San Angelo began in the late 1860s across the North Concho River from Fort Concho, which had been established in 1867. Bart DeWitt, a settler from San Antonio, bought 320 acres across the river from Fort Concho and began to build a town. He named it in honor of his wife, who had died in San Antonio. Her name was Carolina Angela de la Garza. Typical of early frontier town, San Angelo was characterized by saloons, prostitution, and gambling. Contributing to the early growth of San Angelo were Fort Concho, an ample supply of water, ranching, agriculture and the coming of the railroads. The fort brought a steady flow of money from the soldiers' pay, which in turn brought traders, merchants, and others who catered to the needs of the soldiers. The first legitimate business, a combination general store and saloon, was opened by William S. Veck. San Angelo was located at the juncture of the North, South, and Middle Concho rivers and was surrounded by farms on the east and ranches on the west. The town's economy, therefore, became more diversified than that of many other frontier settlements.

During the cattle boom of the 1870's, thousands of longhorn cattle were watered and fed along the Concho rivers on their way to market. Richard F. Tankersley had introduced cattle ranching on the South Concho as early as 1864. John Arden and Joseph Tweedy introduced sheep ranching in 1877. Fort Concho and several other forts further south, Fort Stockton and Fort McKavett, fueled the ranching boom by providing a major market for cattle and sheep. Prior to the forts being established, cattle had been driven as far as California to be marketed.

And, Fort Concho's military hospital was the only hospital in the area until the first civilian hospital was established in San Angelo in 1910.[46]

San Angelo became the county seat as the result of a widespread flood in 1882, which destroyed the smaller town of Ben Ficklin, the original county seat, just a few miles downriver. There's an interesting story behind this.

The town of Ben Ficklin was named after the Virginia gentlemen who helped establish and run the Pony Express in the 1850s in the Concho River area. After the Civil War, he obtained a contract to deliver mail between San Angelo and El Paso. In 1869 he bought land three miles from Fort Concho and a stablished a stage stand at a crossing of the South Concho River, which later became the town of Ben Ficklin.

The town soon became a rival to San Angelo for the political and financial control of Tom Green County. Because it was a transportation hub in the era of stage travel, solid citizens like ranchers, professional people, and merchants, moved there. It was a proper and safe place to live, compared to San Angelo, which was a 'military' town. Many of the establishments in San Angelo provided services to the soldiers stationed at Fort Concho, including the usual diversions such as saloons, card houses and bordellos. In 1875, there was an election to determine which town would become the county seat of Tom Green County. Even though more people lived in San Angelo than in Ben Ficklin, election shenanigans helped the smaller town win.

But they hadn't counted on Mother Nature. Floods were a fact of life in the Concho Valley. In an ironic twist, the good people of Ben Ficklin were devastated by an epic flood in 1882, while the rougher crowd in San Angelo escaped major damage. The rain-swollen South Concho River swept downstream at a pace that swept up people, livestock, and houses. The 1882 flood marked the end of Ben Ficklin as a rival to San Angelo. Following the devastation, the 'respectable' citizens of Ben Ficklin moved to San Angelo, which then became a boomtown and the county seat. The 1880 census showed the population had climbed to over 3,600.

San Angelo became a major shipping center with the coming of the Santa Fe Railroad in 1888. Communication with the outside world was provided by the telegraph and telephone. The telegraph came with the establishment of Fort Concho. The San Angelo Telephone Company was established in 1899. The town has been served by the news media since its beginning as the town "over the river." James Kibee was editor of the *Concho Times* from 1880 to 1884. The first hospital was a post hospital constructed at Fort Concho in the 1870s.

Fort Concho, whose earlier presence had fostered much of the growth of San Angelo, was closed within a decade of the defeat of raiding Apaches in that part of Texas. The last federal troops left and the flag lowered when the fort closed on June 20th, 1889.[47]

The Concho valley was also the southern end of the Buffalo range, and this had attracted large numbers of buffalo hunters, who shipped hundreds of thousands of Buffalo hides by wagon from the San Angelo area. This activity, along with the various cavalry regiments at Fort Concho led to the decline and migration of Indians from this part of Texas.[48]

A less detailed but more exuberant description of the area, and San Angelo in particular, appeared on the front page of their local newspaper in September, 1888. It boasted:

Reasons Why Tom Green County is destined to be the banner county of the state and San Angelo one of the foremost cities in Texas: Tom Green County's altitude is 2000 feet above the level of the sea. The healthfulness of her climate challenges comparison with that of any in the United States. The statistical report of the army and navy shows the sick list at Fort Concho to be considerably smaller than that of any other post in the Union. She has 2000 miles of waterfronts, a large area already under successful irrigation, which is capable of being increased at comparatively small cost to an enormous extent.

The yield of small grain from her valleys challenges comparison both for quality and quantity with any in the world.

Existing orchards testify of the superior quality of her soil as a fruit producing country. In addition to the usual varieties of fruit raised in other parts of this state, experiments have proved that her almond and olive culture will in the near future prove a source of great revenue.

The late Dallas Fair demonstrated to the satisfaction of all visitors the superiority of her forage plants.

The fact that the price of her stock cattle averages from $1 to $3 more per head than many other sections of the state demonstrates the quality of these denizens of her prairies.

The receipt of 2,000,000 pounds of wool at San Angelo alone, during the season of 1887, will convey some idea of the importance of sheep husbandry in Tom Green County.

Her population, cosmopolitan in character, have demonstrated their enterprise and public spirit by the manner in which San Angelo, the county seat, with her numerous public improvements, consisting of waterworks, ice factories, schools, bridges, etc., were built up.[49]

10. Ranching in Irion County, Texas

So, no matter what version of the area you choose to believe, the Irvin clan chose this area to settle down and raise a family. Here was a land which seemed to provide everything a settler might wish for in west Texas at this time in our Nation's history. But those times were not always easy. There was a drought in 1886 that was described as one of the driest and worst in the history of that area[50]. If their ranches had not bordered the Middle Concho River, the Irvins might have needed to move on, as many others in the area did. The winters were also quite severe at this time.

The environmental hardships faced by pioneers in the county at this time were primarily the occasional droughts and floods, as well as wild fires. Winters could be cold but heavy snowfalls were rare, given the low average rainfall and warmer temperatures of this part of Texas. Flooding was the major cause of hardships in the Concho River area and remains so to this day. But wildfires always remain a threat.

Nathanial and Levina's family continued to expand. Most of their ten children were born in this part of Irion county. Their birth records list their birthplace as San Angelo. San Angelo is the nearest large town, about 15 miles due east of Arden, and had the only hospital in the area. Whether the children were born at the hospital or at their home, all births from that part of the county were recorded in San Angelo. That was evidently the case back in New Mexico Territory, too, because both Tom and Daisy Irvin had been listed as born in Silver City, the closest large town to Lake Valley. However, it's likely that most ranch births in those times were home births, with family or neighbors nearby who could help out.

Following the birth of their second daughter, Willia, Nathanial and Levina Irvin had four more daughters while at their ranch in Irion County, Texas. Mayme was born in 1886, followed by Elsie in April, 1889, Evelyn in 1890, and Agnes (or Agatha), in 1892.

Their children were initially either home schooled or may have attended a small school established in private homes during this time. Records are hard to come by, but Irion County established a school district in 1892, which included two schools at the county seat of Sherwood, a small town about twelve miles south of Arden, and one school in Arden. The school population for Irion County at this time was estimated at 200.

There was a one room school house in Irion City, a town that is no longer listed on any records or maps. The town was located on the northeast side of the Middle Concho river several miles upstream from what is now Arden road. This would have been just a few miles from the Irvin ranch, close enough for the Irvin's children to attend easily during their stay in that area. The Irion County Brand Registry from those years noted that PB Irvin, whose cattle brand was something that looks like 7ZL, listed his residence as Irion City. It took me a while to figure out where Irion City was located because there is no record of the town today. I assumed that Irion City and Arden would have been very close to each other, but couldn't be sure until Joyce Gray, the de facto historian of Irion County, provided the following information, "Irion City and Arden are very close together, about 10 to 12 miles apart. Irion City was a wild and wooly place that frequently had to have a Ranger come by. All that remains of that city is 2 foundations which have been used by the oilfield crews for years."

Following is a description of the Irion City school, as submitted by Madina Clark, who was a student at the school:

Irion City, once a thriving community of ranch and farm people, was located about 18 miles northwest of Mertzon near the Middle Concho river. The school house was probably built in the latter years of 1800, a one room frame building, painted white. It was heated by a wood-burning cast-iron, box type heater. The first ones to reach school in the mornings usually started the fire. A windmill nearby furnished water which was brought in by buckets. There were outdoor "Johns," his and hers. The teacher and students did the janitorial work. Grades one through ten were taught. Recess, noon, etc. were announced by a little hand bell that set on the teacher's desk. Baseball, marbles, hide and seek, pop the whip were some of the favorite games.

Most of the teachers were single and lived in one of the homes near the school building. The J.T. Burns residence was home for several of them. Children came by foot, buggy or horseback. Two boys, who lived nine miles up the Concho river, walked to school each fall until Christmas and were usually the first ones there. During the Christmas holidays their daddy, Mr. Ford, set up a tent on the school ground for them to live in during the winter months. They went home on weekends.

Teachers' salaries ranged from $25.00 to $75.00 per month. In 1891 and '92 the amount of money apportioned to the school was around $175.00 for four and a half or five months school term...

Irion City School was discontinued in 1921 or 1922.[51]

What was Levina Irvin doing at this time, between child births and helping her older children with their lessons? The life of the pioneer women of this area has been described as follows:

Life for the pioneer woman was never easy but it was a life of gratification, bare of all selfishness and pettiness. Her family was usually large and her daily chores time consuming. Cooking in quantity with crude facilities and a limited supply of food, making all the clothes for her family and keeping her house were routine but keeping her family's clothing clean was the major project.

Before people began to dig wells, the family washing had to be done at the creek. The clothing was first wet in the stream, then placed on a log from which the bark had been removed and beaten with a club. It was then rinsed in the creek and spread on the grass or bushes to dry. Later when larger utensils became available, the clothing was boiled. Often the roots of the sacahuiste or other desert plants were dug, peeled and placed in the boiling water; they produced a suds-like lather. Handloads of mesquite leaves were added when they were available as they were thought to whiten and brighten the wash. The sudsy lather of the desert plants was also considered to be very beneficial for washing the hair.

On house-cleaning day, all beds, bedding and unused clothing were hung out of doors to 'sun' and 'air'. Walls were swept down and floors scoured or thoroughly cleaned.

The early homemaker used the bark and roots of trees for coloring cloth and clothing. The bark of the pecan and walnut produced tones from tan to brown; the roots of the chaparral bush produced a bright yellow and those of the algarot, an orange tone. The fruit of the mulberry made a bluish purple.

Tallow candles lighted the early homes until they were replaced by kerosene lamps.

Wood was the only fuel used throughout the area for many years.

The use of the sewing machine became common in the late 1880's. Prior to that time, all of the clothing for the family was made by hand.[52]

Nat and his father PB were still supporting their families primarily by raising cattle and they were doing pretty well at it. They even made the news in the capitol city of Austin, over two hundred miles southeast of their ranch. That city's newspaper quoted the following short notice from the *San Angelo Standard*, "P.B. Irvine [sic], one of Tom Green's main and most solid cattlemen on Main Concho, was in the market this week and reported cows and grass in good shape. He sold 80 head of twos to Tol Rutledge at $11. He thinks there is a bright future in store for the cowman."[53]

Prices for cattle did vary, however. A few years later, prices had dropped, according to that same newspaper. "Cattle are booming. Hold your steer for stiff prices. P B Irvin of Middle Concho has refused $8 for his steer yearlings."[54]

To put these dollar amounts in context, here are the valuations set by Irion's Board of Equalization in 1890, "Cattle, first class (three years or older), $10; second class, $7.50; and third class (stock cattle), $6." At the same time, saddle and work horses were valued at $20, and sheep from $1.50 to $3, depending on breed. Land holdings were valued at anywhere from $1.25 to $20 per acre, depending on such factors as irrigation, distance from water, whether it was enclosed, etc...

Rocky Creek branch of the Middle Concho River tributary, near Irvin's ranch, Irion County, TX

The earliest records that I've located for the Irvins in this area are the Tom Green County Tax records from 1884. These were initially brought to my attention by Jessica Tharp, a student researcher at Angelo State University in San Angelo. At my request, she had graciously searched for Irvin in their microfilm archives. These records show that in 1884 P.B. Irvin & son's cattle herd numbered five hundred, valued at $12.50 a head, an exceptional value, and twelve horses and mules valued at $40 a head. At this time, they owned no goats, sheep or hogs. Their ranch land consisted of three 640-acre sections, one valued at $1.50 per acre and the other two valued at $1.00 per acre, all purchased from the Southern Pacific Rail Road (SPRR). The parcel that fronted the river was taxed at the higher rate. Under the category of Carriages, Buggies and Wagons Etc., they owned two, valued at $200. Their miscellaneous property was valued at $100 and they declared $1800 cash on hand. Their total valuation at this time, if you do the math, was $11,070. It's unlikely that they made this much money from livestock, alone, in Lake Valley. They must have also made money from their silver mine claims.

The Irvins weren't wealthy--but by the standards of those times, they were well off. Remember that in those times, settlers raised most of their own food, sewed their own clothes, built their own homes, and weren't paying for utilities like water, electricity and gas, waste disposal, telephones, and the like. They used water from wells or rivers and streams, illuminated their home by candle and kerosene lantern, cooked with wood fire, buried or recycled their waste, and communicated face to face. Cash was mostly used to purchase dry goods such as cloth, shoes, sugar, flour, salt, pepper and cookware, as well as tack, farm implements, occasionally seed and feed, and ammunition for hunting. Along with farming, most ranchers hunted, fished or raised their own meat, and did their own butchering and preserving by smoking, drying or salting.

Living like this, $1800 cash on hand was a sizeable nest egg.

Later tax records from Tom Green County all show that the size of the Irvin ranch continued to grow. In 1885, they owned five sections of land, all purchased from the Southern Pacific Railroad. Their money on hand decreased to $500, their miscellaneous property increased to$1150, their horses and mules decreased to eight and their cattle herd decreased to 400. Their additional land was probably financed by cattle sales, and their miscellaneous machinery purchased with cash on hand. By this time, few ranchers reported much if any cash on hand, knowing that it would be taxed.

According to the 1886 tax records, they expanded their operations to include hogs. Their land holdings remained the same but they now owned 15 hogs, along with their 400 cattle, and their miscellaneous property had increased to from $1150 to $1550. They declared no cash on hand. Maybe none on hand, but perhaps stuffed in an old boot somewhere?

The next tax records that I located were those of Irion County, 1889, the first tax year for this brand-new county that had just been carved out of the much larger Tom Green County. That year, PB Irvin & Son had five sections of land, 6 horses and mules, 2 conveyances (buggies, carriages or wagons), 800 cattle, 1025 sheep, 30 hogs and $1500 in miscellaneous property, with a total valuation of $10,441. Theirs was now a very sizeable ranch and well-stocked. They claimed no 'money on hand', nor did most of the others listed on that page. Their total evaluation had dropped some, even though their herd was larger, because cattle prices had decreased. The Irvin cattle at this time were only valued at about $2.63 per head! Possibly because of decreasing cattle prices, the Irvins had made the decision to try their hand at raising sheep, as well as doubling their number of hogs.

PB Irvin was now 54years old and his son NH 'Nat' Irvin was 30. Nat's son, Tom, was almost 10, certainly old enough in those times to be of some help with the ranch chores. The Irvin's had come a long way from their simple start in Bee County back in 1861. At that time, NH was just a two-year-old and PB's only holdings were a string of seven horses and a small herd of just 25 cattle, with no land ownership listed.

As their holdings grew, Nat and Levina's family also continued to expand. After six daughters in a row, Nat and Levina finally had another son. Powhatan Bowen (always referred to as 'PB', Jr.) was born on February 9, 1894. He was the last of the Irvin children to be born in Irion County, Texas.

Author's microfilm work station in Dr. Ralph Chase West Texas Collection room of Houston Harte University Center, Angelo State University

So, what else were the Irvins doing in Irion County besides ranching successfully and having children, equally successfully? My only sources of information were occasional articles from *The San Angelo Daily Standard*, the local regional paper at that time. The newspapers are not yet available online but microfilm copies were made available to me at the Chase West Texas Collection, located in the Huston Harte University Center on the campus of Angelo State University. Those news articles provide a glimmer of the Irvin activities and the role they played in the development of this pioneer settlement. Following is a chronological listing of news and excerpts from that newspaper which referred to the Irvins during their stay in that area. (This was a very small newspaper at the time, often only four pages, so page numbers are not provided.):

May 17, 1884. This was the earliest article about the Irvins and confirms their earliest year in Tom Green County. PB Irvin is listed among those appointed to help lay out some of the first county roads. "Commissioner's Court meets; juries appointed to lay out county roads. J. Miles, J D Etheridge, P B Irvin, P C Lee and C B Metcalfe were appointed a jury of view to lay out a first-class road from San Angelo to the west side of Tom Green county, in the direction of Ft. Stockton, the county seat of Pecos county." At the same time, two other juries of view were appointed to lay out similar roads leading north and leading south from San Angelo. Clearly there was a need for this because San Angelo was becoming the hub of local marketing.

October 4, 1884. Irvins are included in a list of cattlemen in Tom Green county. The relatively short list includes Irvin, P.B. & son. Nat and his father were continuing their partnership in cattle ranching which began long before their move to and from New Mexico Territory. This is not surprising because Nat was an only child and was apparently very close to his parents. There is no mention of A. D. Irvin, who evidently migrated to Arizona from New Mexico Territory when PB and NH Irvin and their families migrated back to Texas.

Sept 5, 1885. Wealthy individuals and corporations of Tom Green county; names, property values: "The following names and figures are taken from the Assessor's rolls from the year 1885, and lists both individuals and corporations that pay taxes in the county rendered at from $5000 and upwards." The list of approximately 100 individuals and corporations includes such notables as Mrs. Katie Arden, one of the wealthiest individuals, at $34,320. Most individuals ranged from $5000.-$15,000, whereas a few corporations (usually cattle companies) exceed $100,000. Irvin, P.B. & son were listed at $9830, near the middle of 'wealthy individuals'. One of the highest listed corporations at $110,000 was the Berendo Stock Company.

Their wealth, relative to other individuals in the same area, makes me believe that PB Irvin and his son, Nat, must have done quite well in New Mexico Territory. What I haven't been able to determine is if they built this wealth by selling cattle or by selling mining claims. Given the amount of money that eastern investors were throwing at the mining ventures in Lake Valley at that time, I suspect that the Irvin's achieved most of their earnings from the latter.

June 19, 1886. Business transacted by commissioners' court: "Ordered that election place for voter precinct 17 be changed from J.D. Etheridge's ranch to P.B. Irvin's ranch on Main Concho river." PB Irvin was now entering into local politics and was apparently respected well enough to make his residence a gathering place for local voters. This article was followed by another on September 25 of that year, listing P.B. Irvin as presiding officer of voting precinct 17. Given the size of the voting population in the area at that time, this honorary sounding title most likely was bestowed on the owner of whatever ranch was named a voting place. But it must have looked good to PB to see his name thusly titled in print in the region's only newspaper--which had a rather wide readership.

February 5, 1887. Grand Jurors are listed. P.B. Irvin tops the list of 15 others listed at Grand Jury, followed by three lists of Petit Jurors for the 1st, 2nd and 3rd weeks of District Court, which included 36 names, all different, on each list. These lists, containing well over one hundred names, represent a good cross section of that area and include many of the earliest settlers. The Irvin patriarch apparently had a strong interest in civic affairs and was willing to dedicate his time and energy to serve his fellow citizens. At this time, his extended family included three very young granddaughters, Daisy, Willia (known as 'Willy') and Mayme. His grandson, Tom, now six years old, may have been starting his first year of school.

February 12, 1887 P.B. Irvin and N. H. Irvin stayed at the Nimitz Hotel in San Angelo. The Nimitz was the grandest hotel in San Angelo. There were many other, less expensive places to stay. It seems that PB Irvin and his son preferred to travel first class.

According to another article in same issue, PB Irvin was to be empaneled on the grand jury, an indication that he continued to remain active in civic affairs.

May 14, 1887. The Commissioner's Court Meeting, Road Construction and Improvements, Ordered that $100 be appropriated to improve the San Angelo and Camp Charlotte Road under supervision of W.F. Holt, with Nat Irvin from the west side of the Arden pasture to west bank of canyon 3 miles west of Johnson's Station, and Jim Snodgrass from there to Charlotte, as overseers.

August 20, 1887. PB Irvin and son again appear on the 'most wealthy' tax list. There had been a major economic recession and most individuals and corporations experienced a significant decrease from the Sept 86 'most wealthy' list. Mrs. Katie Arden's valuation, one of the wealthiest individuals listed, had dropped to $24,540. The microfilmed issue was difficult to read but it appeared that Irvin's valuation had dropped to $6990.

November 19, 1887. PB Irvin stays at the Nimitz Hotel again, in San Angelo. It's unlikely that the Grand Jury was still in session since February so this may have been a shopping trip or involved sales transactions.

February 18, 1888. "Commissioners Court holds February session. The report of W.F. Holt, supervisor of roads in commissioner precinct No. 4 was read and approved and the following overseers appointed: from the N line of prs no. 4 where the Knickerbocker road crosses on Main Concho River, to Knickerbocker, Virgil Ryan; thence to Sherwood, George Scott; from bank of Main Concho to Sherwood, Ed McDonald; from Main Concho road to Charlotte, Nat Irvin and Todd Rutledge; from the Lucas farm on Spring creek to the intersection with Dove Creek road, Jim Johnson." I'm not quite sure what a road 'overseer' does, but assume they kept an eye on road conditions and notified the supervisor if there were any problems, such as flood damage, major obstruction, etc. The roads had to be satisfactory for the travel modes of that time; horse or mule drawn wagon and horse drawn buggies.

April 28, 1888. The report of regular term of district court included the following, "Ordered by the court that J.B. Taylor, John H. Ryburn and P. B. Irvin be appointed jury commissioners. The following thirty-two bills were brought in by the grand jury during their session: one for robbery with assault; two keeping a disorderly house; one assault to murder; one theft of a mule; one passing as true a forged instrument; two theft of horse; three theft of cattle; one theft of property valued at $37; one aggravated assault; two selling diseased meat; three permitting gaming in house; one receiving stolen property; twelve other indictments. Nineteen of the above cases were transferred to County Court, being classified by the District Court as misdemeanors." So, PB Irvin not only served on grand juries, but also served as jury commissioner, a responsibility not granted lightly.

September 15, 1888. The Irvins are listed among 'heavy taxpayers' of Tom Green County. Under assessments of $5000 upwards, year ending Jan 1988, Irvin, PB and Son are listed at $8400. One of the wealthiest individuals, Mrs. Katie Arden, is listed at $23,380. Highest corporations, various cattle companies, are listed at just over $100,000, and the average individual at approximately $8000. This represents an increase for the Irvin's, even though one of the wealthiest taxpayers, Katie Arden declined again from the previous year.

March 9, 1889. An article on livestock and range notes states, "There were 55,330 horses shipped from San Antonio this year. J. R. Nasworthy sold 50 head of steer yearlings to M. B. Pulliam at $8. per head. P.B. Irvin has sold all his two-year-old steers, about 100 head, to M. B. Pulliam at $11." PB Irvin either drove a hard bargain or had exceptional steers, or both. He always seemed to get a better than average price.

March 16, 1889. Under Personal Items, "P.B. Irvin, a cowman of Rockey, was in the city yesterday." I don't suppose that every cowman who comes to San Angelo gets their name in the newspaper, so PB Irvin must have been a citizen of some note. This is the first time I've seen his ranch location listed as Rockey, but that was a local designation for his location on the middle Concho River just west of the town of Arden.

August 3, 1889. P.B. Irvin is appointed as a commissioner in Irion County. "Jos. Funk has resigned as commissioner of Irion County, and P.B. Irvin has been appointed in his stead." PB appeared to be quite involved now, becoming a commissioner of an entire county. Irion at this time was a brand-new county, carved out of the much larger Tom Green county just months previously on March 7, 1889.

August 31, 1889. Under Local News, "P.B. Irvin of Middle Concho, one of Irion County's sterling cowmen, made the STANDARD a pleasant visit Tuesday."

114

In case you ever wondered why cattle of that time and place were referred to as 'long horns', this same news column noted that "Bill Macnab brought in a big pair of beef horns this week from Dove Creek. They measured four feet four from tip to tip and twelve inches around the base." If you check the records, you'd find even larger horns were measured. According to Wikipedia, some of the very longest steer horns measured over one-hundred inches, tip to tip. If you are standing up close to a longhorn, especially with no fence between you, those horns are quite impressive.

February 22. 1890. P.B. Irvin is doing well enough to hold out for a higher price, according to this short note, "Cattle are booming. Hold your steers for stiff prices. P.B. Irvin of Middle Concho has refused $8 for his steer yearlings."

March 8, 1890. As it turns out, PB finally accepted the price he had turned down in February. This note was listed under Stock News, "Mr. Tankersley this week bought 400 steer yearlings from W. S. Veck, P. B. Irvin, Mark Tankersley and Cal and Jack Davis for $8 per head. These are all A 1 yearlings and he will pay $8 for a thousand more of the same class of cattle."

June 21, 1890. PB tried travel by train according to this note under Personal Items, "P.B. Irvin went south on the Santa Fe Sunday morning." This trip remains a mystery. Was this a business trip? A visit to relatives? The only rail line I can find that went south from the hub in San Angelo proceeded southwest, the first stop being Sherwood, the Irion County seat. However, Sherwood could just as easily be reached by horseback or horse drawn carriage. Maybe PB just wanted to see what train travel was like? His life story does suggest that he was an adventurous soul and this might have been his first opportunity to ride 'the iron horse'.

November 29, 1900. PB apparently stopped by the newspaper office during a visit to San Angelo, according to this note under Personal Items, "P.B. Irvin, one among our first subscribers and a prosperous cattleman of Middle Concho made the STANDARD a pleasant little visit Thursday." Lots of information in this single, folksy line. PB was one of their first subscribers, he obviously liked to read and was interested in the news, and he was recognized as a prosperous cattleman by the editor.

March 14, 1991. This note under Personal Items indicates that PB's ranch was located in a part of Irion County known locally as Rockey, "P.B. Irvin of Rockey was in the city Monday".

Another item under that same column noted there would be a new market opening up for cattle and gives an indication of how large the market is, "W.H. Godair has leased a 100,000-acre pasture in the Indian Territory near Tulsa, and will stock it with Tom Green County steers. He will begin shipping from San Angelo about the 25th. M.B. Pulliam shipped five car loads of cattle via the Santa Fe to the Nation today. This is the largest shipment made this season." The cattle business in this area was apparently still significant but large-scale ranching was the most lucrative.

June 20, 1891. This brief article suggests that Nat was searching for another source of water besides the nearby Concho River, "A driller named Orlando, while drilling a well on Nat Irvine's ranch, on Middle Concho near the new post office of Arden a few days ago, struck a vein of fine water at 66 feet, which in less than two hours, raised to within eight feet of the top of the well. With the proper casing, this could be made a flowing well. The *Standard* congratulates Nat on his good fortune." A bit of irony here. Today that whole area is cluttered with well-heads for oil that was discovered long after the Irvins were gone.

June 27, 1991. This article about the Commissioner's Court indicates that PB Irvin was still active in county affairs, "Be it known that on Monday, the 8th day of June, 1891 at 10 O'clock a.m. there was begun and holden a called 'session' of the Honorable Commissioners court of Irion County, Texas.

Present and presiding: Hon. J. M. Carson, county judge; W. L. Locklin, commissioner pre. No. 1; J. H. Ryburn, commissioner pre. No. 2; Fayette Tankersley, commissioner pre. No. 3; P. B. Irvin, commissioner pre. No. 4; W. N. Elliot, sheriff, E.C. McDonald, clerk."

At this meeting, the commissioners discussed a number of items, including approving the expenditure by the sheriff of $5.40 for feeding prisoners. They also adopted tax valuations of various properties such as: irrigated lands, $15-20 per acre; first grade steer cattle, $10 per head; Saddle horses $20, stock horses

$15, hogs $2; and sheep, first grade, $3. These valuations hadn't changed much from previous years.

September 12, 1991. Steer wasn't the only kind of stock sold in the area, according to this item under Stock News, "Last Saturday, R.O. Smith for J. B. Cherbino, sold five bucks to P.B. Irvine, at $20 and $25 a head." Both male deer and goats are referred to as bucks. I'm supposing that it was goats, for milk and cheese. Deer could be hunted easily enough.

Another item in that same column suggested that some stockmen were beginning to leave this area, "Mr. Tom Rudd, who has been one of the most successful stockmen in West Texas for years, will start in a few days from his ranch at the head of South Concho, 1000 head of cattle to his new ranch on the Pecos, thirty miles south of Pecos City. His fine seven-section ranch at the head of the river is too small for his business and he now offers it for sale. The *STANDARD* regrets losing Mr. Rudd and his excellent family from this section and wishes them much prosperity in their new home." This also provides further evidence that the wave of the future in cattle ranching was to increase the scale of production. Some small ranchers were selling off to larger ranches and moving on.

August 27, 1892. Sometimes PB made the news in ways that he may not have intended, "P.B. Irvin's team, left unhitched, ran down Chad and into a freighter's wagon. P.B. Irvin left his team unhitched at the Montgomery hotel Tuesday and it took a notion to take in the town. The record was broken coming down Chadbourne street, and the frightened animals ended up smashing into a freighter's wagon standing in front of Mile's stable. Mr. Irvin's wagon received several contusions and to add to his troubles the city recorder charged him $10 for not reading the hitching ordinance."

That was the last news article that I was able to locate from the microfilm records of the *San Angelo Daily Standard* for the Irvin's in that area.

Why were the Irvin's no longer in the local news after this date? It required a careful study of Irion's local tax records to answer that question. Local taxes are paid by all residents of that particular county. If there's no record of their paying taxes, this suggests that they may no longer live there.

Tax records from Irion County in 1895 still list both PB Irvin and son, but in the 1896 tax records, only NH Irvin is listed. The 1896 records show that NH Irvin now owns only four sections of land, three purchased from the railroad, and the fourth purchased from his father, PB Irvin. He also owned 12 horses and mules, 400 cattle, 5 hogs, 2 buggies or wagons, and miscellaneous items valued at $750. These holdings were considerably higher than any other persons listed on that same page. His total taxable property was $6682.

So, where was PB Irvin? I discovered a clue from previous family tree research on birth places for some of the Irvins. A few births were listed as taking place in Fisher County, Texas. So, I did a search of Fisher County tax records for this time period. Sure enough, PB Irvin shows up on the 1896 tax records from Fisher County, which is approximately 100 miles northeast of Irion County. That record lists PB Irvin, with 115 cattle and 9 horses and mules--but no land. There is no listing for his son, NH Irvin.

Why had PB moved part of the Irvin herd to Fisher County? Records from that time show that he wasn't the only rancher leaving Irion County. In 1890 there were 118 farms and ranches in the county. Fourteen of these were larger than 1,000 acres but most holdings were relatively small holdings, averaging around 1600 acres, about two and a half sections. The United States census counted 870 residents that year. However, by 1900 the number of farms and ranches declined by more than half, to fifty-two. Population dropped to 848.[55]

There was a major reason for this exodus. The scale of cattle ranching during that time was increasing dramatically in order to make it financially feasible. Small ranchers were being bought out by investors and entrepreneurs. The Suggs brothers had come to this part of Texas in the mid 90's with very large resources after the government had ordered all cattlemen off the Indian Territory. They purchased a number of ranches with cattle west of San Angelo, totaling about half a million acres. This became one of the largest ranches in Texas.[56]

One extreme example of just how large cattle ranches could become is the famous XIT ranch. In 1882, in a special legislative session, the Texas Legislature struck a bargain with a Chicago syndicate with mostly British investors, who agreed to build a new Texas State Capitol in Austin in exchange for 3,000,000 acres of land in the Texas panhandle as payment. The ranch stretched 200 miles along the border of New Mexico Territory and included all or part of ten counties in Texas. The fencing of this land with barbed wire required whole railroad cars full of staples. The ranch started operations in 1885, and at one time had as many as 150,000 head of cattle within its 1,500 miles of fencing. In order to provide sufficient water, the ranch erected 325 windmills and 100 dams across its land. Unfortunately, this ranch did not prove profitable for long because cattle prices crashed in 1886 and 1887.[57]

Major flooding of the Concho River area in 1894 could have been another factor. And years with too much rain were often followed by periods of drought and concurrent wildfires. Cattle prices were declining. Whatever the reasons, a rancher's life in that part of Irion County was definitely becoming more difficult. Smaller ranchers were forced to sell out and move elsewhere.

So, PB had moved a small part of the Irvin herd further north scouting for better pasture, and also to be closer to Abilene, the largest cattle market and shipping center in in this part of Texas. Abilene had been established by cattlemen as a primary stock shipping point on the Texas and Pacific Railway back in 1881. In fact, the town was named after Abilene, Kansas, the original endpoint for the Chisholm Trail.

PB must have realized that his current location in Arden was no longer suitable for a small cattle ranch. Fisher County, less settled, was an unknown. Resettling there would be a gamble, but it may have seemed his only choice.

11. Ranching in Fisher County, Texas

What would ranching be like in this new area? There was the primary advantage of any newer area, more available land. But cattle ranchers were now competing with farmers, and the competition would only get tougher.

Here is a brief description of Fisher County, based on the *West Texas Historical Association Yearbook of 1930.* Like Irion County, Fisher County is in the Rolling Plains region of central West Texas. It covers about nine-hundred square miles of grassy, rolling prairies. The elevation ranges from 1,800 to 2,400 feet. The northern third of the county is drained by the Double Mountain Fork of the Brazos River. The southern two-thirds, where the Irvin's located their ranch, is drained by the Clear Fork of the Brazos. Over half of the land in the county is considered prime farmland. The vegetation, typical of the Rolling Prairies, features medium-height to tall grasses, mesquite, and cacti. Cedar, cottonwood, and pecan trees also grow along streams. The climate is similar to Irion County's, subtropical and sub humid, with cool winters and hot summers. The average annual rainfall measures twenty-two inches, and the average annual snowfall is five inches.

In general, Fisher County was quite similar to Irion County. But this area was settled decades later than the area around Arden, probably because of the Commanche problem and because it was farther still from earlier settlements. A few buffalo hunters passed through the area in the early 1870s, but not until 1876, when the legislature separated the county from Bexar County, did the first permanent settlers arrive.

The new county, named for Samuel Rhoads Fisher, a signer of the Texas Declaration of Independence, remained sparsely populated and was not organized until 1886. Most of the early residents were cattle ranchers, who were attracted to the area by its abundant grasslands and available water. The census of 1880 reported 136 inhabitants. Only four of those who responded listed their occupation as farmer; the remainder were connected with the livestock industry. A post office, was established in 1881. Roby was one of the first registered townsites in 1886.

Railway construction began in 1881, when the Texas and Pacific Railway routed an east-west branch through the southeastern corner of the county. Cheap land, and improved access to markets made possible by the new railroad connection, lured many new settlers to the county. Between 1880 and 1890 the population grew more than twentyfold, from just over one-hundred to almost three thousand.

However, many of the new settlers were farmers, who began plowing and fencing the prairie. In 1880 there were only three farms in the entire county; in the 1890's that figure had grown to over three hundred! One result of the dramatic rise of the farming economy was the gradual decline of ranching. The earliest farmers in the county planted such subsistence crops as corn and wheat. But in the 1880s cotton was introduced, and by the early 1890s, corn, oats, and wheat were being grown commercially. Wheat and cotton eventually became the dominant agricultural product of Fisher County.

The Fisher County Plat map shows the Irvin ranch was adjacent to the main fork of Elm Creek (now called Clear Fork), a tributary of the Brazos River, and to the small hamlet of Hobbs. This is somewhat less than 10 miles WNW of Roby, the largest nearby town and the county seat.

Roby, Texas was a typical ranching town with a population of only 300 in the 1890 census. Like the rest of the county, the little town was in a 'boom' period and its population was over 700 by 1900. A brief history of Roby relates that in 1898 the first bank was chartered and the Roby school district was formed. The Irvins' new location here was much like the situation they had encountered more than a decade earlier near Arden.

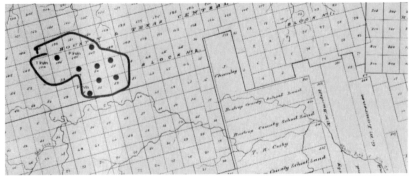

Irvin ranch sections shown on portion of Fisher County, Texas plat map

The plot of land Powhatan chose for their new ranch had several advantages. There was a main tributary of the Brazos, Elm Creek, adjacent to the Irvins' original land grant, and a smaller tributary just north of their later land grants. This would have provided the water needed for grazing herds of several hundred cattle.

The distance from the Irvin ranch near Arden to Abilene was over 100 miles. The distance from their new ranch in Fisher County was just over 40 miles. This new location would save the Irvins two to three days when driving their cattle to market.

The tax records from Irion County in 1897 still only listed NH Irvin, with the same land holdings, but his herd of cattle is now 600 and his miscellaneous assets decreased to $300. It appears he was selling off some farm machinery and buying more cattle, in preparation for leaving Irion County. His total tax valuation now totaled $8730.

Sometime during this move, Nat and Levina had another son, this one named after his father. Nathanial Hawthorne Irvin was born in Fisher County, Texas, on March 5, 1897. Levina was probably staying with Nat's parents at the time of her delivery.

Subsequent tax records provided information about the progress and completion of the Irvins move from their Irion county ranchlands to a new location in Fisher County, Texas. The 1898 Fisher County tax records now listed both NH Irvin and PB Irvin. NH Irvin owned no land, but had 14 horses and mules. PB Irvin owned 228 acres of land, 7 horses and mules and 200 head of cattle. NH must have left most of the Irvin herd in the care of a neighbor while moving his family north and setting up quarters at the new ranchland his father had settled on. But at that time, his father's land holdings weren't nearly large enough for their entire Irion herd.

Fisher County tax records from the following year, 1899, show that NH had acquired a small parcel of valuable river land (based on its valuation) and now had 11 horses and mules and a herd of 300 cattle. His father PB Irvin now owned 1328 acres, slightly over two sections, as well as 7 horses and mules and 250 cattle. It appears that the Irvins had now completed their move north to new ranchlands.

Ironically, just at their years-long move was completed, the ambitious and crusty old Irvin patriarch and pioneer, Powhatan 'PB' Irvin, passed away. He died on June 13, 1899 at the age of 63, and was buried in a small, isolated cemetery ten miles west of Roby, in a small hamlet now named Sardis. This was the church cemetery of the local Baptist church. PB Irvin's wife Mary, according to her obituary, was a church-going Baptist for most of her life "a member for more than 75 years", so it's likely that Irvin family attended this church, and that would explain why PB is buried in the graveyard adjacent to it.

Sardis Cemetery, just east of Irvin ranch and a few miles west of Roby, Texas. PB Irvin's tomb is the large brick structure centered within the signpost.

When I visited the Irvin ranch site and PB's gravesite, I had lunch at the local café in the nearby hamlet of Hobbs. The café is located in one of the original schoolhouse buildings. This would have been the very same building where some of my Irvin ancestors attended school. I spoke with the proprietors. They had not lived there during that time but seemed pleased to meet a direct descendant of one of the ranchers who had. No free lunch, though.

As untimely as his death might seem, PB Irvin must have died happy, believing that he had successfully relocated the Irvin clan and their herd to seemingly better pastures. And it must have made both PB and his wife Mary very happy to see their only son raise such a large family to carry on the Irvin name as the twentieth century was closing.

As it turned out, Nat and Levina weren't quite finished growing their family. They had one last child, another son. Ivan Ray 'Boots' Irvin. He was born in Roby, Texas on June 12, 1900, almost a year to the day after PB's death.

Nathanial and Levina Irvin now had 10 children. And Nat's widowed mother, Mary, was also now living with them. They were all facing a brand-new century together. They supplemented their numbers with a hired hand, Oscar M. Davidson. According to the 1900 US Census for Precinct 3, Fisher County, Texas, he was white, age 24, occupation 'stock driver', from Louisiana, and living with them. Nat would need help, now that his father was gone and most of the kids were busy getting educated. That same 1900 census, also notes that most of Nat and Levina's children were in school at that time, including Tom and Daisy, who were then 20 and 18 years old.

It's possible, given their ages, that Tom and maybe even Daisy attended college in nearby Abilene. Simmons College (later to become Hardin-Simmons University) was founded in Abilene in 1891. Many years later, when I lived out at the camp with my grandparents Tom and Irene, Tom seemed to know a lot more about rocks and minerals and chemistry and geology than a cattleman would normally pick up on his own. He never spoke of his education background but his vocabulary and general knowledge were certainly that of a well-educated man.

I was unable to locate any newspaper accounts about the Irvins during this period but Fisher County tax records provided

124

clues about their welfare. Tax records from 1900 show that NH inherited 1280 acres of land (2 sections) from his deceased father, PB. Those records showed that he now also owned 18 horses and mules and 650 cattle (and, no sheep, goats, hogs or dogs). Not a bad way to start the 20th century.

The following year, tax records show Nat's land holdings had more than doubled to nearly five sections (3,068 acres) but his string of horses and mules had decreased to twelve and his herd of cattle was now only 400. Evidently, he sold off some of his herd and acquired more land, maybe with an eye on future growth or because the cattle needed more grazing area than their previous holdings provided. Maybe grass was sparse because of drought? This part of west Texas has a history of droughts. The first droughts are recorded in 1870, then again in the years 1885 to 1887. However, 1900 was an especially wet year[58], so there should have been ample grass for grazing. Maybe he had to sell some of his herd just to meet expenses.

Records from the Texas General Land Office show that NH Irvin sold a parcel of land down in Irion County to an ML Mertz in 1901. That was probably the Irvin land holdings near Arden, which he apparently didn't put up for sale until he'd moved all of the herd up to the new ranch in Fisher county.

Fisher County tax records for the following year, 1902, show Irvin's ranch is still the same three-thousand plus acres, but there are a few more horses and mules. His cattle herd has now decreased to only 300. This was also the first year that NH Irvin's oldest son, Tom (my grandfather), now twenty-two years old, is listed on any tax records, even though there's no property of any type associated with his name.

He might not be a man of property, but Nat's oldest son, Tom, had other things on his mind. He had found the love of his life.

12. Tom Irvin Marries

At this time in Irvin's story, I'd like to focus a bit on Nat and Levina Irvin's oldest child, my grandfather Tom Irvin. He was the first of their ten children to marry and start a life on his own. He was now a young man and likely aspired to a ranch of his own, but not without the companionship of a good woman. Now he had found her—or perhaps it was she who found him.

On December 21, 1902 Nathanial's son, Thomas Hiram Irvin married Mary Irene Bulloch. Their marriage was recorded in Roby, TX because that was the county seat, but it's likely that they actually married at the Irvin ranch. Tom was twenty-two years old and his bride Mary, who was usually called by her middle name, Irene, was only seventeen. Irene Bulloch, like her husband, was also a first-born and also the first of David Thomas Bulloch's twelve children to marry. They would have had much in common.

Even if just the immediate families attended, their wedding would have been sizeable, what with Tom's parents and his nine siblings, as well as his grandmother, along with however many Bullochs attended. Tom's wife Irene had eleven siblings and probably a few aunts, uncles and cousins in that part of Texas. Can you just imagine what a grand party those two families must have enjoyed at Tom and Irene's wedding! The first child to marry in both families.

Most of what I originally knew about my grandmother Irene Bulloch's ancestry was obtained from a letter she had written my mother about her ancestry.[59] Irene mentioned that her uncle may have been a governor of Virginia (or possibly Georgia). Her family was from Scotland, with some Irish mixed in. She mentioned a possible connection with President Theodore Roosevelt. Supposedly her father, red-whiskered newspaper editor David Thomas Bulloch, was related to Martha Ann Bulloch, Teddy Roosevelt's mother.

That connection with one of my favorite Presidents interested me, but I was somewhat skeptical. Well-meaning relatives pass on such stories for generations with nothing to go on except similar last names, approximate ages and only a general idea of where their ancestors came from. So, I did a little research. I found a James Dunwoody Bulloch, June 25, 1823 to Jan. 7, 1901, from Georgia, and he had a half-sister, Martha Bulloch, daughter of James Stephens Bulloch of Roswell, GA, who was married to Theodore Roosevelt, Sr. in 1853. Theodore Roosevelt (later President Roosevelt) was born in 1858. The dates are consistent within a few years, but most of the Bullochs Irene was descended from were from North Carolina, not Georgia. Also, I found no close family connections to Roosevelt's mother Martha. So, I'm not at all sure that Teddy Roosevelt really was a close relative, but I'd like to think so.

My grandmother Irene Bulloch's family apparently settled in Roby in the early 1890's, where her father produced the town's newspaper. I found this information from this news article about her father's death:

> Roby Aug. 14—Roby and Fisher County are in deep mourning over the loss of one her most highly esteemed and honored fellow citizens, Mr. D. T. Bulloch, editor of the Roby Banner, and for fifteen consecutive years, district and county clerk, died Monday morning at 2 o'clock. Some two months ago Mrs. Bulloch's health required a visit to Fort Worth, where Mr. Bulloch remained with her for three weeks, and upon returning to Roby he brought with him in his system the germ of that dread disease, typhoid fever. He soon took his bed and after a month's severe suffering was released from all earthly suffering.
>
> Mr. Bulloch was not much of a speaker but a fine actor. No man in the county had his name on more notes and those in need were never turned off if it was in his power to assist them.
>
> He leaves a wife and a number of children and an aged father and mother to mourn his departure.[60]

Ironically, I couldn't find the *Roby Banner*, or any other newspaper listed for Roby in the two largest online newspaper archives during that time period. Consequently, I had very little to rely on except for tax records.

Subsequent tax records continued to provided evidence of where the Irvins were and how they were doing. The 1903 and 1904 Fisher County tax records still show Tom Irvin, now married, as owning no property, but the holdings of his father, NH Irvin, had increased in 1904 to 5,008 acres, almost eight sections. That's eight square miles of ranchland! The number of horses and mules remained unchanged at fourteen and the herd of cattle was still at 300 head. Most likely Tom and Irene were living with his father at the Irvin ranch west of Roby during the first few years of their marriage. Tax records were essentially the same for 1905 and 1906; no change in land holdings or stock, and Tom Irvin still listed with no holdings.

Everything changed in 1907. The Irvins were no longer listed in the regular tax records. The only tax records I could find for Irvins in 1907 was a 'supplemental roll of unrendered property', and NH Irvin is no longer listed. TH Irvin (Thomas Hiram) is listed with but a single line and shows no taxable holdings. NH Irvin must have left Fisher County sometime in 1906.

Why?

I'll return to that matter shortly, but want to continue with Tom's family.

Fortunately, the town of Hamlin, just twenty miles northeast of Roby, began printing a newspaper in 1906 which provided a clue as to the whereabouts of Tom Irvin and his new family. A front-page column reported that, "Mrs. Tom Irvin visited with her aunt and uncle, Mr. and Mrs. S. W. Thomas at Aspermont this week."[61] Aspermont was just a short ride north of Hamlin.

Another article, this one from a Farmington newspaper the following year, reported, "Thomas Irvin, who was here from Hamlin, Texas for a visit with his folks NH Irvin and family, left Saturday for his Texas home. While here, he and his father took a few days trip into the mountain country northeast of Pagosa."[62] The town of Pagosa was a popular trout fishing area nearby in southern Colorado.

So, in 1906, about the time his father moved his family to New Mexico, Tom and Irene Irvin, who had decided to stay in Texas, were living in or near Hamlin, Texas.

128

Why would they have moved to Hamlin? Why not travel to New Mexico with Tom's father and the rest of the Irvins? Maybe, at least partially, it was because Irene's family still lived in the area. It's also possible that they moved there because Hamlin, though not the county seat, was becoming the rail center for that area.

The arrival of the railroad was announced in 1902, and the first train arrived in 1906. It's no surprise that the city was named for W. H. Hamlin. He was a railroad official of the Kansas City, Mexico and Orient Railway. This line reached Hamlin in 1906 and was followed by the Texas Central Railroad within a few years and then by the Abilene and Southern Railroad in 1910. The population had boomed to nearly two thousand by the 1910 census. Roby's population was only about eight hundred at that time. Tom probably moved to Hamlin to find employment because there's no indication in the tax records that he owned any cattle in 1906. There may have been no opportunities in the nearest town, Roby. But Hamlin was booming.

Because it was bypassed by rail service, Roby's future wasn't too promising. When my wife Rosemarie and I visited Roby in November of 2011, parts of the city were almost like a ghost town. A significant number of abandoned business buildings and residences were gradually disintegrating with age and disrepair. However, the courthouse where we found the marriage application of Tom and Mary (Irene) recorded was surprisingly modern--but only half the offices were occupied, and the only other visitors we saw there were also doing family history research. The farms nearby were either abandoned or barely surviving because the region was still suffering from drought conditions.

The Irvin's leaving their Fisher County ranch had been a wise decision! Roby may be headed toward the same fate as Llano and Arden and Lake Valley, towns the Irvins had previously left in search of a better life. Towns which are now just ghost towns.

Tom and Irene wasted little time in starting their own family. Their first child (my uncle), named Thomas Bulloch Irvin, was born on December 19, 1903, just shy a few days from one year after their marriage. The birth probably took place at the Bulloch home in Roby. Less than two years later, my mother

Iris Irene Irvin was born on September 21, 1905. Tom and Irene had their third and final child, my aunt Ruth Phyllis Irvin, two years later on September 24, 1907. All of their children's births are recorded in Roby, Texas.

Tom Irvin was still listed in the Fisher County tax records for both 1908 and 1909, but both tax records showed TH Irvin with no taxable property. There are no Irvins listed in the Fisher County tax records after 1909.

Tom and Irene Irvin's Marriage Record. Sometimes the only way to obtain such records is to visit the local courthouse and photograph them yourself. (County Courthouse, Roby, Texas)

13. Better Prospects in Farmington, NM

Returning now to Nat Irvin. Sometime back in 1906 Tom's father had made the decision to sell off his ranch and move his family to Farmington, New Mexico Territory. Why would he move his family all the way from west Texas to the northwest corner of New Mexico Territory at this time? It was a very great distance for those times and would require many weeks of travel under difficult conditions.

1894 Sandstorm over Midland, TX, not far from Fisher County (NA 162)

There are good reasons why they must have decided to leave Fisher County. They were much the same reason that they had left their ranch in Irion County. The drought that began in the late 1880's certainly might have made both farming and ranching in west Texas more difficult, but it hit cattlemen the hardest. They depended on enough grass for their herd. Nat Irvin was increasing the size of his ranch but decreasing the size of his herd during this time. The selling price for cattle also dropped during this time. All of this is consistent with drought conditions. Farmers could irrigate their fields when there wasn't enough rain. So, farming, especially cotton and wheat, was becoming the primary occupation in Fisher County by this time. The introduction of barbed wire and the associated range wars over free passage and water rights that accompanied this transition would have made stock raising more difficult. In this new century, times were changing for this part of Texas. Nat Irvin may have been frustrated by these changes and realized that it was time to move on, not just to another cattle ranch but maybe even to a new way of earning a living. The 1910 census for Farmington, New Mexico no longer listed his occupation as a 'stock raiser' but instead as 'own income'.

What did he do with his 300 head of cattle? The Irvin family were moving to an area better known for farming than cattle raising, so it makes no sense that they would undertake that long and difficult trip driving a sizeable herd of cattle. But there was no evidence that he sold his herd in Texas. Did he drive his herd into New Mexico and sell it at cattle markets along the way?

That wasn't the only question I had. Just when did Tom's father, Nat Irvin, actually leave Texas for New Mexico? And why Farmington?

I'm pretty sure that I know when he left Texas, because he arrived in Farmington by spring or summer of 1906. The local newspaper, the *Farmington Enterprise,* describes NH Irvin as a Farmington resident in a list of investors of the Farmington Oil and Gas Company, filed October 23, 1906.[63] It's pretty likely that he'd been in Farmington at least a few months undertaking such an investment.

Another clue as to when they left Texas was the marriage of Nat's second oldest daughter Willia. She had fallen in love with Waller Tomlinson, a Texas land developer. They were married on December 3, 1905. He was twenty-five years old at that time, and Willia was twenty, and they now had their first child on the way. Waller and Willie Tomlinson were to remain in west Texas for the rest of their lives.

I would guess that Nathanial did not move his family to New Mexico until after Willia's marriage, and probably not until spring, 1906. This way the Irvins could all be together for Christmas one last time, and it would also avoid the rigors of winter travel.

The 1910 Census for Farmington, New Mexico, posed another question. Nat's third oldest daughter, Mayme, was not

132

listed with the rest of the family. Neither was she listed in any of the news articles which mentioned his other children. Where was Mayme?

I didn't have an answer to that question until I'd nearly completed this book. After a long and careful search, I found her listed, in the 1910 Census for Bellefourche, in Butte County, South Dakota. She's named as the spouse of Alabama born Thomas A. Jordan, who is working as a Tinner (someone who makes things or repairs things made of tin or other light metals) in a hardware store. They had two boys, the oldest born in Texas and the youngest born in South Dakota. This same census shows she was married four years. So, she must have married in 1906, shortly after her sister Willia married.

So how did Mayme end up in a small town in South Dakota? As it turns out, Bellefourche had recently become a major shipping point for cattle from the west to Chicago's stockyards. There was a well-used cattle route from San Angelo, Texas that followed the Pecos River north past Fort Sumner in eastern New Mexico, through eastern Colorado and up to Cheyenne, Wyoming. From there, it branched off to other destinations, including South Dakota. That small town was a major terminus of cattle drives from west Texas.

This knowledge provided a plausible answer to what became of Nat's herd of cattle. The dates and locations are consistent with the circumstances. It's just possible that Nat had decided to trust his cattle to a drover who could sell them up north for a much better price than he could get in west Texas or in New Mexico. Mayme would have been almost twenty years old in 1906, old enough to marry. She apparently met one of the cowboys, Tom Jordan, working for a major drover and married him. And, as a new Irvin son-in-law, he could look after the Irvin cattle during that drive.

When her husband left on that long drive, Mayme could have stayed behind with either her married sister or her married brother. At the end of the cattle drive to Bellefourche, Tom Jordan found a good job at a hardware store and that's where he and Mayme decided to make their home.

I'm thinking that's what Nat did with his cattle. He'd certainly get a much better price for them up north where they were destined for eastern markets. When the drive ended, and the cattle were sold, his new son-in-law Tom Jordan would send Nat the money from the sale.

If Nat didn't have to drive a herd of cattle all the way to Farmington, the trip would be much less difficult. Less difficult but certainly not easy. They were still a family of ten, including young children and an older widow. And this would be the longest trip they'd ever made.

I'm not sure of the route by which they traveled but any of the routes in use at that time would have required weeks if not months to travel that distance. It was a trip of at least 700 miles, which involved crossing major rivers and circumnavigating mountain ranges. They likely entered the San Juan valley by way of Largo canyon, the usual route for settlers of that time.[64] This trip would have involved leaving the Rio Grande and traveling north-northwest from Albuquerque. If they made that trip in the Spring, there would be numerous springs and tributaries along that route to supply water for their livestock.

At first, I was unable to find out just how they traveled that great distance. They would certainly have taken some livestock even if they weren't driving a large herd. Did the Irvin clan pull a wagon loaded with supplies and a buckboard loaded with family? Were most of the family on horseback?

Later in my research, I ran across an article in the *Farmington Daily Times*, one of their regular columns entitled "Frontier Days in New Mexico" by Mary Hudson Brothers.[65] The article mentions that the Irvin family owned a Bain wagon back in 1908 or 1909. This particular wagon was manufactured in Kenosha, Wisconsin and was quite popular among settlers of that period. Typically, the wheels measured 52" on the back and 44" on the front. The box width was 38" with a length of 10' 6". A wagon this long and deep could easily carry enough gear and provisions for a long journey and was easily covered. The relatively narrow wheel base made it easier to navigate those early roads, some which were little more than a wide trail.[66]

Every rancher and farmer who could afford one had a wagon for transporting feed and equipment as well as their family. These wagons would last for many decades if properly maintained. Because Bain wagons had been available since the 1850's, it's likely that the Irvins may have even bought this wagon during their earlier ranching years in Bee or Llano county, Texas. They might have used the same 'family wagon' for their travel to Lake Valley, then back to Irion and Fisher Counties in Texas, and finally to Farmington. But it's certain that they made this last, long family trip by horseback and wagon, possibly two wagons. Not by stage or by rail. Not an easy move, under the circumstances, but Nat's daughters were raised on a ranch and could help drive what stock they took with them. Even his sons PB and NH, now age twelve and nine, respectively, were old enough to help. At their young age, just imagine the adventure!

However, returning to the main question, what was the big attraction of Farmington? Why would Nat Irvin leave his ranch and sell off his cattle then put himself and his family at risk by traveling such a great distance into territory that was new to them?

Apples!

As it turns out, in the early part of the 1900s, apples became a prime crop for the local farmers in Farmington. This small town in the northwest corner of New Mexico was in the middle of an agricultural boom. Local newspapers were widely and enthusiastically publicizing the virtues of the area.

Up until 1905, Farmington had remained pretty relatively isolated so there was a limited market for the produce of their fertile river valleys. The nearest train service was located north in Durango, Colorado, a full day by stage and two days by wagon. However, on September 19, 1905, the long-awaited Denver and Rio Grande Railroad arrived, making the 50-mile trip from Durango to Farmington after first passing through the county seat in Aztec. It was called the "Red Apple Flyer", and the wide gauge train ran six days a week, transporting fruit and hay to a much-expanded market via Durango.

It's almost certain that Nat would have heard of or read some of the articles circulating in the area newspapers of that time. They were extolling the benefits of this area in the some of the most glowing descriptions you can imagine. Following are just a few examples that appeared in multiple issues of the *Farmington Enterprise* during 1905:

> San Juan County is located in the extreme northwest corner of New Mexico, containing about 100,000 acres, or about the same size as the state of

Connecticut. It is larger than Rhode Island and Delaware combined.

The county has more rich natural resources than any other county in New Mexico or the greater west. There is much embodied in this assertion, but it is true. The county has the finest water supply of any county in the west. The Animas, San Juan and La Plata Rivers all have their source of supply in the Rocky Mountains of Colorado. And the Animas and San Juan Rivers have their source in the highest mountains in regions of perpetual show. Hence the source of water for these Rivers is unfailing and everlasting.

The land that's in the valleys and on the mesas and divides between these three rivers is just as rich and productive as can be found in the west and hundreds and thousands of acres of it can be irrigated by the waters of these numbers. Not one-third of the land now under actual irrigation is utilized or actually being cultivated.

The coal fields which will in the future do more toward contributing to the great wealth and prosperity in San Juan County than any other resource is simply marvelous. The experiments of the experienced coal experts have shown that so far as known, there is not another section of country in the United States of the size of this county, that has more coal within its limits than is found here. San Juan County, New Mexico, offers more and better opportunities at this time for safe and profitable investments and for men with either much or limited capital to get better homes than any other county in the entire west. Now is the time and San Juan County is the place for the active industrious man who wants to secure a home at very reasonable rates, that in a few years will make him independent. Remember that fortune knocks but one time at your door and she is knocking and beckoning you on to the most favored region of the great southwest.

Farmington is: the metropolis of San Juan County, the center of the best fruit country on earth, the present terminus of the Denver and Rio Grande railroad, on the surveying line of the southern Pacific, which is building from the south and will give you through line to the Pacific Coast. Located at the junction of the San Juan, Animas and La Plata Rivers, in the center of the largest coal fields in the world and the best waters section of the west, and between the great precious metal producing sections of Colorado and Arizona. It is a town of homes and homeowners. Its buildings are old and owned very largely by those will occupy them. This is indicative of the possibilities of both town and county. Many who are now homeowners here have made these homes by their labor in these values.

Farmington has: a flour mill, electric lights, canning factory, three churches, a fire department, piped water works, ideal climatic conditions, an altitude of about 4500 feet, a population of about 1000 people, a two-story brick schoolhouse, broad shady streets and driveways, splendid brick business and residential buildings, a telephone exchange with long distance connections, a fine City Hall and many prosperous up to date business houses, and hustling energetic residents who believe in keeping up with the times.

Farmington needs: men with capital who will come in and help develop the country, men who will assist in advertising the town and the possibilities of the surrounding territory, and industries with a payroll.[67]

The following year, *The San Juan County Index* newspaper (of Aztec, NM, just east of Farmington) continued to publicize the merits of this area:

Lying to the south of the high La Plata mountains of South-western Colorado, among the valleys of the San Juan, Las Animas and La Plata rivers, is San Juan county, New Mexico with mesa and valley lands snugly fitting among low, cedar-covered hills peculiar to this locality. The soil is light sandy loam, and a heavier adobe, rich in plant food, and the hills and mesas are covered with a wild growth cedar, sage brush and grass. The population is almost entirely American, with schools, churches, etc.

The elevation at Aztec is 5,600 feet, and the climate is mild the year around. In winter the frost never

137

goes deep and tender fruit does not winter-kill. The snowfall is not heavy, as a rule, and seldom lays long. In the springtime rains are usually of short duration and vegetation appears several weeks prior to that of the eastern slope of the Rocky Mountains. The watershed of San Juan county drains into the Pacific Ocean. In summer the sun is hot and the growing season long, hut the nights are cool and the breezes from the snowcapped peaks 50 miles to the north, are refreshing, even on the hottest days. In the fall, the harvest of golden grain, fruit and vegetables is abundant and sure. Fruit raising is the leading industry. Apples, pears. peaches, prunes, plums, apricots, grapes, cherries, nectarines, small fruits and berries, alfalfa, com, wheat, bailey, oats and all kinds of vegetables produce the finest of their kind. These products are all watered by the rivers above- mentioned and the water supply is abundant the entire year and never failing.

With the advent of the Denver & Rio Grande railroad standard gauge branch from Durango into this country, has come an opening for many products which could not stand the wagon transportation. At Durango and Silverton, Colo., are found markets for much that is produced here, but this county has never been able to supply the demand for poultry, eggs, butter, strawberries, blackberries, grapes, etc. from these cities. Our apples are in great demand on account of the extraordinary keeping qualities, fine flavor and excellent coloring. Dallas, Texas, Chicago and other cities send buyers each fall into this county to get all the apples possible Thorough spraying for the coddling moth has made our apples wormless and perfect...

All the essentials necessary to make a wealthy community are in evidence in San Juan county. New Mexico. The population is about 5,000, with newcomers arriving constantly, and the two principal towns of Aztec and Farmington are thriving.[68]

After reading or hearing about such glowing reports, I can see why Nat Irvin was willing to pull up stakes in west Texas and re-settle in this part of New Mexico Territory! Unlike the

138

empty, rolling, drought-stricken plains of west Texas, his children would be growing up in a place where they could take advantage of seemingly endless opportunities. Here was a place that was extending an open and most enthusiastic invitation to anyone interested in participating in, and benefiting from, the rapid growth of this part of New Mexico.

Also, the Homestead Act had opened much new land to settlers there who were willing to live on it and develop it. Even more land was made available in this part of New Mexico after the Jicarilla Apaches declined an extensive area just east of the Navajo reservation and chose to stay in north-central New Mexico instead. Most likely all of these developments were a factor in Nat's decision to make that long and difficult trip.

Raising cattle in west Texas had lost its charm. Nat Irvin was now a prosperous, middle-aged rancher who wanted a better life for his remaining, unmarried children. Times had changed and he was ready for a change, as well.

14. Life in Early Farmington

When the Irvins arrived, Farmington was still a small town. It was the mid-1870's before it even became a settlement. The 1890 census showed only 138 people.[69] Settled originally by pioneers who came down from Animas City, Colorado, the town's location at the confluence of the La Plata, Animas, and San Juan Rivers fostered the growth of farms and ranches. It became the largest town in San Juan County by 1900. The town incorporated on July 15, 1901. The population of Farmington by 1905, about the time the Irvins arrived, had reached 750.[70]

The town was just beginning to modernize. They began operating their first electrical power company in 1902, powered by an irrigation canal watermill 100 hp generator, which supplied 32 customers.[71] A telephone exchange was installed by the Colorado Telephone Company in 1903.[72]

Farmington's Main Street at this time, like most small settlements in the southwest, was a mixture of wooden and adobe false-front buildings, some sharing common walls. There were single-story buildings with covered boardwalks and a few two-story brick stores. By 1901, there was a bank, dry goods store, grocery, and a fruit evaporation plant. In 1902, William Hunter, of Hunter Mercantile, donated a park at Orchard Avenue and East Main Street, with a one hundred-foot well at its center. Hunter Park became a center for civic and social functions with local parades starting or ending there. By 1903, there was a two-story City Hall that housed the telephone company, with the fire department and jail at the rear.

Downtown Farmington 1909 (courtesy Farmington Museum)

The Irvin's first home in Farmington was once the town's only schoolhouse, a one room adobe building. This one-room 18 by 24-foot building was built in 1879 by a group of citizen volunteers who had donated the building materials. At that time, it had served as a school, a church and a general meeting place, a common practice in early settlements.[73] It was located on the F. M. Pierce homestead on Main Street, halfway between Wall and Court avenues. The Pierce family built their two-story home around the schoolhouse after a new school building was built.[74] The Irvin's modified and added to the structure to accommodate his large family.[75] The 1910 census showed that Nathanial H. Irvin owned the home outright, that it was a house, with no mortgage, and that it was on Main Street.

Farmington and the surrounding area were still populated at this time by a large number of somewhat nomadic indigenous people, mostly Navajo. In 1868, the 3.5 million-acre Navajo Reservation had been established. It covered half of San Juan County's 5,560-square-mile area and extended west and northwest of Farmington's present city limits into Arizona, Utah, and Colorado. The Navajos were an important part of Farmington's livelihood, providing a significant customer base and labor market, as well as making the area more attractive to visitors and tourists because of their unique lifestyle and their outstanding weaving, pottery and silver-turquoise jewelry.

Nat Irvin was not only an adventuresome man; like his father, he was also ambitious. He wasted no time getting involved in Farmington's business affairs. During his first year in Farmington, he joined financially with a handful of other residents to undertake the first major efforts to explore for oil and gas in the Farmington area.

At this time, no major wells had been drilled but there had been several minor discoveries of both gas and oil in the area. Sometime around 1896, Sylvester R Blake, had hired a driller to provide him a water well on his farm just south of Farmington. They found gas at a shallow depth and quit drilling. Old timers said there was a pond near the well which ice skaters used in the winters, and they'd light the gas leaking from that well to stay warm.

Blake was motivated by this finding, so he hired a geologist to pick the next drilling site. They put together a simple coal-fired cable tool rig and began operations at the new site but were only able to sink a shallow well before they ran out of money.[76] Determined to continue, Blake formed a group of Farmington investors. He and six other townsmen formed a corporation called the Farmington Oil and Gas Company. A large article in the *Farmington Enterprise* described the corporation in detail, mentioning that this corporation would be involved in the exploration, production, storage, refining, sale and distribution of oil, gas, coal and whatever else they might uncover. It named the seven founders as NH Irvin, WA Hunter, CE Stivers, SR Blake, J Allen Johnson, SM Pierce, and CJ Carlisle. A million shares were being offered at 10 cents each. Blake was the largest investor in the group, at $1100 and NH Irvin was the second largest investor, at $400. The total initial investment capital was $2200.[77]

Blake bought an old drilling rig in Colorado and they began operations later that year, drilling a well on his property. They encountered gas at depths of 240, 390, 700 feet and especially at 1160 feet, where they encountered thick sands of trapped gas. Encouraged, they continued drilling deeper, later encountering seams of coal, water and brine with globs of crude oil mixed in. Maybe there were larger and richer reservoirs further down.

Drilling was a slow and difficult process. Especially back in the days when the drill, a cable-tool rig, was actually more like a pile driver. A long heavy metal shaft with a bit on the bottom end is lifted and dropped, again and again, gradually penetrating deeper and deeper, usually with the help of liquid. Bits wear out and have to be replaced. At a certain depth, drilling must wait while casing is lowered and pounded in place. This keeps the well hole open. The deeper the hole, the more time this takes, as the string of drill pipe and the depth of casing becomes longer and longer. One of the worst things that can happen, other than a human injury (common on drilling platforms) is that the cable attached to the drilling tools will break. This makes it difficult or impossible to retrieve the tools and they are expensive to replace. Fishing the tool out of the bottom of the hole, or partway down where it may have jammed, requires special equipment. More time and expense. Often, it's cheaper to just quit that well and move on to another—if you can afford it. Many could not afford it.

This is what happened to Farmington Oil and Gas Company. At a depth of about 2700 feet the cable broke, the tools were lost and the drilling stopped. Estimates put the potential yield of that well at one-to-two million cubic feet of gas/day but there was no way to exploit it economically after the tools were lost. This would have required the expensive and time-consuming process of 'fishing' for the tools with no guarantee they'd be recovered. It was a gamble—and they lost. However, and this was important, their well demonstrated the potential of very rich gas deposits in the area, and was a harbinger of the gas and oil boom in the decades to come.[78]

At the time, this must have been a huge disappointment to Nat, but, at his core, he was a farmer and rancher, not an oil man. This would not be his last venture into drilling for oil and gas, but for now he was taking on a new role, adapting to 'city life' in this rapidly growing community. Convenient rail transportation made marketing easier and more profitable. Small businesses were multiplying, farms and orchards were expanding and there was a continuing influx of settlers. Most of the new arrivals were responding to Farmington's relentless advertising efforts, extolling the merits of this area.

The town responded to the needs of its rapidly growing population. Their first hospital was established in 1907 from what was previously a ten-room home.[79] They opened their first drug store that same year. They opened their first bank around

1910. Altogether, Farmington's Main Street now had three general merchandise stores, a bank, a post office, a newspaper, a drug store, two saloons, and ten specialty stores, all with electric lights. Also available were two lawyers, one physician, one dentist, and two insurance sales offices. And there was the new Allen Grand Hotel located north of Main Street on Allen Avenue with a livery on West Main. There were also local sawmills and brick manufacturing facilities to provide building materials.

The Irvin children seemed to thrive in this new environment. When the Irvin's first arrived in Farmington in 1906, three of Nat's daughters, Daisy, Elsie and Evelyn, were already young women at ages twenty-four, eighteen and seventeen. The three girls were apparently quite close and shared a number of adventures and activities together. The following account, which took place in 1907, was written forty-five years later by one of the Irvin girls' close friends, who would later become Evelyn 'Eva' Irvin's sister-in-law:

HALLOWEEN WAGON PARTY NEARLY ENDED IN TRAGEDY BACK IN 1909.
Just a little story on some Farmington Halloween doings along about 1908 or 1909. I am not absolutely certain which date, just to assure the youth of today, they don't possess a corner on all the original ideas of a different escapade on black cat and witch night. This one was thought up by the Irvin girls as they were spoken of at the time, and a guest of theirs, Evans Woods, a young man from Texas, whose family had just moved to Aztec.
Aztec was advertising a big masquerade ball on Halloween night, and a group of young folks looking for fun listened to Mr. Woods tell us what a Gala event this was going to be. The first problem was transportation and we soon gained Mammy Irvin's consent to use their big Bain wagon which had helped transport the Irvin family from Roby Texas to Farmington. The Beaux's of the girls of the group, when they heard of the plan, agreed to rent a couple of teams from the Allen Livery Barn, fill the wagon box half full of hay, and after that decision the party was on in Grand Style.

The party consisted of John Graham and Daisy Irvin, Fred Carson Sr and Elsie Irvin, Charlie Brothers and Eva Irvin, Dalcie Hudson and Mike Wales, Hattie lock and May Rush with Jim Pierce, and last but not least was Evan Woods and I. Evans, fresh from Texas, decided to show the bunch how they drove in the Lone Star State, so he and I occupied the big spring seat, as we got on the way making knots along the dirt road.

Everybody was called on for a ghost story, and the party was gay and spooky as we munched apples and candy, as each tried to outdo the other with wild tales. Just as we turned north, into the lane east of the old Utton place, where the road was smooth and sandy for a long stretch to the east of the Gower place, Evans decided to indulge in some fancy driving and stood up and popped the long whip, emitted a few Texas Cowboy yells, winding up with, "Three cheers for the bonnie blue flag that bears a single star", and the four horse team was doing their best to deposit us in Aztec in record time.

Suddenly just opposite the giant maple tree stand along the old Utton fence, the team swerved, as the leaders tangled with some object in the road, the driver had neither seen or heard. There was a melee of horses, and another vehicle, and a few wild curses, demanding to know what we thought we were doing. Luckily no one or the horses were hurt and Evans succeeded in stopping and quieting the team with the aid of Charlie Brothers and John Graham, both fine horsemen who ran up and grabbed the horses by the bits. The other party turned out to be George Hutchison, who still lives where he did then, about a mile-and-a-half further on up the road. He was on his way to town to band practice, when suddenly he found a horse trying to occupy the seat beside him, and the other horse of the lead team was tangled up in his buggy, but the Bain wagon was intact and after a few minor repairs to the harness, we went on our way.

Yes, we made the dance, had a gay time and got home safe and sound, trembling in our boots for fear of what our parents would do and say when this story was out. I remember Sis and I got a good talking-to and our Alibi was the age-old one, "Oh, we weren't doing anything bad, just chasing goblins and having a little Halloween fun". Oh yes, I forgot to say we all had a mask in our pocket, which we hastily donned, when we weren't dumped out, with a wagon and charging team on top of us, which could have very easily been the result of our wild drive. A number of those present still live here in Farmington and I can see them grin if they read this. Cross my heart it sure 'nuf happened, just ask some of those I mentioned.[80]

That must have been some party. As it turned out, all three of the Irvin girls eventually married their dates from that evening.

The three 'Irvin girls' were apparently quite talented. They were now performing in plays and playing piano. I have no idea where or how they would have learned such skills nor how much schooling they had before moving to Farmington. They had been raised all their life on a cattle ranch with no large towns nearby. There were schools, of course, even if it was just a one-room school house, but pianos and theaters must have been scarce. It's possible that they learned these skills during their first year in Farmington. Living in a town now, there was certainly a wider audience to appreciate their performances.

At the Farmington Opera house, Daisy and Elsie had leading roles in a one act play and also participated in a Burlesque production that same evening at which their sister Eva played the piano. The proceeds from this evening of entertainment went to help finance an Episcopal church. They performed the same production later at Aztec, the next largest town in the county, about half the size of Farmington. Here's what the Farmington papers said about the Aztec production.

The entertainment given at Aztec last Saturday by several of the young ladies of this place was as pleasing an atmosphere as when given here, was fairly patronized for so short a season of advertising, and only two days – and was well received by the audience. The ladies repeated the drama and burlesque as was given here recently, and the following musical program was rendered...

The Aztec citizens are a clever lot of people, whom we found courteous and obliging, as the young ladies had compassion on us and took us along, and we enjoyed the trip hugely. Supper was served at the New American hotel by host H L Lair who formerly lived in Durango Colorado. He is a genial fellow, has built a fine 24 room building of stone and brick with numerous porches and shade trees around it and is using his best endeavors to give Aztec a first-class hotel. Owing to lack of time we had no chance to do much visiting but managed to say hello to our former Denver friend Wilson and Mr. Mullins, the late director of the Farmington band. Jay T. Green, proprietor of Greens Hall where the entertainment was held, is a courteous gentleman and was kind to his patrons, but we would suggest that he had the hall piano cleaned and tuned, that it's discordant strains may not fall so harshly on one's musical ear. Otherwise things moved along nicely and Mr. Green was clever in his business dealings. The young ladies sustained their reputation as pleasing entertainers. The trip was made by bus and buggy and quite a number remained after the play to trip the light fantastic.[81]

That Farmington building hall which was dubbed the Opera Hall, served as a meeting place for live performances and other presentations. Later, in 1912, it became a movie theater, showing silent movies Tuesday, Thursday and Saturday for ten-cents per ticket.[82]

It was during this time that Tom Irvin, Nat's oldest son and first-born, left his family briefly and traveled alone from the small hamlet of Hamlin, Texas to see his parents and siblings in Farmington. While there, he and his father took a trip into the mountain country northeast of Pagosa Springs, Colorado. During their time together, Nat apparently convinced his son to bring his young family to Farmington as quickly as he could manage. Tom returned to Hamlin after only a short visit because his wife Irene was pregnant with their third child.[83]

The following year, early in 1908, Nat Irvin made a brief foray into local politics and ran for the local office of Town Trustee. Municipal politics was rather new here because Farmington had only incorporated in 1901. There were only two parties at the time, the Business ticket, or 'Wet's, and the Citizen's ticket, or 'Dry's'. Wet and Dry referred to those in favor of, and those opposed to drinking alcoholic beverages. There were considerable efforts at this time around the nation to abolish such drinking altogether. There were at least three temperance organizations in the Farmington area. And Aztec's city council was already moving toward shutting down saloons in their town.

Nat was one of ten candidates running for five seats on the council. As a good Irishman would, he ran on the 'Wets', ticket. The Wet's ticket won three seats, the Dry's ticket won one, and the fifth seat was a tie. Unfortunately, Nat was shy one vote of being in the tie.[84] However, at a town council meeting later that year, one of the newly elected trustees resigned. Following a motion for his nomination, Nathanial Irvin was unanimously elected to fill the position. Nat was now a member of the Farmington Board of Trustees![85]

Just a few months before being elected, Nat had sat in the audience of Farmington's only grade school and watched his youngest daughter Agnes sing 'School Days' solo at her 8th grade commencement. Hers was a graduating class of ten, up two from the previous year. Farmington was growing. But it still had a long way to go. The high school in Farmington had only graduated their very first class the previous year. Class size? Two seniors!

Not all of his daughters were behaving as Nat may have wished. He was likely a bit displeased when his daughter, Evelyn ran off and married a local boy, Charlie Brothers, and didn't tell her parents until afterwards. Evelyn Irvin, or Eva as she was known, had just turned eighteen. The local newspaper reported the event with a positive slant:

> Charles Brothers and Eva Irvin stole a march on their parents last Tuesday evening and were married by the Rev. R, U, Waldraven. After the ceremony they broke the news to Mr. Brothers and to Mr. and Mrs. Irvin and although coming a little unexpected, no one was displeased with the match and their respective fathers were seen to wink when they thought nobody was watching them. The young couple left Wednesday for Durango and will probably be back the third to go to

148

Aztec where Charlie will play ball. The many friends of Mr. and Mrs. Brothers wish them all kinds of luck and prosperity.[86]

Charlie Brothers gave a dance on the following Saturday in honor of his new wife. Eva was the first Irvin child to marry in New Mexico and the third marriage in Nat's family of ten children. And this was only the family's second year in Farmington!

How much did it cost back then for a young married couple to purchase various provisions when setting up in a new home? In the same issue of *Farmington Enterprise* that announced Charlie and Eva's wedding, Staplin's, a local general store, offered the following lists of items on sale. For a mere five cents, you could buy any of the following: a large kettle cover, bottle of sewing machine oil, vegetable brush, ordinary bread pan, spring mouse trap, or a wire egg whip. For ten cents, they offered: large sized scrub brush, Gem Pan-6 hole (a muffin pan), enameled cuspidor, four hook hat rack, pair iron brackets, Mason or Bell jar opener, screen door spring, vinegar faucet, paint brush, or any of the popular novels. And, for fifteen cents, they offered: a large dishpan, stew kettle, revolving flour sifter, individual tea pot, western linen writing tablet, milk strainer or a large wash pan.

Staplin's also advertised a One Dollar Special, wherein you'd receive $1.50 worth of staple articles, all bundled together. The items included were: can of corn, package of oat meal, package of corn starch, package of mincemeat, can of jam, can of oysters, can of Anderson's soup, box of Nabisco, box of crackers, can of baking powder, box of Uneeda Bisquit, and two boxes of matches. At the end of this list, their newspaper ad reminds the reader that, "$1 Spot Cash buys the lot". Imagine what you could buy with a ten spot!

And, if Eva and Charley Brothers decided to splurge and dine out, they could enjoy a dinner of, "good food and plenty of it", at J.W. Kight's Home Resturant [sic] on the north side of main street.

But we're talking small potatoes here. Nat Irvin had decided it was time to start making real money. Early that

September, he sold off some of his land holdings, 16 acres of orchard land just southwest of town, to a Mr. S R Garritson of Loveland, Colorado for a price of $52.50.[87] Just three weeks later the newspaper reported the following land purchase by Nat Irvin. "During the past week, J F McCarty sold 80 acres being the east one-half of his home farm which lays about two miles east of Farmington to N H Irvin for $8000. The entire 160 acres was purchased by McCarty a few years ago for $12,000 and since that time he has made numerous and valuable improvements. The dividing up of this property between these progressive men means that still further improvements will be made on both portions."[88]

Nat was evidently getting into the land business. He must have used some of the money from selling a parcel of his land west of town to purchase land east of town. He planned to divide this purchase into five and ten-acre tracts and sell them in that shape 'so as to further assist in the settlement and improvement of the valley'.[89] It would likely improve his own fortunes as well. There was widespread interest in land ownership in this part of New Mexico at that time. Nat was contacted by some venture capitalists in Oklahoma who planned to visit the area and learn more about the prospects.

But all this land purchasing and development was becoming tedious to a cattleman and rancher who was more comfortable when outdoors on horseback. Nat decided that he was due a vacation after all this land development activity. The paper reported succinctly, in the vernacular of those times, "N.H. Irvin left this week for a month's trip to the mountain. Hunting and fishing will afford amusement."[90] The paper reported a week later that he and his friend, Henry Freeland and his hounds were having a fine outing and wouldn't be back for some time. Two weeks later they returned with a bear as their hunting trophy.

So, now this cowpoke from Texas is bear hunting in the Colorado mountains, with hounds yet, and returning successfully with a bear hide. What will it be next?

He lost no time once he returned. He'd been smitten by the lure of land investment. The following week he posted an ad in the newspaper.[91]

Nat Irvin's Ad in Farmington Enterprise, Oct 30, 1908

The same paper reported that Nat had just returned from another hunting trip with Charles McKinney (no mention of a bear this time).

Nat must have done pretty well on his land venture. Just two weeks later the paper listed him as one of only a few dozen Farmington citizens who'd made cash contributions toward the construction of a brand-new bridge in the city across the Animas

River. Nat's old drilling partner, Sylvester Blake, was also listed as a donor, and his hunting buddy, Henry Freeman, helped out with the labor.[92]

This new Animus River bridge just south of Farmington was quite an impressive achievement, built entirely from local donations and labor. It was a 150-foot-long wood and iron truss bridge anchored on either side by concrete pilings ten feet tall. It was fourteen feet wide with a four-foot walk for foot passengers and four-foot high railings on each side. The floor planks were three inches thick. It was built to support loads as heavy as twelve tons and to withstand flooding, even to the point of submergence. It was a Farmington landmark and rightly made front page news.

Unfortunately, the bridge was very short lived. A few weeks after its completion, a luckless cattleman tried to drive a herd of cattle across it and the bridge collapsed. The local paper described the incident as follows:

> ANIMUS BRIDGE GOES DOWN. Big Bunch of Cattle Was Too Much for Newly Built Bridge. Late Saturday morning, November 21, shortly before noon part of a herd of cattle being driven south, crashed through the new Animus bridge. The first span on the north side of the river went down and two of the four one-inch truss rods on each of the other two spans were broken, and other damage was done. A few of the younger stock were injured.
>
> There were nearly a thousand cattle in the herd of Geo. Nash and Wm. Pucket of Montezuma and were being taken south to winter pasture. The owners had some local people help them drive the herd through Farmington and had intended not to cross the bridge. When they got to the river the first section of the herd started up on the bridge and they could not be turned. A big bunch of them got on the first span. Opinions differ as to how many; some witnesses say as many as 100 head, other witnesses say not more than 50. They stopped on the first span, or many of them did, and that span collapsed. The cattle that were on the bridge, and did not go down with it, went on across to the other side

and two truss rods on each of the other spans were broken.

This is the bridge that was built by private subscription, and those who contributed toward building it immediately took legal proceedings against the owners of the cattle. They were put under bond and their cattle were attached. They made an offer of $150 cash to pay for the damage done on the bridge and it was accepted after a few days, and all legal proceedings were withdrawn. It was thought by some that the damage was greater than this, but those who had the matter in charge decided it would be better to settle the case and get the repairs made, rather than spend money and time in the courts.[93]

Building a much-needed bridge wasn't Nat's only effort to make his newly adopted city a better place to live. Newspapers from this time regularly included the minutes of the monthly town meetings, and they suggest that Nat Irvin was always in attendance and an active participant. In the same news edition that carried the list of donors for the new Animus bridge, town meeting minutes reported Nat Irvin recommending that they study the feasibility of replacing Main Street's plank sidewalks with cement walks of uniform width. The motion carried unanimously. This was at a time when horses and wagons greatly outnumbered automobiles but it was becoming apparent that this might soon change.

The temperance issue also continued to be an important matter. In November the city council began raising the fees one had to pay to operate a saloon, making the practice prohibitively expensive. On April 30 of the following year, the council called a special meeting, held in the city clerk's office at 8PM 'for the purpose of considering EJ Walter's application for retail liquor license.' Nat Irvin moved that the application be tabled indefinitely and a resolution, which also prohibited anyone else from opening or operating a liquor saloon in Farmington 'for any period whatsoever', was passed unanimously.[94]. This became law on August 4, 1909. Because that saloon was the last one remaining in the county, San Juan County became the first dry county in New Mexico Territory.[95]

It turns out that while Nat Irvin was involved in shutting down one of Farmington's entertainment centers, another Irvin was entertaining the townsfolk in a different way. Right next to the newspaper column titled "Farmington Saloon Closed" was an article titled, "Farmington's Young Talent". At a fundraising event for the library held by Farmington schools in Allen Auditorium, fifteen-year old PB Irvin wowed the crowds with his rendition of the song, 'Dixie Kid', which "was the hit of the evening, and when he responded to the encore with a short couplet, 'Goodbye Booze', he made a reputation as a black face comedian that he has the ability to keep up." A fitting accompaniment to his father's action at the Town Council. Although, as it would soon turn out, young PB Irvin might better have payed closer attention to the lyrics of his popular encore.

As one would expect, closing down the town's saloons didn't necessarily stop the local citizens from drinking. The May 28 issue of the *Farmington Enterprise* described an incident where Marshal McFadden and NH Irvin noticed a commotion at the cannery following the show letting out on Saturday. When they walked over to investigate, they found a keg of beer on tap and a crowd of men 'partaking of it freely'. An arrest was made the following day of a local who apparently was brewing the beer illegally.[96]

Never one to sit still for long, Nat Irvin decided to see the Seattle Exposition that summer. He set off for an extended visit to Washington state with his fifteen-year old son, PB, and his twenty-year-old daughter, Elsie. This trip must have been quite a treat for both of them, though Elsie probably had the chore of managing PB during their travels. And as you will soon learn, PB Irvin was not an easy one to manage.

Nat had traveled to Oregon earlier in the year, returning with word that it was 'fine country'.[97] And no sooner than he'd returned from Washington, he set off for Ignacio, Colorado in order to publicize opportunities in Farmington and bring investors from that area to his home town. For those times, that seems like a lot of travel in one year.[98] I can only surmise from all this travel that Nat Irvin was now, by any measure, a prosperous man.

Nat's son, PB, was apparently achieving a measure of success with his school work at this time. He was elected vice-president of his class's literary club. The club met every other week and it was described as an important part of their school work.[99] And life wasn't just about studying for PB. Later that year he spent Thanksgiving weekend in Bloomfield, a small community a few hours ride east of Farmington. He rode there with a school chum, Bruce Sullivan, so that they could attend a special Thanksgiving Dance.[100] I find it fascinating that such seemingly ordinary activities were routinely reported in the local newspaper.

Nat's youngest son, nine-year-old Ivan Ray took part in a school play that merited a sizeable story in the local newspaper. The play was performed at Allen Hall, Farmington's multi-purpose facility for popular performances and meetings. The play was titled, 'Cinderella in Flower Land' or, 'The Lost Lady's Slipper'. This production was apparently a big deal because the performance was done on a Friday evening so that all the townsfolk could attend. Little Ivan, I should add, wasn't exactly the leading man. He played a raindrop. ([101])

His older sister Agnes had a more significant role in a high school play performed in Allen Hall on a Friday evening later that December. The play was titled "The Black Knight" and was based on Ivanhoe and Robin Hood's adventures. She played one of Robin Hood's followers, which had to be a bit more demanding than playing a raindrop. Accompanied by piano and soprano, admission to the play was set at thirty-five cents or fifty cents, depending on age.[102]

Not to be outdone by their talented younger siblings, Elsie Irvin, now twenty-one and Daisy Irvin, twenty-seven, were elected officers of the Order of the Eastern Star. Elsie was elected Conductress and her older sister Daisy an Associate Conductress. Officers were installed at the Farmington Masonic Lodge at the end of the year.[103]

So, it seemed that Nat's propensity to take part in community activities had been passed on to his children. This was likely the norm, at a time when there was no TV and no cellphones. After school work and home chores were done, participating in plays and organizations provided some of the only opportunities to socialize in a small town.

In the summer of 1910, another of Nat Irvin's projects came to fruition. He finally got a cement sidewalk in front of his property. The local paper described the project as follows:

Iness and Jerris are laying cement walks in earnest this week. Monday morning, they commenced at NH Irvin's property and are working west along the north side of Main Street. They have a concrete mixer operated by a gasoline engine and are also employing a large force of men, so are able to lay walks quite rapidly. As they come to the end of street crossings, they will only complete half of the job, leaving a strip of open roadway for the use of wagons. The remaining part will be finished on the return trip up the other side of the street. Their work has the appearance of being first class in every respect. The town board is now figuring on the creation of another cement walk district. This is the right idea. Walks should be laid all over town.[104]

As with most small towns in the southwest at this time, Farmington' streets were meant primarily for horses and horse-drawn conveyances, not automobiles. Typically, these were carriages of various designs such as buckboards or buggies for passengers, and horse or mule drawn freight wagons for commerce. Although a small number of automobiles did exist this early, they were few and far between in this part of the country. One of the first automobiles owned by a Farmington resident was John Hubbard's 1909 High Wheel International. It's easy to see why people referred to these early automobiles as 'horseless-carriages'. This one looked very much like a buckboard with no traces for a horse.[105]

Nat Irvin was striving for much more than just paved sidewalks. He had served on a committee appointed by the city earlier this same year to study the feasibility of bringing more railroads into Farmington. There was strong interest in bringing in a new rail from the south, connecting with Southern Pacific railroad in Gallup. You'll recall there was already rail from the north, connecting Durango, Colorado to Farmington. A rail from the south would greatly facilitate the transport of coal, timber and minerals. Unfortunately, it would prove to be too difficult and expensive to build. Also, at this time, there was still no easy access from Farmington to Albuquerque or to the territorial state capitol in Santa Fe. Farmington, for all its riches, was still somewhat isolated.

It was at about this time, probably early 1910, that Nat's oldest son Tom moved his family from Hamlin, Texas to Farmington. At this time in history, they most likely still traveled by horseback and horse drawn wagon. They would have traveled north along the Rio Grande to Albuquerque and then proceeded northwest to Farmington, via the Largo Canyon route described earlier. Because Tom had visited Farmington from Texas back in the summer of 1907, he'd have had no problem choosing the best route. The best travel time would have been spring.

Tom Irvin and his family are listed in the May, 1910 Census as renting a home farm on Main Street in Farmington. Tom was now thirty and his wife Irene was twenty-five. Their three children Tom, Iris and Ruth are listed respectively as six, four and two years old.

By 1910, the population in San Juan County had reached 8,504, which included an estimated 2,500 Navajos. Navajo families often camped out of wagons on Broadway in order to trade in Farmington, which was still the largest town in the county with a population of nearly one-thousand.

At a time when most settlers in this area still did not have telephones in their home, the 1911 *Farmington City Directory* did list Nathanial H Irvin, rancher, with his wife Levina in parentheses. It also listed Nat's daughters Daisy and Elsie Irvin and his mother Mary Irvin, as the widow of P. Bowen Irvin. The separate phone listings suggest that they all lived in separate dwellings or at least separate rooms of a large home. Immediately following Nat's listing, a Thos. Irwin, rancher was listed but with no spouse shown, so I can't be sure that it was actually Tom Irvin, but it most likely was, with that typical misspelling of Irvin.

The *Farmington Enterprise* noted that on May 5, 1911, Tom Irvin purchased a quit claim deed from a Winnie Spath. A few months later he filed a notice of intention to make proof. This was categorized as Coal Land under Desert Lands Act. It's not clear if he was purchasing this land just for a ranch, or to use it commercially in some other way. It did not appear to be just an ordinary homestead, purchased in order to build on and farm. The land, made up of three adjoining parcels totaling 156 acres, was located just north of the Farmington-to-Bloomfield road, about two-thirds of the way to Bloomfield from Farmington. That road paralleled and was just north of the San Juan River. I

157

was never able to determine if Tom Irvin lived on that land. He may have used it as rangeland or rented it out or maybe just sold it later for a profit.

There were yet other land transactions involving the Irvins. Later that month, Nat Irvin signed over a piece of his land to John Graham, and John Graham also received a piece of land from his parents. There was a very special reason for those particular land transfers. On Saturday, October 1, John Graham, with Nat Irvin's oldest daughter Daisy by his side, drove up in front of Reverend Jackson's house on Orchard Street. With her sister Elsie as bridesmaid and John Carson as best man, Daisy Irvin and John Graham were married by the Reverend in a quiet ceremony on his front lawn. Daisy, Nat's oldest daughter, was just a few months shy of thirty-years old. I expect that Nat and Levina Irvin gave a long sigh of gratitude and relief when she and John finally tied the knot.[106]

According to their wedding article, they had left on their honeymoon immediately after their wedding. Hopefully it was to higher ground. Just a week after they were married, Farmington and the surrounding area experienced a catastrophic flood.

As one might expect in an area where three rivers come together, there's always the chance of major flooding, especially when there are numerous high foothills and mountains just a short distance north. Melting snow in the spring and summer thunderstorms sometimes produce too much runoff to be absorbed. Just such a major flood occurred early in October of 1911, working its way south and then west through Aztec, then Farmington and Shiprock. It was a flood that took lives, washed away homes and destroyed farmland, roads and bridges. Front page stories of the *Farmington Times Hustler* reported, "TERRIBLE DESTRUCTION OF LIFE, PROPERTY AND CROPS. Three Lives Lost and 150 Miles of River Bottoms Devastated." "San Juan and Animas Rivers Highest Ever Known in the Memory of Oldest Residents. Houses, Lands and Bridges Swept Away. The county of San Juan has just gone through the worst experience in its history since the coming of the white man."[107]

This particular flood was the result of an unusually heavy and prolonged rainfall that covered an extensive area. As runoff poured into the rivers in southern Colorado and northern New Mexico, the rivers soon overflowed their banks and in a matter of hours, the San Juan and Animas had reached depths ten feet above their banks. Twenty-five miles of railroad tracks were swept away east of Durango and every bridge in the county was destroyed except the suspension bridge at Aztec. Even the brand-new bridges in Farmington was destroyed by the flood.

All of this destruction had a major impact on trade and commerce in the county that did not return to normal for another year. At least 50 ranchers and farmers were wiped out completely, losing dwellings, stock and farmlands. Given the enormity of the flooding, the miracle is that only three lives were lost.

Early Farmington had also suffered significant damage from fires. Back in January of 1910, a fire on the 100 block of East Main street destroyed nearly every business on the south side of the street. This represented a considerable portion of Farmington's downtown businesses, including; Andrew's Store, Hunter Mercantile, Times Hustler (newspaper office), I.N. Ball Furniture, Staplin Mercantile, Evans Jewelry Store, Hunan's Palace of Sweets, Hubbard's Real Estate, Current's Barber Shop, Clark's Real Estate, Dr. Reece's Office, and Cline's Bakery.[108]

In spite of these two major catastrophes, daily life in Farmington proceeded pretty much as it always had. As 1911 was drawing to a close, Agnes Irvin, along with two others, won special praise in the local paper for her role in the high school's Christmas play production at Allen Hall. Their performance was described as 'particularly pleasing'.[109]

And, Farmington newspapers continued to describe their fair city in glowing terms. Here's a list of what are referred to as 'a few facts worthy of note':

> Farmington has no saloons, is incorporated, it has a city park, it has a creamery, it has a brass band, it is an altitude of 5000 feet, it has five churches, it has a steam laundry, it has two good hotels, it has two National Banks, it has a board of trade, it has a $4000 town hall, it has a population of 1200, it is lighted by electricity, it has a rail line, it has a piped water system, it is at the junction of three rivers, it enjoys almost perpetual

sunshine, it is the commercial center of the county, it is the center of the county telephone exchange, it's in the center of the greatest fruit belt in the southwest, and it has the best schools of any town in Northern New Mexico including a complete high school course.[110]

They should also have included that Farmington had an Opera house, a movie theater-- complete with a pianist, a brand-new bridge and *paved sidewalks* on Main Street! Farmington was, in its own small way, still growing and prospering. By 1911 it had more than twice as many businesses as Aztec, the county seat. Those two towns often competed on one thing or another, but Aztec would never again approach anywhere near the population of their sister city.

Still, Farmington remained somewhat isolated. Even though there were a number of railroad lines by this time in New Mexico, it still took 3 days by rail to travel from Albuquerque to Farmington. This was because there was no direct line from Albuquerque to the northwest part of the state. A rail traveler would first go north to Santa Fe, spend overnight, then to Antonito and spend another overnight, then west to Durango for a third overnight before traveling south the next day by rail to Farmington. Efforts to build more rail lines had not succeeded. So, travel by road, whether by horseback, stage, or wagon, remained the only choices.

A horse drawn wagon took at least a week to travel from Albuquerque to Farmington. Travel by stage coach would have taken two full days, assuming an average speed of five miles per hour and twelve hours of travel per day. That's about as long as any passenger could endure the bumpy and uncomfortable ride.

To the city fathers of Farmington, that new contraption, the automobile, was beginning to look like the transport of choice. By 1915, a new roadway under construction would allow an automobile to drive from Albuquerque to Gallup to Farmington in about 12 hours.[111] That road trip today, a distance of roughly 110 miles, takes less than two hours on a modern, mostly four lane, paved highway.

15. New Mexico Becomes a State

The year 1912 began with a most joyous event. On January 6 the Territory of New Mexico was granted statehood into the United States of America, making New Mexico the 47th state in the Union. They beat out Arizona (which had once been a part of New Mexico Territory) by just one day. Statehood had finally occurred, but only after many years of wrangling in Congress and numerous efforts by officials of New Mexico Territory. So, this would be a year of celebrations throughout the new state.

Farmington, NM 1912. Some Irvins might be in this picture. (courtesy Farmington Museum)

People celebrate in different ways. This Irvins were no exception. You may recall that the Irvin daughters sometimes had a way of surprising folks when it came to marriage. Elsie Irvin, now twenty-two years old, pulled just such a surprise. While returning from a trip to Texas in early May of 1912, she diverted from her route and stopped in Albuquerque. There she met her Farmington boyfriend Fred Carson. Was this a chance meeting or was it planned? Regardless, they married each other then and there on May 2. This was apparently a surprise to all their friends and family. Serving as bridesmaid and best man to Daisy Irvin's marriage last year may have helped inspire those two to wed, just as soon as the time seemed right. And, this year, while everyone was celebrating statehood, seemed like just the right time. Because these two were both quite popular in Farmington, their wedding made the front page in the local paper.[112] Fred Carson was the oldest son of a Farmington pioneer, William Carson. William was born in Farmington shortly after it became a town and continued the family tradition of operating trading posts on the Navajo reservation.

Now it was Elsie's younger sister's time to shine. Farmington High School was graduating their largest class ever, eight seniors, and Agnes Irvin was one of them. The senior class included six girls and two boys, all of them from families who were well known in the Farmington area. The high school made this year's graduation a special event for the whole town. The newspaper gave it front page center coverage. It was held at the town's Opera House on a Friday evening and even charged a small admission to 'help cover the cost of the high school's piano'.

The extensive program included an Invocation, Salutatory, Class Poem, Orations on 'Life' and on 'Heroes of Science', a Class Will, an address by Reverend Higby, and a Valedictory. There were also several orchestral numbers which included a solo, two duets and a quartet. That's quite a show for just eight seniors! Agnes Irvin and her classmate Bessie McDonald sang a duet, 'When We're Together'. Agnes also sang in a quartet, along with Bessie and two brothers, Harry and Louis Woods, who were not seniors. The paying audience certainly got their 25-cent admission's worth! The senior class had been feted at a banquet at Hunter Hall the previous week by the high school's 11th grade class and high school alumni. Graduating from high school in those days was a really big deal.[113]

In addition, shortly before graduation, Agnes volunteered to serve on a committee of the G.A.R. (Grand Army of the Revolution) to help prepare for the celebration of Decoration Day. The G.A.R. was a fraternal society made up of veteran's family's who'd served in the Union military during the Civil War. Decoration Day was a predecessor to today's

Memorial Day. It was a day set aside to honor those who had been killed in the Civil War. Agnes was on the committee to solicit cut flowers, a major part of the upcoming celebration. The newspaper described the town's May 30 celebration as follows:

> The exercises held here on Memorial Day occupied the entire day and evening. They were the most enjoyable ever presented in this town and were witnessed by the largest crowd ever assembled here on such an occasion. The old soldiers followed by the Odd Fellows and Rebekah's marched to the cemetery in the forenoon and with appropriate ceremony decorated the graves of all the old soldiers and Odd Fellows. In the afternoon, a great crowd gathered in the large auditorium of the Methodist church and was entertained by the band and vocal music of which the pupils of the Shiprock Indian school gave the most enjoyable recitations and an exceptionally able address by Rev. R. U. Waldraven. The meeting adjourned to Allen's Hall at 8:00 PM
>
> Before the program was resumed, Allen's Hall was packed for standing room and many who came afterwards had to turn away. The great attraction was the singing of the Indian boys and girls from the Shiprock school. Superintendent Shelton and his wife with the head of the teaching corps, Miss Vandergift, brought up a chorus of 26 voices made up exclusively of the pupils of the Shiprock Indian school and the music they rendered was a surprise to all who heard them. We venture the assertion that there is not another school in San Juan County that could come anywhere near competing with them in this line.
>
> It was brought out in the Governor's message that New Mexico had furnished a greater percent of her population to the war than any other state or territory and the enthusiasm shown in the celebration surely was indicative of this fact.[114]

A few months later, Agnes traveled to Aztec to attend the San Juan County Teachers' Institute and take the teacher's test. She was a young lady on the move.[115]

Early in October, John H Graham, Daisy Irvin's father-in-law, rounded up his herd of sheep from an area close to the nearby village of Blanco and brought them in to Farmington. He and Nat Irvin then sold their combined sheep herds to a buyer from Durango, Colorado. Nat had been reluctant to raise sheep in Texas, but in this part of New Mexico, there was always a good market with the Navajo as well as the nearby town of Durango.[116]

Having completed his ranching activities, Nat Irvin and his hunting buddy, Henry Freeman, decided to go bear hunting again, early in December. This time they took Nat's son-in-law, Charlie Brothers along. Maybe Nat figured if he couldn't shoot his latest son-in-law Fred Carson for eloping with his daughter Elsie, he'd shoot a bear instead. And maybe he intended to show young Fred what a fine marksman he was, and that it would be best to stay on the right side of his new father-in-law.[117]

If the year 1912 had ended without further event it would have ended near perfect, but this was not to be. When Nat Irvin returned to Farmington (no word this time that he brought back a bear trophy) he was likely still in a mood to shoot a Carson. But this time it was Fred Carson's younger brother. Nat's now sixteen-year-old son PB had been thrown in jail along with his friend Lauren Carson for intoxication, disorderly conduct and drinking under age! The two of them were scheduled for a grand jury hearing and an investigation was underway to see who sold them the liquor, which was now illegal.[118] This may have put a bit of a damper on the Christmas holidays at their home, but on balance the Irvin family had much to celebrate at the close of 1912. Now they were proud citizens of one of the forty-eight United States of America.

The following year, life pretty much returned to normal. It's well known that prohibiting the production and sale of alcoholic beverages never prevented all that many, who were so inclined, from drinking. The Irvin family was no exception. Just a few short months after PB Irvin was arrested for drunk and disorderly conduct, his older brother Tom apparently also had a bit too much to drink. Marshal McJunkin arrested Tom Irvin (my grandfather!) on a cold Saturday night for drunk and disorderly conduct and locked him up in the town jail. But, unlike PB, Tom was 32 years old and had a wife and three children to worry

164

about. He wasn't about to spend the night in jail. During the night, he broke the leg off a table and, using it as a pry, he broke the bars to his cell and went home to his family. Not only did this story make the front page of the local paper; there was also an article about a temperance rally on the same page.[119]

It's not clear what happened to Tom Irvin after he broke out of the jail, so maybe not much came of it. I was unable to find any future article on the matter. The marshal may have decided to just take a lesson from that breakout and install heavier bars in the cells. And to keep more distance between inmates and tables.

This wasn't Tom's only run-in with the law since he'd moved his family from west Texas to Farmington. He'd been scheduled to appear at a court hearing early in January of 1912 on a charge of assault and battery. The complaint had been filed against him by Dave Anderson, proprietor of a local restaurant. The outcome of the trial, if it was held, remains a mystery. Maybe Nat Irvin's oldest son had the inside track with the law in Farmington. It was clear from other news articles that the Irvins and Mcjunkin's were close socially.[120]

It didn't usually turn out as well for Tom's much younger brother, PB. Just four weeks earlier, PB was fined five dollars and expenses for disorderly conduct and profanity in the street. That story also made the front page.[121]

It's worth noting that the day after the *Farmington Times Hustler* reported that PB was fined, the other town newspaper, the *Farmington Enterprise*, ran the following tongue-in-cheek story, lamenting how all this law enforcement was stifling the citizens of Farmington:

> Last week the town board appointed R. H. McJunkin to oversee the job of cleaning the streets. Mac now has a force of men at work cleaning up things properly. Having also been appointed marshal, about the first thing out of the band box Mac pulled one of our boys for using profane language in the presence of a ladies. If he keeps up this gait, we are afraid that we're going to be mighty lonesome as the 1:00 AM serenades are apt to have to cease. Why can't well enough be left alone? Must all the joys of life be done away with simply because there's such a thing as law, and because

someone wants to enforce the same? What will Farmington come to if the marshals tried to enforce all the laws we have here? How can we get along without our little drink to open the day with, or the midday tonic or the after-supper refresher? We only take a thimbleful at a time, but we don't see why we should be deprived of that. Must our recreation of gambling go also? We could do without these pleasures, of course, but things are most certainly coming to a pretty pass when an American citizen cannot say what he pleases on the streets. If the ladies don't like to hear our manly profanity, they should stay home. Think of arresting an American for swearing, and in this a free country. Surely, surely, we are fallen.[122]

Nevertheless, the City of Farmington voted later that year to remain 'dry' for another four years by issuing no licenses to liquor emporiums. The mayor thanked both newspapers for their support in this endeavor.[123]

The Irvin boys were certainly spirited, if you can forgive the pun. It may have been more than coincidence that their sister Agnes left for Texas at about this time to visit her sister Elsie for a couple of months. It's likely she was fed up with the unruly behavior of her brothers and she probably didn't care much either for the gossip about it that she must have overheard at her women's meetings in Farmington.[124]

None of these family goings-on seemed to dissuade Nat Irvin from continuing to pursue his fortune. He decided to invest his time and money, once again, in the search for gas and oil. He was one of the biggest investors (tied with others for second largest) from Farmington in a new start-up corporation, The San Juan Basin Oil Company. There were dozens of investors from Farmington, as many from Santa Fe, and others from northern New Mexico, including Albuquerque, over a dozen from Colorado and one from as far away as Washington state. They managed to raise enough cash, a bit over $8000, to purchase their own modern drilling rig and associated equipment and planned to begin drilling as early as August.[125]

Agnes Irvin, in the meantime, had returned from her Texas visit to spend a few weeks in Gallup, New Mexico. She then traveled to Albuquerque where she enrolled in the Albuquerque Business College to study a combined program of courses. The Irvin women, is spite of their menfolk's shenanigans, were continuing in their own productive pursuits. Tom's wife Irene earned a bit of fame, instead of notoriety, at the Albuquerque State Fair in October. A box of fancy Jonathan apples that she and Mrs. Frank Brothers had packed won a blue ribbon. What's more, they'd originally been packed for sale and not for show at the fair. Even so, their apples beat out the competition and won first prize. Farmington's fame as a prime source of fruit was continuing to grow and people like Irene Irvin and Mrs. Brothers deserve credit along with many other hardworking growers and pickers.[126]

Farmington Times Hustler carried a quote from the *Albuquerque Herald* early in 2014 extolling the economic benefits of growing apples. Responding to concerns that the planting of more apple orchard in New Mexico might lead to overproduction, the *Herald* article states,

> Such a thing as an overproduction of apples is not possible save as a result of inefficient distribution. And our means and methods of distribution both are improving with every year. The use of apples is increasing both at home and abroad. Millions of bushels can be taken care of in cold storage for indefinite periods. Millions of dollars' worth can be exported annually. The demand is almost unlimited. No man in New Mexico need fear to plant apple trees. The far-seeing farmers from the state who live in regions suited to apple production, and this includes practically the whole of our irrigated territory, are hurrying to get apple trees into the ground. Modern methods of smudging practically guarantee the crop. The apple tree of good variety, property planted and tended, is about the best investment any landowner can make. Is almost as safe as a government bond; and many times more profitable.[127]

Whereas there seemed to be no problem with overproduction of apples in Farmington, the same could not be said for the production of newspapers. Farmington lost one of its two newspapers this year, the *Farmington Enterprise*. The retiring publisher and editor, Frank Staplin, was accompanied to Durango by Orville Ricketts, the man who would eventually become the editor of the town's remaining newspaper, *Farmington Times Hustler*.[128] The latter paper reported, "Orville Ricketts went up to Durango, Saturday, accompanying Frank Staplin that far on the latter's homeward journey. There are some who think that after reading the last leading editorial in the Enterprise he felt so depressed that he had to go to a town where there were much better opportunities for enthusing than in a dry town like Farmington."[129]

His newspaper wasn't the only local business that shut down that year. Nat Irvin's latest investment ran into financial difficulties. Drilling was stopped at the San Juan Basin Oil Company's fledgling well. The gentleman in charge of the drilling quit and left for another drilling job in British Columbia because the corporation could no longer cover expenses. However, the corporation remained hopeful that money could be somehow be raised and drilling could be continued[130]

Nat's family had suffered another loss earlier that year. Levina's father, Hiram Ricketson, had died on April 20th, 1914. He was buried in the Oxford, Texas cemetery, near where Levina had grown up and later met and married Nat Irvin. Her father left 'Vinnie' (as he called her) and Nat $2000 in his will. That money may have helped keep the drilling going.

As for the younger generation, life proceeded right along, as they pursued their interests and talents. The *Times Hustler* announced a new Uplift Program, a community literary group that would meet at the school house Monday evening. Activities would include a mix of sing-alongs (Swanee River), oral presentations and musical presentations, including Agnes Irvin and her old school mate Bessie McDonald, once again singing a duet together, to close the evening activities. The following week's paper commented that Agnes and Bessie sang beautifully. Those two must have had some real talent if they were still being asked to sing together at local functions. At that same meeting, the case was made that young people needed more social outlets and that "our community must, instead of maintaining so many lodges and churches, might better spend the same money on a public library with gymnasium attachments."[131]

The young folks did have their occasional social events, such as the one provided at the home of a Miss Lucille Devlin in May of that year. That particular event was described by the

Times Hustler as, "a dainty two course lunch consisting of salad, pickles, sandwiches, coffee, cake and strawberry sherbet was served. Dancing was engaged in until a late hour." No mention of any alcoholic beverages but included in the guest list were Agnes Irvin and Bessie McDonald.[132]

For young folks, there were now also moving pictures, usually Tuesday and Saturday nights, at Allen's Theater or Opera House as it was often called. The film titles and other difficulties suggest that this was not always an activity which would appeal to the younger generation. Even if a young man had actually gone so far as to take a date to a Saturday night movie with a title like, "Manger to Cross", they might arrive only to discover the film hadn't arrived. *Times Hustler* describes one such circumstance.

> The moving picture film entitled "From the Manger to the Cross", which was to be given at Allen's Hall tonight, has been delayed. The following telegram explains the cause. 'From SF to the opera house, Farmington, New Mexico. Exhibitor who had booking Manger to Cross previous to yours has run away with same and has not been apprehended. Therefore, do not figure exhibiting this picture until you hear from us. We will advise you within the next day or two by wire, date which you can examine the production.[133]

It's apparent that viewing a motion picture back in those times in a small isolated town was not quite as simple as streaming a movie on your smartphone today. Those cannisters of film had to travel hundreds of miles by coach or wagon or horseback, as the case may be. Live performances, such as musicals and plays, remained the norm.

There were other outlets for youthful energies. The Fourth of July celebration was always popular. The local fairgrounds held a variety of competitive races on that date. The *Times Hustler* described Farmington's 2014 July Fourth as follows,

> In spite of the rain which prevailed during most of the afternoon and evening of the Fourth, the program of sports was effectively carried out. In the morning the

Boy Scouts of this place played a well-matched ballgame with the Indian lads of the Methodist mission. The game resulted in a score of 6 to 5 in favor of the Farmington youths.

1:30 o'clock saw a large crowd gathered at the fairgrounds. A number of visitors came down from both Aztec and Durango to spend the day, and some agreeably surprised to see so many Navajos in town. One older Indian celebrated by dressing up in the garb of Uncle Sam, much to the amazement of the crowd. His outfit was complete with stovepipe hat.

The first event was a 100-yard dash in which Durango easily took first place. Fruitland was second. The time was slow, due to the muddy track. The next event on the program was a quarter mile horse race. P. B. Irvin crossed the line in 29 ½ seconds, with John Brown a close second.

The boys all ran their hardest in the potato race which followed. The two on a half-mile Indian relay race was a humdinger. The three teams were well matched and the result was doubtful up to the last minute. Very much in contrast was the white man's race of the same distance. As that race had clearly been fixed, nothing but jeers greeted the winner.

One of the most laughable of the afternoons events was the boys sack race. The way the contestants slipped and rolled around in the mud was just perfectly killing. Three Indian squaws proved their fleetness of foot in the 50-yard dash. The time was almost 40 seconds. The chicken pulls, one for Indians and one for whites, were held during the afternoon.

The ballgame between Fruitland and Farmington was slow and rather uninteresting. This, however, not the fault of the players, who did the best they could under the circumstances. The grounds were sloppy to begin with and the almost constant drizzle made them worse as the game progressed. The game resulted in a fifteen-to-one victory for Farmington.

The final event of the afternoon was a 5-mile marathon between William Scott-the man in overalls- and a runner named Peterson from Durango. This race

170

promised to be one of the best of the day, and was well run for the first 1½ mile. But on the fourth round of the half mile track Peterson gave out and dropped, leaving Bill to finish the race alone. In the evening a number of Indian dances were put on for the benefit of the visitors and the day was ended by a display of fireworks.[134]

Horse racing was always popular, of course. Apparently PB Irvin, like his father, and his grandfather before that, was a pretty good horseman. A quarter mile horse race, especially on a muddy track, requires exceptional skill on the part of the rider as well as the horse. PB had grown up on a cattle ranch and I'm pretty sure that his father, Nat, would have seen to it that he rode a horse properly. It's likely that his big brother, Tom, showed him the way.

As it turns out, winning a horse race just wasn't excitement enough for PB. Later that same year, he and two other boys decided to burglarize the town depot on a Monday night in November, by breaking in through a window. They then broke into the money drawer but all the money had been put in the safe. They did, however, find a half a barrel of bottled beer in the room, which they took from the premises. Marshal Stokes hunted around and found the beer hidden down below the depot. Watch was kept the following night and the three boys were caught going after the beer.[135]

Georgia Salmon Irvin holding son George Bolin Irvin c. 1917

However, a year or so later PB Irvin's life took a totally different tack. He discovered that there are other pleasures in life besides drinking and boisterous behavior. He fell in love. He began courting Georgia Salmon, the attractive young daughter of George Salmon, a prominent rancher and citizen in nearby Bloomfield. There were indications that this was not a union favored by Mr. Salmon, but Georgia had taken a liking to this somewhat rambunctious young man and wasn't to be dissuaded.

They were married on May 12, 1916. PB was twenty-two years old at that time and Georgia had just turned sixteen. There was no mention of their wedding in the local paper, so their wedding was probably arranged quickly and wasn't a lavish affair. Neither was it a 'shotgun wedding', however, because their first child was born ten months later. They started life together at PB's ranch in Bloomfield. The Irvin family had gained a fine new daughter-in-law, the first since Tom's wedding to Irene in Texas almost fifteen years ago. And, it must have pleased Nat and Levina greatly that PB had finally settled down. Or, at least, so they thought.

Nat Irvin's setback in drilling a few years back for oil hardly slowed his efforts to provide for his family. In addition to land speculation and his ventures into oil and gas exploration, he was still a stockman, and apparently doing well at it. In July of 1916, several prospective buyers came down from Pagosa Springs, Colorado to look over his cattle. One of them was the brother of Willet Brown of Hunter Mercantile in Farmington. Colorado was a good market for Farmington ranchers because it was a great deal easier to ship cattle east from Colorado.

Maybe Nat had to sell off a few head because he was still on the delinquent tax list for the previous year.[136] Based on the number of delinquents in the various districts, paying taxes promptly wasn't that popular in Farmington during those times. The lists of names owing taxes consumed several full pages in the local pages each July and continued to do so for a number of editions following.

Or, maybe Nat Irvin was selling cattle and late paying taxes because he was interested in buying himself one of those new motorized vehicles. The *Times Hustler* carried an article in March of 1917 stating that he'd just driven back from Gallup in a brand-new Dodge car which was a 'dandy looker'. Four cylinders rated at 24 horsepower, and steel wheels. The Dodge, considered one of the best cars at that time, wasn't even available until late 1914 and sold for a hefty price averaging over $800, depending on the model. It probably sold for more than that in Gallup, adding in the freight cost from the Detroit plant. For perspective, some building lots in downtown Farmington were selling then for as little at $400. Nat must have been doing OK financially in order to buy a new car, still a rarity at that time and place. There weren't enough folks buying cars locally at that time for Farmington to even have its own car dealer.[137]. Folks were regularly selling horse-drawn buggies then in the local papers. In fact, at this time, the so-called Farmington Auto Company was only a transportation service. They made weekly automobile trips to Gallup, charging $15. per passenger.

Nat drove his new Dodge back to his home in Farmington with two friends, Larkin Beck and R.H. McJunkin, the same McJunkin who'd arrested his son, Tom, just a few years back. Apparently, that arrest caused no lasting hard feelings. I would guess that Nat started badgering the city fathers shortly after this to start paving the roads. He wouldn't want to bang up his brand-new expensive Dodge bumping around all those pot holes or dragging bottom while driving in the deep ruts on Farmington's dirt roads.

He must have enjoyed driving. He didn't wait long before showing off the advantages of his new car. The following month he drove W.D. Bell up from his meat shop in Gallup to spend Easter at the Irvin ranch. I would imagine that by then, Nat was sporting a pair of driving goggles, which were available at Hunter's Mercantile for as little as 25 cents.[138] I can almost visualize him driving up and down Main Street, honking at friends and waiting patiently for folks to cross the road in front of him. And cussing the horse-drawn conveyances to move aside.

16. U.S. Enters World War I

When World War I erupted in Europe in 1914, President Woodrow Wilson pledged neutrality for the United States, a position supported by the vast majority of Americans. Britain, however, was one of America's closest trading partners. Several U.S. ships traveling to Britain were damaged or sunk by German mines, and in February 1915 Germany announced unrestricted warfare against all ships, neutral or otherwise, that entered the war zone around Britain. A month later a German cruiser sank a private American vessel. President Wilson was outraged. The German government apologized and called the attack a mistake.

But the outrages continued. On May 7, the British-owned *Lusitania* ocean liner was torpedoed off the coast of Ireland. Of the 1,959 passengers, 1,198 were killed, including 128 Americans. The German government maintained that the *Lusitania* was carrying munitions, but the U.S. demanded reparations and an end to German attacks on unarmed passenger and merchant ships. Germany pledged to see to the safety of passengers before sinking unarmed vessels, but in November they sunk an Italian liner without warning, killing 272 people, including 27 Americans. Public opinion in the United States began to turn against Germany.

Early in 1917, Germany, announced the resumption of unrestricted warfare in war-zone waters. Three days later, the United States broke diplomatic relations with Germany. Just hours after that, the American liner *Housatonic* was sunk by a German U-boat. On February 22, Congress passed a $250 million arms appropriations bill intended to make the United States ready for war. In late March, Germany sunk four more U.S. merchant ships.

This had gone far enough. In spite of his initial resistance and pledge to keep our country out of the war, President Wilson called for a declaration of war against Germany. On April 6, 1917, the United States officially declared war on Germany. On June 26, the first 14,000 U.S. infantry troops landed in France to begin training for combat.

Our nation's entry into the war produced no lasting headlines in Farmington newspapers at the time, although editorials in the *Times Hustler* supported President Wilson because he entered the war to uphold democratic ideals. Quoting from the front page of the *Times Hustler* of April 19, 1917, "…Woodrow Wilson has shown himself the greatest statesman and social philosopher of all ages. Other men have led nations to war to increase their power, glory and wealth. No other statesman has so irrefutably connected his country with the peace and democratic aspirations of the world."

Otherwise, life remained pretty much the same for most of the local residents. Life for the Irvins was still just the usual ups and downs. Nat's son, NH was involved in an underage drinking case that went to court, along with a friend, Sidney Tice. Tice was given a light fine but it was dismissed for good behavior. The man who gave them the liquor at his residence, J.W. Burch, was fined $100. NH, who was only 18 years old at the time, apparently got off with just a reprimand.[139] There was no reportage of what he might have encountered at home, but it's not likely he got off quite so easy.

Nat Irvin has just celebrated his 58th birthday and was probably feeling pretty good, otherwise, about how things had turned out. He'd been settled for over ten years now in what must have seemed the garden spot of the world. He had a fine, large family, some still living at home and most of the others married and living nearby. He'd been successful in his land speculations and his stock raising and farming, and rubbed elbows on a regular basis with the town merchants and politicians. His home must have been a large and very handsome place because now he was even hosting weddings, some of which were not even his relatives. The *Times Hustler* describes one such occasion, "Rev. L.W. Gunby performed the wedding ceremony for James Guy Lanier and Miss Leta Ellen Rippey at the Irvin home. The couple lives at Aztec. Quite a number were present at the wedding, which was held out under a bower of blossoms."[140]

Not bad for a cowpoke from west Texas who started out for New Mexico Territory back in the late 1870's with nothing to his name but a young wife and a spirit of adventure.

All this good fortune apparently had little effect on how timely Nat, or his son Tom, or for that matter, quite a few other townsfolk, paid their various taxes. Both Nat and Tom were listed in the local paper as being delinquent in Bloomfield Irrigation District Maintenance taxes for the previous year 1916. Of the more than one-hundred properties listed on just one page of twelve, most individuals listed owed $30. or less. However, Nat owed about $180. and Tom about $60., which gives you some idea of the relative size of their holdings compared to most of Farmington's residents.[141]

In spite of all the trappings of civilization, Farmington, was still a frontier town and this part of our country was still the 'wild west'. Horses and cattle were still being stolen. Enough so that ranchers like Nat found it necessary to post a running notice in the newspaper, warning prospective cattle rustlers:

> NOTICE This is to give notice to the public that no person or persons have a right to sell or offer to sell any cattle in the following Brands: T & K on left thigh, T on left shoulder, H on left side, G on left hip. Anyone selling or offering to sell stock in the above described brand will be prosecuted to the full extent of the law. This, the 19th day of June, 1918. N. H. Irvin.[142]

In August of that summer, Nat decided to get away from it all and took his son-in-law Tom Jordan fishing with him all the way up to Silverton, Colorado, a distance of about 150 miles. The Animas River headwaters in that area, fed by an average of four-hundred inches of snow annually, were famous for trout. Fly-fishing was the preferred way to catch them. Even though Silverton is high up in the mountains at 9300 ft. altitude, it was accessible by rail, because of mining activity there. One could take the train from Farmington north to Durango and from there switch to narrow gage and chug right up into the tiny mountain town of Silverton. The scenery alone was worth the trip, but to a fisherman, there were none better than those big rainbow trout. According to the paper, 'they caught plenty of fish and had a fine time'.[143]

Idyllic as life might have been for some, there was a major war going on at this time. The United States Congress did not have a large army when it declared war on Germany so it had to resort to the draft. The Selective Service Act during this time had three periods of draft registration. The first, on June 5,

1917, was for all men between the ages of 21 and 31. The second, on June 5, 1918, registered those who attained age 21 after June 5, 1917. The third registration was held on September 12, 1918, for men age 18 through 45. By this time many had already joined the service from San Juan County. Many more had registered for the draft.

The *Times Hustler* routinely published listings of those who registered for the draft. Twenty-year old Nathan (NH) was listed on September 26, 1918. His oldest brother, Tom, who was now thirty-eight years old and was married with three children, had registered just a week earlier on September 12. His older brother PB had registered back on June 5, 1917 at the age of 23, 'married with one child, age one'. All of the Irvin boys had registered but one. Ivan 'Boots' Irvin, Nat's youngest son and last child had only just turned eighteen that year, but now he would also be registering and eligible for the draft.

Thankfully for all, the war ended on November 11, 1918. The November 14 issue of the *Times Hustler* headlined it as follows, "PEACE. The greatest war in history ended Monday morning, November 11, at 6 o'clock, Washington time, after 1,567 days of horror in which virtually the entire world was convulsed." Even though the U.S. did supply troops to the war in a significant way until 1918, by the end of the war over two million Americans had served on the battlefields of western Europe and more than 50,000 lost their lives. Although many residents of Farmington served, only seven Farmingtonians died of combat in the First World War.

As it turned out, none of the Irvin boys were drafted nor enlisted into military service during the War. This was partly the luck of the draw, and partly because of their age or marital status. Nat himself had also missed serving in the military, because he was too young during the Civil War. He could certainly claim, however, to be a combat veteran of the Apache wars!

17. The Post-War Years

The war had inflicted casualties far beyond just those who were killed or wounded in battle. Lack of sanitation, food and shelter, and the mixing of many peoples from various locations, provided ideal conditions for the spread of disease. That last year of the war and the year following was even more deadly because an epidemic of the Spanish flu. It was spread widely around the U.S. and the world by returning soldiers. An estimated 675,000 Americans died of influenza during that pandemic, ten times as many as in the world war! Of the U.S. soldiers who died in Europe, half of them fell to the influenza virus and not to the enemy. Influenza was taking its toll in Farmington as well. This account by Mike Maddox describes the impact of the Spanish Flu epidemic on Farmington:

On January 30, 1919, the Farmington Times Hustler reported that there were over 400 cases of the flu in the area served by Farmington's physicians. It was a huge number considering that in the 1920 census, the population of the Farmington precinct was 1304 people. According to the National Archives, the worldwide flu epidemic of 1918 and 1919 "killed more people than any other illness in recorded history." The outbreak in the spring of 1918 was mild, but when it returned in the fall, the strain was deadly. Victim's lungs filled with liquid and many suffocated to death. In many instances, pneumonia was listed as the cause of death, but it was more often, than not, a flu-induced pneumonia.

That autumn, Dr. Arthur Monroe Smith made trips to remote areas on the Navajo reservation to treat flu patients. Despite his efforts, hogans across the reservation lay abandoned with their deceased residents inside. The seeds for the climactic deluge of influenza were planted during the Christmas season of 1918, when folks traveled home to see Ma and Pa and attended crowded church services and other holiday events. If they did not carry the flu to Farmington, they took it back home with them. Nationwide one out of every four persons contracted the flu. In late January 1919, all of San Juan County's schools were closed. Up in Durango, 140 students had the flu and students in several entire grade levels were told to stay home.

The first week of February may have been the worst week in Farmington. On February 6, 1919 the Times Hustler reported nine influenza related deaths: Minnie Durnell, age 18, she was the valedictorian of Farmington High School in 1918; Mrs. Roy Watters passed after giving birth, her baby died one day later; Alfred Hubbard, age 26, he left behind a wife and child; Charles Warrant left behind a wife and four children; Willa Martin Wynn, age 34, she was married on June 3, 1919 and left behind her husband and a baby boy; Arthur Edgar, age 37; George Hudson, age 19; and lastly Isabelle Stewart, age 29. The week before, the Times Hustler reported six deaths. (That is 15 deaths just in Farmington in two weeks. By contrast 34 people have died so far in all of New Mexico during the 2017-2018 flu season.)

In early February, Dr. Smith had a physical breakdown due to his unceasing work in combatting the epidemic. He was laid up for three days. One fifth of the world's population contracted the flu and 50 million died. World War I, which coincided with the epidemic, claimed 16 million.[144]

The Irvin family, like so many others, felt the impact of the great influenza epidemic. An article in the Feb 6, 1919 issue of Times Hustler mentioned that a Mrs. Agnes Brame took the train from Silverton, Colorado to Farmington in order to help care for the Irvin family and their siege with the flu.[145]

This period of extended illness may have motivated Nat Irvin to move his family temporarily to a warmer climate. Two weeks later, the Times Hustler reported, "The N. H. Irvin family left this week for California, where they plan to remain until June. They will make the trip overland in two big cars. The

Harry Peisen family moved Tuesday into the N. H. Irvin home on Main street."[146]

This would have been an extremely ambitious undertaking at that time, given the distance, lack of service stations and quality of the roads. It may have been too ambitious. The following week, the paper carried this short statement, "The N. H. Irvin family who left for California the other week, came to grief in the mud flats on the reservation and partly wrecked their car, it is reported."[147] There was no report after this as to whether they continued to California or returned to Farmington. I hope they were able to continue on successfully. It would please me greatly to know that they visited the state that just thirteen years later would become my birthplace.

The following year, tax records showed that Nat made significant improvements to his property, possibly either to rent it or to put it up for sale, based on this local news article, "The R. A. Wade family has moved into the N. H. Irvin home on Main St."[148]

National problems that could not be dealt with easily during the war became issues again, once the war had ended. Two of these problems had been especially divisive; whether or not alcohol consumption should be illegal, and whether or not women should be allowed to vote. These were topics of much discussion and debate among the states at that time. Even some of the younger Irvins participated in the discussion. The February 5 *Times Hustler* mentioned that Tom Irvin (son and oldest child of Thomas H. Irvin) participated in a mock state convention on these topics at Farmington High School.[149]

Congress and the states ultimately settled the issue by amending the Constitution. Both the 18th amendment, Prohibition, and the 19th amendment, Women's Suffrage, became effective in 1920. Young Tom Irvin was a member of the senior class by that time, and a member of the high school's Literary Society. He was Nat Irvin's first and oldest grandchild and the first to graduate from high school. That fall he began his studies in mining engineering at the New Mexico School of Mines (Now New Mexico Tech) in Socorro.

Whereas his grandson seemed to be doing quite well, some of Nat Irvin's sons seemed, at times, to be on a totally different track. His son and namesake, NH, appeared to be following in the tracks of his older brother PB. An article in the September 30 *Times Hustler* states, "Last Saturday Sheriff J C Wynn arrested NH Irvin, Jr and George Lang, who were charged with breaking into the cellar of Jess Harwood and taking about 25 gallons of wine and grape juice, 25 jars of canned fruit and two auto tubes..." Nat Irvin had long since discovered that it wasn't always that easy to raise a family, but PB and NH seemed to pose the greatest challenge.[150]

PB seemed to be doing much better now. The year 1920 ended on a fairly happy note with PB and Georgia Irvin dining at her father George Salmon's home on Christmas, along with another couple.[151] It looked like PB was now even getting along with his in-laws. Married life appeared to have a stabilizing influence.

Unfortunately, if such was the case, it was short-lived. Just two Christmases later, PB knifed a man over a minor argument, nearly killing him. The *Times Hustler* reported:

> At a dance at Bloomfield Christmas night, Glen Lane, a stepson of Charles Holly was seriously wounded by PB Irvin. The report is that the two were quarreling over some feed for stock and a fight started when Irvin pulled a knife and cut Lane in the neck, arms and body. Dr. M.D. Taylor of Aztec was called to attend Lane and found the wounds very severe but no arteries had been severed although it was little less than a miracle that they had not been. Lane will recover if no complications set in. Irvin was arrested and was released on a $2000 bond.[152]

As if that wasn't bad enough, just a few months later, PB's life pretty much hit bottom. His young wife Georgia died, leaving him alone with two young sons. Her obituary read as follows:

> The deceased, Georgia Agnew Irvin, youngest daughter of Mr. and Mrs. George Salmon was born in Bloomfield March 19, 1896, and passed away after a short illness April 29, 1923. All her young life and school days were spent in the vicinity of Bloomfield. She always saw the bright things in life and was ever cheerful

and brought sunshine to those she came in contact with. On May 12, 1916 she was united in marriage to P.B. Irvin and from this union two sons were born. Bowen, aged six and Ray, three. She was always a loyal and devoted wife and mother and in her last hours her thoughts were for the care and education of her children. Besides the immediate family, husband and children, she leaves to mourn her loss, father and mother, also sisters, Mrs. Eloise Salmon, Mrs. Winnie Finch, and young brother Joe and also grandmother and grandfather, Mr. and Mrs. P.M. Salmon.[153]

I could find no other information about Georgia's illness. I can't help but wonder if she just died of a broken heart. How horrible it must have been for her, that her own husband almost killed a man at a Christmas party in the very town she grew up in. The circumstances of her death are haunting.

Nat's oldest, my grandfather Tom, seemed to fare much better. His son was now in his final year at college. And, just few months after his brother PB had lost his wife, Tom Irvin's oldest daughter, Iris Irvin (who was later to become my mother) graduated at the head of her high school class in 1923. A front-page article in the local paper mentioned it was the very first class to graduate from the new school building. And, it was the largest class that Farmington high school had ever graduated. There were twenty-three graduates.[154]

Farmington High School 1927(courtesy Farmington Museum)

TOM IRVIN
Basket Ball, '20
Wilsonian Literary Society, '18
Club Hispaña, '19
Literary Society, '20
"A College Town," '20
Assistant Business Manager of Nan-
iskad, '20
"As a wit, if not the first, in the very
first line"

Tom Irvin, class of 1921

IRIS IRVIN
"To do easily what is difficult
for others is the mark of talent."

Delphian Literary Society, '21
Los Vivos '21-'22-23
Glee Club '21-'22-'23
Basket Ball '21-'22
Economics Club '22-'23

Iris Irvin, class of 1923

*Ruth Irvin, 1920's, going
fishing*

Not to be outdone, Iris's younger sister Ruth made news in the same issue. Her story, however, didn't make the front page. A tiny article on the last page stated that she had injured her shoulder when she jumped from a moving car. End of school year hi-jinx? More likely, just Ruth being Ruth. My aunt Ruth, as I remember her, was always a bit of a character, loved adventure, and tended to act impulsively. Still, jumping out of a moving car?!

And speaking of moving cars, there were now various plans to build a two lane 'highway' from Gallup to Farmington via Shiprock, hopefully to be completed by harvest time. That turned out to be optimistic because of the numerous routes proposed.

Nat Irvin started the year 1924 being 'laid low at his home on East Main St. with pneumonia'.[155] To add to his misery, just a few months later, his son, PB plead guilty to the charge of assault with a deadly weapon. He was sentenced on June 2, 1924 to two-to-three years in the state penitentiary in Santa Fe.

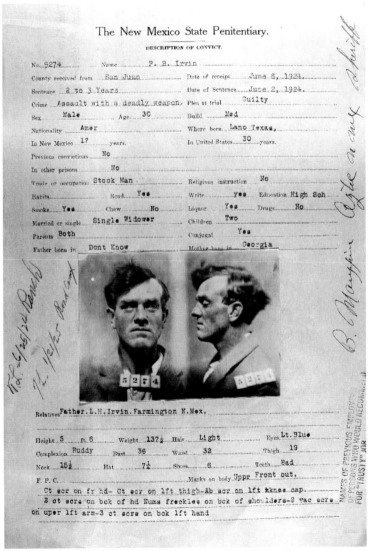

P. B. Irvin is convicted and sent to NM State Penitentiary

On a brighter note, his newly graduated granddaughter Iris Irvin found a job teaching at Kirtland High School in April, replacing the position vacated by Miss Hendrikson.[156]. A few months later, his granddaughter Ruth Irvin was listed as among the best typists in her typing class, based on a standard test provided by Underwood Typewriters.[157] She was also elected secretary-treasurer of the high school senior class of 1925.[158]

Some of Nat's sons might occasionally have caused him grief, but some of his grandkids seemed to be turning out pretty well.

The next year, some land held by Nat Irvin and others near Bloomfield was leased by a drilling company which planned to drill for oil in that area.[159] Natural gas had been discovered in this part of the county and was being distributed in the early 1920's, but most drillers were prospecting for oil, not gas. The discovery of commercial amounts of oil twenty miles west of Farmington in 1923 had set off a rash of exploratory drilling in this part of San Juan County. It wasn't long before wells were producing huge amounts of oil. Continental Oil Company laid pipeline to a new refinery in Farmington in 1925. Farmington did not become an oil 'boom town' at this time, however. Economic setbacks which would occur during the Great Depression, and the area's limited accessibility were formidable roadblocks to any major energy resource development. The local oil industry remained mostly speculative and exploratory. Some local businessmen invested in oil leases, betting on the future. Others operated small drilling rigs as wildcatters. But Farmington's economy would continue to rely primarily on agriculture for the next few decades.

During this time, Tom Irvin's oldest daughter, Iris, continued to pursue a career in teaching. She completed a summer course for teachers in 1925 at Las Vegas, NM.[160] That course work helped land her a job teaching at nearby Largo, NM. Largo was only about fifteen miles east of Bloomfield but was quite isolated. It was little more than a cluster of homes located a few miles south of Blanco, a town of a few hundred, in Largo Canyon. Her students were probably the children of Hispanic and Navajo sheep ranchers. Her sister Ruth, now graduated from high school, visited Iris in Largo and spent a week with her that November.[161]Those two sisters were always very close, even though their personalities were widely different.

Nat's son N.H. jr. continued down the path of his older brother, P. B. The June 18 *Times Hustler* reported, "In the case of the State vs N.H. Irvin, Jr., charging him with three felonious counts and assault and battery on Juan Trujillo, he pleaded guilty of assault and battery and was fined $25 and given 60 days in jail and the jail sentence suspended."[162] There were no details about the felonious accounts. N.H. jr. was now 30 years old and still single at this time.

Farmington held their first ever Community and Trades Day in late June of 1926. This trade show was put on by local businesses and offered a number of special bargains for those who attended. Tickets were awarded for purchases made at the show. A free movie was also provided to all those attending, a comedy that seemed to be enjoyed by all. Various merchants who'd set up displays had mixed reviews of the event, thought more people should have attended, but it was apparently a very warm day. At this event, Irene Irvin (wife of Tom Irvin), won a number of prizes. First prize was a ten-dollar gold piece; second prize a five-dollar bill; and 5th, 6th, and 7th prizes of one-dollar each. The newspaper mentioned that she had such good luck because of a large number of cash purchases she'd made at the event. Tom and Irene must be making pretty good money.[163] Tom was now in the oil business, operating a cable tool rig out on the mesa south of Bloomfield, where he and Irene were sometimes living while he was working at the well.[164]

Tom's youngest daughter Ruth also made the news this same summer, though it was about misfortune, not fortune. She was injured when a Ford coupe she was riding in overturned near Flora Vista. Ruth was badly bruised, another woman in the car had her arm broken. This was on July 4. It was not determined who was driving.[165] Ruth seemed to have more than her share of automobile accidents, especially given her young age. But, after all, this was the Twenties and young women in our country were feeling their new independence. It could be that they were celebrating their country's independence just a bit too much on that day.

My aunt Ruth's life was about to change shortly. An article in the August 13 issue of *Times Hustler* mentions that a Nick Brink was visiting Bloomfield from the Two Grey Hills store.[166] This young man, so different in temperament from her, would be a most stabilizing influence.

Nick's father, Leonard Peter Brink, had played an important role in New Mexico. After he married Elizabeth Van Eeuwen, they moved to the southwest in 1900. A Christian Reform missionary, Leonard help start the first Navajo high school in Rehoboth (near Gallup), New Mexico where he translated the first portions of the Bible into the Navajo language, no mean task, given the complexity of that language. Leonard Brink's family spent 35 years among the Navajos, first in Tohatchi (1900-1913), then in Toadlena (1914-1925), and finally in Farmington (1925-1936).

His son, Nicholas, known as Nick, literally grew up among the Navajo. He shared a common trait of Navajos. He was quiet and self-effacing. Maybe that's why he found my outgoing and boisterous aunt Ruth so attractive. The son of a preacher meets the daughter of a cowboy turned wildcatter.

Tom's oldest daughter, Iris, was rehired by the San Juan County Board of Education to teach at the rural school in Largo for the 1926-27 school year.[167] An article in *Times Hustler* October 1 mentioned that she came in from school to visit her parents in Farmington over the weekend.[168]She had no car and didn't drive. Such visits would still have been done on horseback. I find it hard, still, to imagine my mother riding horseback nearly twenty miles just to be with her family, but there are old photographs that indicate she knew her way around horses.

This same year, one of Nat's married daughters, Agnes (now Mrs. Byron Bell) came down from Joliet, Montana to visit her father and other relatives in the area. She returned to Montana in November, but while in Farmington had sent a case of apples to friends in Montana and they exclaimed they were the best apples they'd ever tasted.[169]Produce from this area was becoming nationally recognized as some of the country's finest.

A marriage certificate from Missoula, Montana states that Nat's youngest son, Boots, married Effie N. Fox on April 30, 1927. He used the name Bulloch Irvin, instead of Ivan or his nickname 'Boots', neither of which he apparently cared for. He and Effie had two children, Yvonne and Darrell. I had gathered from conversations with my relatives that Boots Irvin enjoyed cattle ranching and he may have moved to Montana with his sister Agnes, so that he could work on a ranch in the 'Big Sky' state. It's possible, too, that he was encouraged to move there in order to avoid the influence of his two older brothers, PB and NH. Boots Irvin never returned to Farmington except to attend a few of his siblings' funerals.

PB Irvin maintained a good record during his incarceration at the state penitentiary. While under sentence he worked on a ranch and later at a road camp. When released he moved in with his parents in Farmington, where his two sons visited him briefly when school was out. They then returned to live with their grandparents, Mr. & Mrs. George Salmon in Bloomfield.[170]. The Salmon's continued to raise PB's boys from this time on. PB earned his living from that time on either working on ranches or driving trucks.

Severe flooding occurred in the San Juan Basin on June 29, 1927. However, the flooding was localized and did not cause widespread damage, compared to the huge flood of 1911. During this same time, Texas businessmen organized the Southern Union Gas Company with pipelines to Farmington that would eventually extend to Albuquerque and Santa Fe. Tom Irvin continued drilling for oil as a 'wildcatter' out on the mesa south of Bloomfield and just a few miles east of the Southern Union Gas Company facility. A wildcatter is someone who drills for oil in unexplored areas, hoping to strike it rich. If the driller is lucky, he often sells or leases the well to a large oil company. Tom was still using an old wooden cable tool rig, even though rotary drills had been around for many years and were much faster. But they were also much more expensive. He also built his derricks of wood, even though the newer ones were made of steel. He always worked hard but he never struck it rich. Nick Brink, also became a driller, who partnered with Tom on some of their drilling sites. There are still producing wells with the Brink name on the lease to this day. But their wells up on the mesa are few in number and produce mostly gas and at a relatively low rate.

Tom Irvin's youngest daughter Ruth married Nick Brink near the end of this year, on November 23, 1927. They were married in Navajo County, Arizona, but claimed to be residents of Mesa, in Apache County, just east of and adjacent to Navajo County. Mesa probably referred to Horse Mesa, which is right at the New Mexico border and just west of Shiprock, New Mexico.

So, why did they marry in Arizona instead of Farmington? It's possible that Nick was working for an oil company that was drilling in that area during that time. Nick Brink listed his occupation as a tool-dresser, working at oil wells in the 1930 U.S. census.

Why wasn't their marriage listed in the Farmington newspaper? A very careful search found no news article about their wedding, even though Ruth's father, Tom Irvin, and Nick's father, the Rev. L.P. Brink were both mentioned frequently in the Farmington news. I can only conclude that Nick and Ruth had a rather quiet, private wedding.

There's a probable reason for this lack of publicity. Their first child, and my first cousin, Iris Laverne Brink, was born on February 23, 1927. I located a copy of their marriage license and checked the marriage date carefully, for obvious reasons. The local paper may not have carried the story because Nick and Ruth's families, both quite well known in Farmington, weren't keen on publicizing that their children hadn't married until eight months after their first child was born! I had not known this until I began writing this history. My cousin never mentioned that she was born out of wedlock, not even to my sister, and they were very close. She should have realized that it wouldn't have mattered in the least to either of us.

In spite of this situation, Nick apparently got along quite well with his father-in-law. He and Tom Irvin worked and later lived together out near one of their drilling sites on the mesa south of Bloomfield.

Tragedy struck the Irvin family in late summer of 1928. The *Times Hustler* reported:

Word was received from Gallup on Sunday that Mrs. Fred Carson, formerly Miss Elsie Irvin, was very critically ill. Mr. and Mrs. John Graham left for Gallup at once. Mr. Graham returned home the same day but his wife remained to care for her sister's children. Sunday evening Mrs. N. H. Irvin Sr., Tom Irvin, and Mrs. Charles Brothers, mother, brother and sister of Mrs. Carson, and Mr. and Mrs. N. Brink went to Gallup. They all returned Monday evening after Dr. Hannet had performed an operation. Monday there seemed to be some hope that Mrs. Carson would recover.[171]

Unfortunately, Elsie died the same day that paper was published and her funeral was covered in the following week's issue.[172]. The service was conducted at Charles Brothers' home in Farmington and she was interned at Greenlawn Cemetery in Farmington. The article reminded readers that her family had come to Farmington in 1905. Elsie's husband, Fred Carson, managed a trading post near Gallup.

Elsie was the first of Nat Irvin's ten children to die, and at much too early an age. She was only thirty-nine. She left behind two young children, a boy and a girl. Fred Jr. was thirteen and his sister, Donna, was only nine. I noticed in her obituary that Elsie's' middle name was Arden. How very special to carry the name of that little town in Texas closest to the ranch where she was born. Her place of birth was listed at Sherwood, Texas. Sherwood had just replaced San Angelo, the county seat of Tom Green county, as the keeper of records for the newly formed Irion County.

That same year, Tom Irvin's oldest daughter Iris met and married a Navy petty officer in California on December 10, 1928. Newspaper articles indicate that Iris taught at Largo, New Mexico, the school year of 1926-27 so she would not have left Farmington before June, 1927. After that, she attended Arizona Teacher's College at Tempe before deciding to move to California. It's not certain when she left Arizona but the dates suggest that she only attended college there for one year. She must have been a very adventurous type to leave her family and home and venture off so far as a young single woman. But this was the 1920's and times were changing. Women everywhere were becoming bolder and more independent.

In Los Angeles, she began her studies at UCLA toward a California teaching credential. She worked as a ticket seller at a theater and also at a nearby dance hall to help pay for her schooling. While working at the dance hall, she met Fred Scanlan, a Navy petty officer on liberty ashore from the aircraft carrier USS Lexington It was only the second aircraft carrier in the US Navy at that time, and carried a full contingent of bi-planes.

Iris Irvin, upper right, with friends in California 1927

Fred Scanlan, on left, with friends in Nanking, China 1924

Fred Scanlan was 25 years old at that time, born and raised in the small Hudson Valley town of Highland Falls, New York. He had completed a few years of high school and attended business school before joining the Navy at the age of seventeen.

His father was in the Army, stationed at West Point Academy, a fort that had become a college to train Army officers, just adjacent to Highland Falls. After enlisting in 1920, Fred Scanlan served mostly in the Philippines and in China (including the Yangtze campaign 1926-27) and by this time was planning to make his career in the Navy. He met Iris Irvin at the dance hall and fell in love with this woman of the West. After a brief courtship, the couple traveled to San Francisco where they married in the historic and beautiful Mission Dolores on December 10, 1928.

Shortly after they married, Fred Scanlan's orders transferred him to the east coast. During that time Iris returned to Farmington and put her teaching skills to work by helping PB's children with their schooling. The Navy was good to the young married couple, and soon re-assigned Fred to shore duty doing recruitment at in Buffalo, NY, not too far from his home town in Highland Falls. Their first child, my sister Patricia Ruth Scanlan was born in Buffalo on April 8, 1930.

They were transferred back to California early in 1933, where dad's carrier was once again stationed. This was just in time to experience the worst earthquake in the state since the 1906 quake in San Francisco. I can only imagine how my pregnant mother must have felt when the tremors began and buildings began to fall. Their second child, Thomas (that's me), was born in Long Beach, California on June 2, 1933. The Seaside Hospital where I was born had been severely damaged by the quake. Most of the outer walls on one side of the hospital were missing. But many city buildings fared much worse.

Returning to Tom Irvin in Farmington, plenty had happened since his daughter Iris had left for California. The area continued to have its own natural disasters, not from tremors but from too much water. The September 25, 1929 issue of the *Farmington Republic* reported, "Tom Irvin in making a trip to Aztec had to detour a circling route almost double the distance. To get by Flora Vista he had to go five miles west and drop down from the foothills. The storm's havoc to roads is unprecedented in the occupation [sic] since the ancients departed."[173] Much of the roadway in this area was still unpaved. Heavy downpours and runoff occasionally washed away whole sections of local roads.

In 1930, Farmington gained recognition as an area of great scientific interest. The local newspaper stated:

> A new branch of the Archaeological Society of New Mexico was formed in Farmington Monday night following an illustrated lecture at the high school auditorium on Prehistoric New Mexico by Dr. Edgar L. Hewett of the School of, American Research. Later a branch of the Museum of New Mexico is to be established here.
>
> Dr. Hewett made the amazing statement that, "Of all the wealth of pottery and artifacts taken from hundreds of ancient ruins in the San Juan Basin, none had found their way into the state museum at Santa Fe except what had been excavated by University of New Mexico students at Chaco Canyon National Monument last summer..."
>
> He continued, "In my travels which have taken me around the world I have not seen a desert scene anywhere that surpasses in scenic grandeur that vista which greets the eye of the traveler on the Cuba-Bloomfield state highway from the Otis trading post past the Huerfano, sacred Navajo mesa, to the wonderful Twin Angels badlands formation which rivals if not excels those of the Painted Desert in Arizona. San Juan county has another great scenic attraction in the little-known Monument valley of weird formations in the fossil fields near Pueblo Bonito historic ruins. Of great interest, are two great fossil beds, one of which lies ten miles northwest of Pueblo Bonito, where perfect specimens of dinosaur fossil mammals are found. Chaco Canyon National Monument will this year be put on one of the direct routes of the Harvey detours, as tourists can see Chaco Canyon, then go to the Aztec ruins and on to Mesa Verde la one trip, thanks to the excellent state highway built last year from Cuba to Bloomfield, with a good road branching off at the Otis trading post to Pueblo Bonito.[174]

What makes all of this particularly exciting to me isn't just that a local branch of this society was formed (The San Juan

Archaeological and Scientific Society) but that my grandfather Tom Irvin was elected to serve on the research committee, along with Orville Ricketts, the long-time editor and co-owner of the *Farmington Times Hustler*!

So, at age 50, this ex-farmer and cowboy and wildcat oil driller who was lucky to survive Apache raids when he was but an infant has now become a scientist, of sorts! It must have made old Nat Irvin pretty proud that his first-born had come so far.

But Nat Irvin also experienced sadness that same year. His mother, Mary, passed away on July 7. Her obituary in the *Times Hustler* read:

Mrs. Mary W. Irvin, mother of N.H. Irvin Sr. died at the home of her son here in Farmington Monday at the age of 94. She was a lovable old lady who made friends of all whom she met.

Mary Williamson Irvin was born in Alabama on February 29th, 1836 and when a little child, moved with her parents to Texas where she lived until 24 years ago last May, when she came to Farmington. Mrs. Irvin had made her home with her son N. H. Irvin since the death of her husband thirty-two years ago. She was the mother of two children, one of whom died in infancy.

Mrs. Irvin had been a member of the Baptist church for more than seventy-five years and had adhered very closely to the tenets of her church, living always a consistent and Christian life. She is survived by her son and wife, one sister who resides in Texas and is more than 87 years of age, nine grandchildren, a number of great grandchildren and five great-great grandchildren.

Altho almost helpless for the last two years her condition did not become critical until Friday and she passed away peacefully on Monday, July 7. She was a very patient invalid thinking more of others work and worry rather than of her own condition.

Funeral services were held at the Greenlawn cemetery Tuesday morning and were conducted by Rev. J.W. Evans, pastor of the Baptist Church.

Many people who did not know Mrs. Irvin personally will remember seeing her at work among the flowers in the Irvin yard prior to her illness and will recall her pleasant smile and cheery greeting. Mrs. Irvin was a great lover of flowers and great quantities of beautiful blossoms were sent to the funeral.[175]

Less than one year later, on June 4, 1931, Mary Irvin's only son died. Nathanial "Nat" Irvin's big heart finally gave out. The cause of his death was listed as arteriosclerosis. The *Farmington Times Hustler* reported on June 5, "N.H. Irvin, Sr., who had lived in Farmington for twenty-five years, passed away at his home here at ten thirty yesterday, Thursday, morning. Mr. Irvin, who was seventy-two years of age had been ill for about a month. The funeral will be held this Friday afternoon at 3 o'clock at the Bero Funeral Home. An obituary will appear next week."

His June 12 obituary follows:

FARMINGTON PIONEER "GOES WEST"

N.H. Irvin, Sr. was born May 30, 1859 in Washington County, Texas. He was married on March 12, 1879 to Lavina Ricketson of Llano, Texas. To this union were born ten children, of whom nine are still living. Mrs. Elsie Carson, a daughter, died three years ago. Mr. Irvin is survived by his widow and eight children: Tom, N.H. Jr., Mrs. Daisy Graham, Mrs. Mammie Jordan, and Mrs. Eva Brothers of this place, Mrs. Agnes Bell of Joliet, Mont., Boots Irvin of Filer, Idaho, P.B. Irvin of Arizona, and Mrs. W. W. Tomlinson of Texline, Texas. All of the children except Mrs. Tomlinson and P.B. were with Mr. Irvin when he died.

Mr. Irvin came to Farmington from Texas in 1906 and has lived here with his family since that time.

Mr. Irvin died at his home here on Thursday, June 4, 1931. Brief services were held at Greenlawn cemetery on Friday afternoon, June 5th, with the Rev. L. P. Brink in charge. Burial was in Greenlawn cemetery.

Levina Irvin, left, with great-granddaughter
Natalie Irvin and mother in law, Mary Irvin.
c. 1929

His New Mexico death certificate was signed by his wife, Levina. She listed his occupation as stockman, raising livestock. Her husband may have farmed and speculated in land sales and oil wells, but to Levina, he would always be that handsome young cowboy she'd met in west Texas. Nat was the last of the pioneering male Irvin's who had to struggle against both Indians and a lawless environment for his survival. His wife Levina, who had shared his life fully, would remain the family matriarch for another twenty-five years.

18. Nat Irvin's Firstborn, Tom

As a boy, I probably met most of Nathanial and Levina's children at one time or another, but I knew his oldest son best. That's because I lived at times with Tom Irvin and his wife Irene, who were my mother's parents. For that reason, most of the remainder of this account will focus on Tom and Irene Irvin and their family.

The years during which I lived with or near Nat and Levina's children were mostly spent at Tom and Irene Irvin's home five or six miles south of Bloomfield, New Mexico. Tom and his son-in-law Nick Brink built what were probably intended as temporary homes for themselves and their families. They had been working together drilling for oil in that area for several years and it made more sense to live near their oil derrick than to drive back and forth to Farmington every day. That trip would have been thirty-some miles, roundtrip, over poorly maintained dirt roads which were sometimes washed away by torrential rains, referred to locally as 'cloud-bursts'.

As I described earlier, their homes were simple, square buildings with plank floors, walls and roofing. The outer walls and roof were covered with tarpaper, an inexpensive form of weather proofing widely used at that time. It kept out the wind, dust and rain, and provided a small degree of insulation from the winter cold. There were three such structures separated from each other by a few hundred feet. Two of them served as homes for the Irvin and Brink families, and a third, one-room structure accommodated guests or crew. That one-room cabin may have served originally as a place for Tom and Nick to stay overnight or get out of the weather during the earlier times when they were still commuting from their homes in Farmington. This compound of tarpaper-covered wooden cabins was referred to as the 'camp' because it was so remote from anyone or anyplace else. And like most camps, there were few amenities. To as

197

casual observer, that cluster of rather primitive structures would have looked very much like a camp.

Tom and Irene's home here, not much more than a bedroom separated from the kitchen and dining area, must have seemed quite primitive after their home in downtown Farmington, but I never heard anyone complain about the lack of telephones, electricity or running water. Nor about the lack of neighbors. They had their daughter and son-in-law with their two small children just shouting distance away.

Nick Brink with son, Paul (Buster) and daughter Iris (Midge) c. 1930

What their 'camp' lacked in amenities, it more than made up for in natural beauty. There was sage, scrub cedar and pinon pine, numerous arroyos and gullies cutting through colorful sandstone, spectacular cloud formations amid deep blue skies, views of snow-capped mountain ranges to the north and east, and views of striking sandstone formations in nearby canyons and Angel's Peak to the south. There were abundant jackrabbits, coyotes, horned toads, mourning doves, quail and hawks, and many other species of wildlife. There were spectacular sunsets, thrilling thunderstorms, and at times when the wind subsided, a serene stillness that filled the open spaces of that location.

Irene and Tom Irvin outside the general store in Bloomfield, early 1930's

I'm not sure just when the Irvin and Brinks moved out to the camp. According to the *Times Hustler* of May 4, 1934, both Tom Irvin and Nick Brink were on the committee for better schools in Farmington, so they were apparently still living in Farmington[176]. However, they were probably both working out on the mesa south of Bloomfield at this time. *Times Hustler* carried a short article in June of that year stating that, "…Tom Irvin of the Angels Peak Oil Company drilling crew had his face bandaged for several days, caused by a piece of steel entering his eye. It is much better now."[177] Angels Peak was about seven miles south of Bloomfield, two miles south of the camp. An earlier article in January stated that, "Tom Irvin and associates have a standard rig nearly completed in the vicinity of township 28, range 10 W. It is probable a deep well will be spudded as soon as the rig is completed."[178] Those coordinates place the well almost due south of Bloomfield, five-plus miles, which would be just about where their 'camp' was located.

There were other clues. An old black-and-white photo shows young Paul and Iris Brink along with my sister, Pat, and me sitting on the running board of a relatively new Plymouth sedan. The background is a sage covered mesa, not somewhere in town. I look as if I'd just turned two years old, so this puts the year at 1935. And, according to the *Times Hustler*, Basin Motors Company Dodge and Plymouth of Farmington sold Tom Irvin a new Plymouth deluxe sedan sometime around July of the previous year.[179]

However, a September article in the *Times Hustler* lists Mrs. Irene Irvin, Tom Irvin's wife, as one of the two-member committee of East Farmington for the Democratic precinct primaries.[180] Perhaps Tom and Nick were still in the process of building the homes out at the camp at this time? The Brink children were elementary school age by now and were probably attending grade school in Farmington.

It's probable that the camp was built in stages, with maybe just the one small cabin, where Tom and Nick stayed when they started drilling operations. Their wives and the children most likely stayed in east Farmington until the children were older and the other two larger cabins were built.

left to right, Paul Brink, Pat Scanlan, Tom Scanlan & Iris Brink, at the camp, c. 1935

Whether or not their families had yet moved out to the camp, by 1936 Tom and Nick were fully involved with drilling activities in that area. The *Times Hustler* noted, "Kutz Canyon Oil and Gas Company, with Tom Irvin as field manager, is

200

straight reaming at a depth of 3100 feet."[181] That's a pretty deep well. They were probably hoping to encounter gas or oil by that time but apparently hadn't. The same article mentioned that, "Southern Union Production Company, operating in the Kutz Canyon district south of Bloomfield, in San Juan County, spudded a well on the Nick Brink lease on April 1." The paper commented, "This well will be watched with considerable interest as it is practically a 'wildcat' but if it proves productive will extend the structure (ed. note: the oil/gas field in that area) a considerable distance."

There was a very extensive article in that same issue of *Times Hustler* about Nick Brink's father, Rev. L. P. Brink, who had passed away on March 24 at the home of his oldest son, Dr. Peter B. Brink in Pomeroy, Washington. The article reminded readers of Rev. Brink's significant earlier contributions in translating hymns and parts of the Bible into the Navajo language, and that he'd made his headquarters in Farmington in 1926 where he resided and worked until the time of his death, stating further that, "… 'L. P.' was the able editor of 'The Christian Indian', a monthly Navajo mission field magazine with a nationwide circulation." The article summarized his contributions stating, "The Navajo trusted him and their trust was never betrayed." A memorial service was to be held in Farmington the following week with several guest speakers of note.[182] Nick Brink's father was, indeed, widely respected by the Navajo.

Later that same year, the September 4, 1936 *Times Hustler* announced a final probate hearing to be held on October 12 concerning the estate of Nathanial Irvin, who had died over five years ago. The probate process in Farmington apparently was no different from elsewhere. It progressed very slowly. Levina was executrix, and the following were listed as heirs: Tom Irvin, Daisy Graham, N.H. Irvin, Eva Brothers, Mamie Jordan, Boots Irvin, Agnes Bell, Willia Tomlinson, P.B. Irvin, Fred Carson Jr., and Donna Carson, Tom Irvin as Guardian of Donna Carson, a minor. These were all the surviving children or their spouses of that grand old west-Texan farmer, cattleman, land and oil speculator, Nathanial Hunt Irvin.[183]

It's possible that Tom Irvin plowed most of his inheritance into his drilling operations. Drilling was an expensive process, requiring extra laborers, specialized tools and a constant supply of metal casing, drill pipe and cable. Sometimes the expenses were legal in nature. The Kutz Canyon Oil and Gas Company, of which Tom and Nick were both members, had to file suit against an attempted 'claim-jumping' on some of their leased oil and gas properties in the summer of 1937.[184]

The inheritance may have helped in other ways. Later that summer, Tom Irvin bought his family a brand-new Dodge sedan from the Basin Motor Company in Farmington. The paper mentioned that he's "breaking the car in for service on the Bloomfield and Kutz Canyon structure roads but a Dodge can take most any kind of road."[185] I wonder what happened to that brand-new Plymouth that he purchased only three years ago? Could it have worn out in that short a time?

That's quite possible. The service roads referred to were unpaved and narrow roads winding their way across the mesa through sage and pinyon pine and numerous arroyos and small canyons, subject to washout during summer rains and full of pot holes and sand traps with ruts sometimes so deep the chassis would scrape. I learned to drive on those 'service roads' (at the age of twelve) and they could be quite challenging. There was very little traffic except an occasional truck hauling water or drill pipe, or a few steers that were grazing in the area who apparently believed they had as much right to the road as an automobile.

Sometime in 1937, the Tom Irvin family and probably the Nick Brink family must have moved out to the camp, because Tom's wife Irene was now listed as one of the alternate judges for the precinct which included the mesa south of Bloomfield.[186]

Nat Irvin's youngest son, Ivan 'Boots' Irvin, made the news in a humorous way later that year. A newspaper in the nearby town of Durango, Colorado stated that he'd been shanghaied in New York City and taken overseas to fight in the Spanish Civil War. He'd then escaped to North Africa but was unable to return home because of lack of citizenship proof. This caused quite a stir in Farmington until it was pointed out that the individual was actually Boots Erwin, who had previously lived in Bloomfield, NM, and was no relation to the Irvin family of Farmington or Bloomfield. Boots Irvin was in Montana at this time.[187]

Tom and Nick, their families now living up on the mesa, stepped up their drilling activities in that area south of Bloomfield. They were contemplating drilling down to a depth of about 5000 feet, hoping to find oil at the bottom of the Mesa Verde strata. They even brought in a consultant from a Denver firm to advise them on this project.[188] That venture apparently was not successful. The following year, an article in the *Times Hustler* stated, "Tom Irvin spent some time in town the first of the week working on details preparatory to resuming drilling for oil again in the Kutz canyon district. The showings of oil encountered in the other drillings in that field in which Tom has been interested encourage him to try again in a more promising location in the vicinity."[189]

Wildcat drillers, who usually lacked sophisticated geophysical means of searching for underground deposits, will tell you that the majority of such drillings end up with "dry holes". But, as I've mentioned previously, that's not the worst thing that can happen. Tom's deep test drilling the following year, part of the Kutz Deep Test, Inc., was closed down at 800 feet with a fishing job.[190] The drill bit and some of the pipe sections it connected to broke off in the well. At this point, they could either pay a specialized outfit to recover the drill bit and pipe, by 'fishing' for it, or just abandons the well altogether. The well was a total loss. The irony is that the same issue of *Times Hustler* mentioned that another well in the area, well no. 9-b, was now producing 4,500,000 cubic feet of gas per day, the largest ever brought in at the Kutz field.

Drilling for gas and oil is a gamble. An expensive gamble. In fact, for all of the time and money that Tom and his father invested in oil prospecting, neither ever struck it rich, so far as I was able to determine. They continued to live in their temporary homes out on the mesa south of Bloomfield but could no longer afford to drill independently as wildcatters. Nick kept working as a driller, but was now working for English Gas and Oil. Tom took a job with the nearby Southern Union Gas Company, inspecting the miles of gas lines that now crisscrossed the high mesa country where he lived. Some areas could only be reached by horseback or on foot.

Natural gas coming up from deep underground is a mix of different gases; methane, ethane, butane, propane, etc., and even heavier compounds, some of which liquify as the gas travels through the pipelines. Condensers spaced along the gas lines removed those heavier compounds. One of Tom's jobs was to drain the condensers. That particular task came with a benefit. The condensate had a high enough octane that it could be used as fuel for low pressure engines like those in his Model A. Free gas would have been a significant benefit at a time when his grandkids were driving back and forth to school every day to Aztec and Farmington. My cousin Midge Brink was now driving that old Model A even though she'd just turned thirteen. Her brother Buster, just a year younger, would soon be driving it, too.

In addition to drilling mishaps, the Irvins had other setbacks which made the news in 1940. The *Times Hustler* carried the following story on the front page:

> P.B. IRVIN JAILED OVER CUTTING FRAY.
> A disagreement which ended in an alleged assault with a knife occurred Saturday night between P. B. Irvin of Farmington and Bill Eaton of the Laplata section. The difficulty occurred on or near the highway where the road to Wood's Country Club leaves the highway. Eaton was brought to a local hospital where nine stitches were found necessary to close one wound and where it was discovered that one cut had entered a lung. Irvin, who was charged with assault with a deadly weapon, was arrested Wednesday at the residence of Wm. Kline south of the San Juan river. Irvin was taken before Justice of the Peace Charles Bolton where he pleaded not guilty and waived examination. He was bound over to the district court under $2000 bond and was in jail at last report.[191]

Apparently P.B.'s previous jail time for knifing someone was not sufficient reminder of the consequences of such actions. He was convicted in April of the following year but got off lightly, considering the seriousness of the injuries he inflicted. Instead of assault with intent to kill, he was convicted by jury of simple assault.[192]

19. World War II

The following year there was bad news for everyone. The December 12, 1941 issue of *Farmington Times Hustler* used a single word for their front-page headline; WAR. In addition to a brief description of the attack on Pearl Harbor, the newspaper carried the full text of President Roosevelt's address to the nation on December 8, his 'day of infamy' speech. The Bloomfield section of the paper noted "Several of our local boys are on the islands the Japs attacked. We are glad to hear Mrs. Tom Irvin has received word her son is safe."[193]

Not for long, as it turned out. Her son, Tom, a mining engineer working in the Philippines at the time, was among the many civilians captured by Japanese soldiers. They were interned in concentration camps at Santo Tomas and Los Banos, both previously universities near the capitol city of Manila.

Bad news continued. In early February of 1942, Irene Irvin was reported as critically ill at her home near Bloomfield, and that her two daughters, Ruth and Iris, would be visiting her from the west and east coasts.[194]Nick and Ruth Brink and their children had moved to Vallejo, CA during the war years of 1941-1944, where Nick worked as a welder and Ruth worked in an ammunition factory. Iris was with her family in Maryland while her husband was at sea in the Atlantic on the battleship Texas. Later in the war, he served in the Pacific aboard the aircraft carrier, *Shangri La*.

Within a few weeks, Tom's wife Irene was on the mend and his daughters Ruth Brink and Iris Scanlan both returned to their families on the west and east coast, respectively. The *Times Hustler* noted in their Bloomfield section on February 27 that Mrs. Tom Irvin was still a patient at the Farmington hospital but was improving.[195] She eventually recovered fully and returned to her home up on the mesa south of Bloomfield.

There was little news about the Irvins after that for several years as the war continued. In late March of 1945, as World War II was gradually winding down, Tom Irvin's family experienced first joy, then tragedy. Tom's wife, Irene, wrote about all of this in a letter dated March 20, 1945 to her daughter, Iris Scanlan in Maryland:

Dear Iris and children,

Thanks very much for your offer of money, but I have plenty. We are better off financially than we have ever been.

Tom had been sick a long time but refused to go to the doctor until it was too late. Dr. Moran said if he had come in six months ago, he would have been all right now but even three months ago would have been just a Gamble. Said he knew when he went in there was no hope. I kept hoping that he would pull through. He suffered agonies and had for a week before we took him in. It was terrible to have to watch him. I stayed every day and Saturday night at the hospital. I was so glad I stayed Saturday night he always hated for me to leave. He knew everyone until just a few minutes before he died. He had a stroke and lived a few minutes after he got so bad. A clot of blood broke in his kidneys killing him and just a little while. Doctor said he had the worst kidneys and bladder he ever saw.

This is a lonesome place now but I'm going to stay as long as the kids are near. If they move away, I will have to leave. Nick wants me to move to their house but I want my own place.

Tommy will be home soon. I don't have an idea what he plans to do but he has to get better before he can work. I will be glad to have him here and Tom was so glad that we heard from him.

I don't think Tom weighed more than a hundred. Tommy said he lost 50 lb. There was a very large crowd at the funeral and more nice flowers than I thought was in Durango. So many people didn't know about it, said they would have sent some. He is buried by little Jackie.

I am doing all right. My blood pressure was high yesterday and I have to go in again this week but I didn't collapse like they were all afraid I would do. Buster stays with me at night. Tom tried to tell me something to tell Buster but couldn't say it.

Mammy was here, sis came over as did Freddie Carson. He didn't hear until 12 and got here at 3. PB came in. We had so much snow and rain that the roads in some places where impossible.

I believe there was more real grief than any funeral I ever saw. He had so many friends. Some of the men cried like babies. Dr. Rice was worse than any man I ever saw. I regret that we didn't just put him in the car and take him in. Nick and midget head hard cases of flu.

I wish I had some good pictures of Tom. Ruth is going to write some letters and I must write to Tommy. It will be a sad homecoming for him. He doesn't know I was sick. We received a card written while he was a prisoner and mailed since Los Banos was freed. He said he received three letters from me, one from you, and one from Larry Robinson. He is in Manila care of the Red Cross.

Hope all of you are well and I am anxious about Freddy. Take care of yourselves. If I get sick or need you for anything, I'll let you know. His bank account was so that I could continue checking.

love from your sad Grandma and Mama

Nat and Levina's oldest son and the first of their children to marry, had died at the relatively young age of sixty-five. Thomas Hiram Irvin was a kind, intelligent man who worked hard all his life to provide a better life for his children. He was a rancher, a farmer, a metal worker and then a gas and oil worker in his later years. He was an amateur geologist and had a love and knowledge of the natural world he grew up in. He also tried his hand at water color paintings of local landscapes in his final years.

Young Tom Irvin's rescue from the Philippines and his father's death were both front page news in the *Times Hustler*:

MRS. TOM IRVIN HEARS FROM HER SON, TOM, WHO WAS RESCUED FROM LOS BANOS. Mrs. Tom Irvin informs T-H that she has heard from her son, Tom, from Manila, the day after he was rescued from Los Banos. He wrote he had lost 50 pounds, but was really eating Army chow. He said the American soldiers were a beautiful sight. He plans to come home soon. The sudden death of his father, Tom H. Irvin here, Sunday, will be mighty sad news for the son when he learns of it.[196]

On page two of the same issue of the *Times Hustler* that announced his son's rescue, there was a full obituary for Thomas H. Irvin. It cited his birth as Jan. 8th, 1886 (incorrect, it was actually 1880) in Lake Valley, New Mexico and his death in Farmington, New Mexico on March 18, 1945, along with just a few other biographical facts. A large number of his family attended the service, including his wife, Irene, his daughters Ruth and Iris, his mother Levina, and many of his married siblings from both out of state and in state. Below the obituary was a special Thank You article to all those who were so kind to Tom during his illness and sent such beautiful flowers. The card was from Mrs. Irene Irvin, Nick and Ruth Brink and family, Mr. and Mrs. Fred Scanlan and family, Tom Irvin Jr. and Mrs. Lavina [sic] Irvin.[197]

Young Tom Irvin arrived home from the Philippines in May of that year. In June, the Irvin family had somewhat of a grand reunion. The *Times Hustler* reported:

> Mrs. Tom Irvin of the Bloomfield section, was a visitor in town Wednesday. She is happy to have her three children home again for the first time in several years. Her son, 'Tommy', was recently liberated from a Japanese prison camp in the Philippine Islands. Tommy was a civilian engineer at Manila for several years before the fall of the city. Three years of life as a prisoner was rather rough on him, but Mrs. Irvin says he has regained his weight and is feeling okay again. Also home on a visit is her daughter Iris, Mrs. Fred ScanIon (sic), whose husband is a Navy officer on an airplane carrier in the Pacific. Her other daughter, Mrs. Nick Brink, has been living at Bloomfield for the past year.[198]

Nick and Ruth Brink and their children Buster and Midge had returned to New Mexico just months before the war ended. Nick resumed his work as a driller with the English Drilling Company. The *Times Hustler* of July 13, 1945 mentioned that Mrs. Tom Irvin was down from her home above

Bloomfield and had mentioned that her son, Tommy, who'd been a mining engineer in the Philippines when captured, is now planning to work in Arabia. He'd be working for the same mining company he worked for in South America, as soon as transportation is arranged.[199]

Tom Irvin, Jr., Nat and Levina's first grandchild, spent only a few month's recuperating at his home in New Mexico. He then left for somewhere in Arabia, where he was employed briefly by American Smelting Company. He sailed back to New York City from Cairo, Egypt on May 19, 1946 arriving on June 10, too ill with tuberculosis to continue working. He traveled to San Diego with me by Trailways bus that summer in order to visit his sister. He died the following year on July 14, 1947 in New Mexico, just a few years before the use of streptomycin and other drugs effective against TB became widely available. Following is part of his obituary from the *Farmington Times Hustler*:

> Tom Bulloch Irvin, son of Mrs. Tom Irvin of Farmington passed from this life July 12th in the Presbyterian Sanatorium at Albuquerque at the age of 43 years and 7 months.
>
> Tom was born in Roby, Texas, and came to Farmington with his parents when still a lad. He graduated from Farmington High School and later from the New Mexico School of Mines at Socorro. As a mining engineer he was stationed in several parts of the world including South America, Central America, Cuba and the Philippines. He was in the latter country when the war broke out and was captured and made a Japanese prisoner in the fall of Manila. He endured with other American boys the rigors and hardships of four years imprisonment, which undermined his health. After the war he returned and, in the hopes, that the climatic conditions would be helpful took up his profession in Arabia, but found the climate unfavorable. He was hospitalized for a time in Cairo, Egypt, and then returned to America and became a patient at the Presbyterian Sanatorium in Albuquerque until his death.
>
> He leaves a mother and two sisters, Mrs. Nick Brink of Farmington and Mrs. Fred Scanlan of

Washington, D. C. While Tom traveled afar, he always regarded Farmington as his home town.[200]

Tom Irvin was the only uncle I ever knew. I never met my uncle on my father's side. So, he and I had become remarkably close, given how little time we spent together. He told me stories about his years in the prison camps that he apparently never shared with his mother or sisters. Like me, he was somewhat of an introvert and perhaps he felt he could share those often horrifying stories with his impressionable thirteen-year-old nephew.

Unfortunately, Tom Irvin Jr. never married. As a consequence, the surname Irvin from this particular ancestral line ended with his death.

Thomas Bulloch Irvin c. 1940

20. The Post-WWII Years

I'll complete Nat and Levina Irvin's family story by recounting just a few more events in the lives of their surviving children and their families. Most of what follows focuses on those that I knew best, the children and grandchildren of my grandfather Thomas H. Irvin, Nat's firstborn.

Paul 'Buster' Brink, my first cousin and son of Nick and Ruth Brink, as you will recall, was very much like a big brother to me whenever we stayed with my mom's parents at the camp. Buster graduated from Aztec High School in mid-term, early1946. He had previously attended Vallejo High School in California when his family was living there working at the shipyards during WWII. He joined the Marines on January 5, 1946. After boot camp in San Diego, he spent the rest of his three-year enlistment at the Marine Air Wing in El Toro, California working as a clerk and officer's aide. He eventually attained the rank of staff sergeant.

Shortly after Buster had joined the Marines, his sister and only sibling, Iris 'Midge' Brink, married Jimmy Smith Jr. of Farmington. Jimmy had enlisted in the Navy just a few days after Pearl Harbor. He had to travel to Durango, Colorado in order to enlist.[201] He was only seventeen at the time. He served in the Pacific until his discharge late in 1945.[202] Iris and Jimmy married on April 11, 1946 at the San Juan Episcopal Church in Farmington, with immediate family attending.[203]

On January 29, 1949, just a few weeks after he was discharged from the Marines, Paul Brink and his father were involved in a tragic auto accident near Farmington. It was reported in the Farmington newspapers as follows:

FARMINGTON CRASH TAKES ONE LIFE. Farmington, Jan 30 (AP) – A Kirtland man was impaled on a hoist beam and killed last night in an auto-pickup truck collision on Highway 55, seven miles west of Farmington.

State Policeman Andy Andrews identified the dead man as Zane Foutz, 21. Three other Kirtland residents in the auto with him were injured.

The injured are Garry Massey, 25, soldier home on furlough, who had serious head injuries; Darlene Williams 17, broken arm; and Lowell Christensen, 19, minor cuts.

Andrews reported Paul Brink and his father, Nick Brink, were in the truck. They escaped injury. The hoist beam was made of pipe. It pierced Foutz' body and the back of the car seat. The side of the auto was sheared off.

Officers worked from about midnight till 2 a.m. to clear away the wreckage.[204]

That road, which connects Shiprock to Farmington, is narrow and winding, with a number of small hills which don't always provide a distant view of traffic ahead. Evidently the automobile overtook the truck at a high rate of speed and the driver was not able to slow down in time. A group of three young men and a woman driving at that time of night might have been drinking but neither article mentioned that alcohol was a factor. Because this occurred in January, there may have been rain or snow or the roads were icy. Whatever the cause, this must have badly shaken up both Buster and his father. It was also a dire precursor of the hazards of their work in gas and oil.

Just a few months later, on April 10, 1949 Paul 'Buster' Brink married Shirley Smith, the sister of his brother-in-law, Jimmy Smith, Jr. They met because their siblings had married each other. He had been dating Shirley back when they were both in high school.

Buster, college admission
photo, 1949

Shirley, high school
yearbook photo, 1947

Buster and Shirley's relationship had not always been a smooth one. In the summer of 1947, while Buster was in California, she quit high school and eloped with a Robert Tate from Colorado. The *Times Hustler* described that wedding briefly as a 'quiet marriage in Aztec' on August 12, after which they left the same day to 'make their home in Texas'.[205] Her father had the marriage annulled and Shirley returned to her classes at Farmington High School.[206] She graduated in 1948 and then attended State Teacher's College in Silver City, NM that fall[207] but returned home in January after just one semester.[208] She married Paul Brink that April. The Farmington paper described their wedding as follows:

> The lovely chapel of the Navajo Methodist Mission was the scene of the marriage for Shirley Smith, daughter of Mr. & Mrs. James W. Smith, and Paul Brink, son of Mr. and Mrs. Nicholas N. Brink on Sunday, April 10 at two o'clock. The double ring ceremony was performed by Willard P. Bass in the presence of the immediate family and a few friends.
> The bride wore an aquamarine afternoon dress with white and gold accessories and her corsage was pink carnations. She was attended by Mrs. Wm. Crowley, a school friend, who wore a navy-blue afternoon frock with pink accents...[209]

The article goes on to mention the best man, the pianist, etc. and those friends and relatives who attended. It also mentioned that Shirley had graduated from Farmington HS and had attended State Teachers College in Silver City, and that Paul had graduated from Aztec HS and just returned from three years in the Marine Corps. They would be living in an apartment in Farmington until the Fall semester began at New Mexico School of Mines, where Paul had been accepted.

So, that fall Buster and Shirley moved to Socorro, New Mexico where he began classes at the New Mexico School of Mines. Paul's parents, Nick and Ruth Brink, visited them in mid-October of that year while returning from Kermit, Texas, where they'd visited Paul's sister Iris and her husband, James Smith, Jr.[210]

Paul and Shirley wasted no time in starting a family. They had their first child, Thomas Dane Brink, during that first semester at Socorro, just two weeks before Christmas on December 11. The birth was a front-page story in the *Farmington Daily Times*, primarily because Thomas Dane was a "fifth generation son", his great-great-grandmother Levina Irvin still being alive.[211] By this time, Paul's sister Iris Smith had a two-year-old son, Michael, and a one-month-old daughter, Nola Corrine.

Nat Irvin' second oldest son, P.B. Irvin, passed away that same year on October 13, 1949. The *Farmington Daily Times* carried a short article, noting that he had died suddenly near Shiprock. The article included a very brief bio, a list of surviving immediate family, and the time and place of his service and internment in Farmington.[212] There was no mention of cause of death.

P.B. had been living on and off with his mother Levina Irvin and had been in poor health, likely a result of hard living and too much alcohol. He was the 'character' of the Irvin clan, very spirited but too often in trouble. But he was also the victim of tragedy, losing his wife so early in their marriage. It probably wasn't easy growing up in a family with six older sisters to boss him around. Although I don't recall knowing PB personally, I think that I would have liked him. We may have met during my visits at Levina Irvin's home, but I was a young boy then and can't say that I remember him. I do remember that his name was often mentioned at family gatherings, not always for the best of reasons. He was the blackest sheep of the Irvin family.

Buster and Shirley Brink had a second son, Charles Donald, on March 13, 1951. Everything seemed to be going well for them, but on May 25 tragedy intervened. Buster's father Nick was seriously burned at a job site near Moab, Utah while saving two others from a burning propane truck which had exploded. One of the passengers had foolishly lit a cigarette. Nick was rushed to the hospital but died the following day from burns over most of his body.[213]. Buster completed his second-year studies at Socorro and immediately returned to Bloomfield to work for English Drilling so that he could help his widowed mother. He returned to college again in September at Socorro.[214]

Just a few months later, the Irvin clan experienced another loss. Tom Irvin's widow (my grandmother), Mary Irene Irvin, moved to Kermit, Texas in September to stay with her granddaughter Iris 'Midge' Smith during Midge's final months of pregnancy. 'Midge' Smith had a second daughter, Sue Ann, on October 4. Midge's visiting grandmother became ill shortly thereafter and died just before Christmas, 1951. At that time, she was only a few hours' drive from the small Texas towns of Ranger and Roby. The Farmington newspaper obit read:

> Mary Irene Bulloch was born June 28, 1885 in Ranger, Texas. She was married to Thomas H. Irvin December 21, 1902 in Roby, Texas. Out of this union was born three children, a son, Tom, who died in 1947, and two daughters, Iris (Mrs. Fred Scanlan) of Mutual, Md. and Mrs. Ruth Brink, of Durango, Colo.
>
> The family moved to Farmington in 1910. Mr. Irvin died in 1945 but Mrs. Irvin had lived there ever since 1910 until September when she went to Kermit, Tex. to make her home with a granddaughter, Mrs. James Smith, Jr. She died in Kermit Dec. 3. She is survived by her two daughters, four grandchildren, five great grandchildren, one sister, Mrs. Ruth Head of Sherman, Tex. and two brothers, Clifford of Little Rock, Ark. And Phillip of Tallahassee, Fla.
>
> Funeral Services were held Thursday at St. John's Episcopal Church. Interment was in Greenlawn Cemetery.[215]

Mary Irene Irvin's two daughters, Mrs. Fred Scanlan (my mother) and Ruth Brink, both attended the services along with other friends and relatives. A card of thanks was posted in the following issue by the Scanlan and Brink families.

Irene Irvin's youngest daughter, Ruth Brink, remarried to a Jack Young. All I knew about Jack was that he was part Indian, possibly Ute, and shared Ruth's love of trout fishing with a fly-rod. They moved to Wyoming for a few years, but their marriage didn't last. Ruth said that "Nick had spoiled her". She eventually left Jack and some of her favorite fishing spots and returned to New Mexico to live close to her daughter. Jimmy and Iris Smith had returned to Bloomfield from his job in Texas and he was now working for a local gas and oil company.

Tom and Irene's oldest daughter, Iris Scanlan, returned to Maryland shortly after Irene's burial services with extreme pain in her groin area. She was checked into Bethesda Naval Hospital and it was determined that she was suffering from advanced uterine cancer. She continued to lose weight as her untreatable cancer worsened. Her family was notified that her situation was terminal and she remained at the hospital until her death on May 19, 1952.

The losses continued. Paul and Shirley Brink had a third child, a girl, Nancy Elizabeth, but she died on November 15, shortly after her birth. The *Farmington Daily Times* noted that a Mrs. Paul Brink from Emery, Utah was discharged from the San Juan Hospital in Farmington.[216] After her release, apparently Shirley and her two sons stayed in Farmington with her parents. A later edition of *Daily Times* noted, "Brinks Leaving. Here for New Years was Mr. Paul Brink, who came to join his wife and children living with her parents Mr. and Mrs. J. W. Smith at 130 N Court Ave. Mrs. Brink came to Farmington just before the birth and loss of their new baby and will return to her home in Emery, Utah with her husband immediately after New Year's Day."[217]

Emery is just an hour or so west of Green River, Utah, near Moab, which is where Buster was working as a driller at this time. His father Nick had worked in the same area for the same employer, Paul English, the head of a Farmington drilling company. With a growing family to support, Buster had left college to work with English Drilling Company before completing his college studies.

From August 23 to September 3, 1954, while I was a corporal in the Marines, I took convalescent leave from the Naval Hospital at Great Lakes, Illinois where I'd been recovering from a serious eye infection caused by a sliver of steel. I drove out to New Mexico and stopped first to visit my cousin Iris 'Midge' Smith and her family. They were living at a gas and oil company's housing complex near their facility at Rattlesnake, New Mexico. This was an isolated area a few miles west of Shiprock. There was a small swimming pool at the compound. It was the perfect place to recover from almost seven weeks in the hospital. And, it was the first time that I had visited my favorite state since the summer of 1947.

It was a relaxing visit but I only visited a few days. After we caught up on family news, there was little to do during the day but swim in the pool because Jimmy was at work all day. I said my goodbyes and drove north to the Green River, Utah area to visit my favorite cousin, Paul 'Buster' Brink, and his family.

In Utah, I visited Buster at the small apartment where he was staying, close to his drilling job. We hadn't seen each other since I was a boy and we talked about our adventures together at the camp. After that, the joy of our reunion soon faded. He was angry and depressed by the recent loss of his father, then his grandmother, and now their only daughter. In addition, he was still upset about having to quit college before completing his degree in petroleum engineering. His reaction to all of this was hurting his marriage, but there was nothing that I could say or do to cheer him up. He gave me directions to his home but didn't go with me because he needed to return to work.

He was no longer the Buster that I remembered. It was with a sad heart that I drove off to his Utah home to meet Shirley and his two boys. I spent several days with his family, taking short hikes and picnics in the area and getting to know Shirley and her two young sons. Dane was only four and Donnie had just turned three, but already they both looked so much like their dad. They had his shock of blond hair and that same impish smile.

Shirley was coping with their situation as well as could be expected, but she felt isolated in this remote area and missed

217

her parents and friends in Farmington. Life hadn't turned out the way she and Buster had hoped. She was still grieving the recent loss of her baby daughter. It seemed to cheer her up some when we sat at her kitchen table and I told her about Buster and my adventures at the camp. She'd heard some of the same stories from Buster.

Spending time in those wide-open spaces of northwestern New Mexico and southeastern Utah was just what I needed after being cooped up so many weeks in a noisy and crowded military hospital. My short visit to that land of high mesas and canyons not far from the Rocky Mountains brought back many happy childhood memories.

That was the last time I would ever see my cousin Buster. I had only been back at the Marine Barracks at Great Lakes for a few months when I received a letter from his wife Shirley. Buster had died in a small plane crash in southern Colorado.

His death was front page news back in Farmington, mostly because the owner of the drilling company and his son were also killed in that flight. The *Farmington Daily Times* first stated:

FARMINGTON MEN REPORTED MISSING ON DENVER FLIGHT. Small Craft Unreported in Denver. Paul English Plane Lands in Durango; Lost for Two Days. Four Farmington men are reported by the Farmington CAA office as missing on a flight between Durango and Denver. Fred VanHook, officer in charge of the CAA station here, said that Paul English, his son, Raymond, pilot Pete Poer and a man believed to be Paul Brink, took off from here Saturday on a flight scheduled to Denver via LaVeta pass. They were flying in the English Beechcraft Bonanza N-5820-C. They cleared the Farmington airport at 9:37 a.m. and landed in Durango at 9:52. Reports from Durango to the local CAA station were that the four men took off from there en route to Denver via Chama and the LaVeta pass. They have not been heard from since.

Another son, Leroy English, said today his father and brother were going to Denver to purchase a truck. He said he has checked various Denver agencies where the couple would go for the truck and reports were the men had not appeared. VanHook said Poer had not closed out his flight plan in Denver.[218]

The paper also mentioned that the Air Force rescue service had been alerted and a search would be instituted. The following day, the paper's headline read, "Sight Crashed Plane on LaVeta." The Air Force search and rescue unit had reported a crashed plane but could not positively identify it. Two ground searches by a sheriff and a rancher from nearby Walsenburg, Colo. also sighted a crashed plane on LaVeta pass, noting that it was in rough terrain at an altitude of 11,000 feet and they were working toward it. There was no sign of life.[219]

The next day's headline story read that the bodies had been recovered and services were pending. The bodies were recovered from the slope of 14,000-foot Mt. Mestas. The wreckage was scattered and only the tail section was intact. The badly mangled bodies of the four were taken to Walsenburg in Huerfano County, Colorado and an ambulance was being sent from Farmington to pick up the bodies because it was snowing too heavily to fly them home. The article noted that Paul English would be greatly missed by the San Juan Basin gas and oil community. The article then noted that Paul Brink was the descendant of a pioneer Farmington family:

PIONEER FAMILY. Mrs. Jack Young, the mother of Brink, who had only moved a few weeks ago from Farmington to Cuba, has been here, since Monday night, staying at the home of her daughter, Mrs. James William Smith, Jr., at 205 N. Behrend, while Mrs. Brink and their two children have been with her parents, Mr. and Mrs. James William Smith, Sr., 130 N. Court avenue. Brink's father, Nick, was reportedly killed about two years ago in a butane tank explosion in Utah while he also was in the employ of the English Drilling company. Brink is a member of a pioneer Farmington family. His grandparents were Mr. and Mrs. Tom Irvin, and his great grandmother, Mrs. N.H. Irvin, is still living here.[220]

Funeral notes in the following day's paper stated, "BRINK, Paul, husband of Shirley Brink. Funeral services will be held in St. John's Episcopal church Friday at 2:30 p.m. Interment will be in Greenlawn Cemetery. Cope Mortuary will be in charge."[221]

It was Cope who had sent the ambulance to Colorado to bring back the bodies.

Paul Brink's obituary appeared in the *Daily Times* a few days later. In the obituary, the person that I had always known as Buster was referred to as "Nock". Was that an error or had he and his father, both drillers for the same company, been known as Nick and Nock? I like the sound of it.

Paul Irvin Brink was born in Farmington May 14, 1928, the son of Nicholas "Nick" and Ruth Irvin Brink. " Nock" Brink departed this world Nov. 13, 1954. Paul Irvin grew to manhood in Farmington and Bloomfield and attended school in Aztec, graduating in mid-term, January 1946. Immediately after graduation he enlisted in the U. S. Marine Corps, serving until January 1949, when he was discharged with the rank of staff sergeant. On April 10, 1949, he was married to Shirley Smith, daughter of Mr. and Mrs. James W. Smith Sr. of Farmington. To this union was born two sons, Dane and Donnie and a daughter, Nancy Elizabeth, who preceded him in death Nov 15. 1953.

He attended New Mexico Institute of Mining and Technology in Socorro for 2 ½ years, returning to Farmington in the fall of 1951 to become employed by the English Drilling company with whom he's remained with the exception of a short period spent in the employment of El Paso Natural Gas Co. until his death. For the past 20 months, he had worked in various parts of Utah. Brink is survived by his wife, Shirley, his sons, Dane and Donnie, his mother, Mrs. Ruth Young of Cuba, a sister, Mrs. James Smith Jr., of Farmington; his great grandmother, Mrs. Lavina [sic] Irvin.[222]

N.H. Irvin, Jr., Nat Irvin's second youngest son, died a few months later, on Feb 22, 1955. The *Daily Times* carried his obituary on the front page:

220

N.H. Irvin, 54, member of a well-known and longtime Farmington family died in San Juan hospital at 5:30 this morning, following a two months' illness. He had been hospitalized two days.

Irvin was born in Roby, Texas but moved to Farmington with his parents when he was a child. He made his home with his mother, Mrs. Lavina Irvin, on the Bloomfield highway.

Other survivors include five sisters and one brother. They are Mrs. John Graham and Mrs. Raymond Kirkendall, both of Farmington; Mrs. Mamie Jordan of Cincinnati, Ohio, who is reported en route to Farmington; Mrs. Willie Tomlinson of Texas; Mrs. Agnes Bell of Rosebud, Mont., also reported as en route here; and 'Boots' Irvin of Washington state.

The body is at the Basin Mortuary with funeral services pending the arrival of relatives.[223]

Barely a year later, in 1956, the indomitable Irvin matriarch, Levina Ricketson Irvin, Nat's widow, and my great grandmother, finally succumbed to old age. With no fanfare nor any front-page news articles, funeral services for this grand old lady and Farmington pioneer were announced briefly in the *Farmington Daily Times* on page 4 as follows:

Irvin, Livina [sic] of Farmington. Mother of Mrs. Byron Bell, Rosebud, Mont., Mrs. Raymond Kurkendoll[sic], Plato, Ariz., and Mrs. John Graham of Farmington. Funeral services will be held Monday at 10:30 a.m., in the Cope Mortuary chapel, with Rev. Alfred Richards officiating. Interment will be in Greenlawn cemetery.[224]

I find it hard to believe that the death of such a long-time resident of Farmington received so little coverage. It could be that Levina had outlived so many of her children, some grandchildren even, that there were few close relatives or friends surviving in the area who might have publicized her passing. Levina was almost 95 years old. She had outlived half of her ten children.

As for the rest of Nat and Levina's children, her third daughter, Mayme Irvin Jordan, died June 28, 1964 in Umatilla, Oregon, a small town of just a few thousand located on the south banks of the Columbia River in north central Oregon. There was no mention of her death in Farmington newspapers. She had never resided in Farmington after marrying, so that's no surprise.

Daisy Irvin Graham, their second child and oldest daughter, died five years later on June 21, 1969. Her death received much more publicity than her mother's, probably because she'd been involved in state politics. The *Daily Times* featured her death on the front page:

MRS. DAISY GRAHAM PIONEER RESIDENT DEAD AT AGE 85. A pioneer resident of Farmington and former state Democratic committee chairwoman, Mrs. John (Daisy) Graham died in San Juan Hospital Saturday morning following a two-year illness. She was 85.

Graham Road, which led to their farm from the Farmington to Bloomfield road, was named for Mrs. Graham and her husband. They also own a cattle ranch near Bloomfield.

A native New Mexican, Mrs. Graham was born Jan. 10, 1884 in Silver City. She moved to Farmington with her parents in 1907. [ed. Note: Census records indicate her birth was Jan 10, 1882, and was probably in Lake Valley, NM]

On Oct. 1, 1911, John and Daisy Graham were married, sitting in a buggy on Orchard St., by Rev. Roderick Colin Jackson, Presbyterian pastor.

Survivors include the husband; a son, Jack Graham of Albuquerque; a niece, Mrs. Natalie Robinson of Farmington, whom the Grahams raised; three sisters, Mrs. Eva Kirkendale (sic) of Farmington; Mrs. Agnes Bell of Columbus, Mont.; and Mrs. Willie Tomlinson of Ingram, Tex. One grandchild and many nieces and nephews also survive.[225]

Three years later, Willia 'Willie' Irvin Tomlinson died in Kerrville, Texas on May 13, 1972. She was the second oldest

222

of Nat and Levina's daughters and the first to marry. She had married a Texan in Texas and never moved out of that state. Because she'd never been a resident of Farmington, there was no mention of her death in Farmington newspapers.

Evelyn "Eva" Irvin Kirkendall died on March 24, 1977. The *Daily Times* carried only a brief obituary, possibly because most Farmingtonians remembered her from her earlier years as Eva Brothers. She'd remarried Ray Kirkendall sometime in the 1950's. "Evelyn Lee Kirkendall of Fairgrounds Road died today at San Juan Hospital. She was 87. Survivors include a daughter, Mrs. Morris Howard of California, and a sister, Agnes Bell of Montana. Funeral arrangements are pending at Basin Mortuary."[226]

It required a lot of searching to find out what became of the youngest of Nat Irvin's ten children, Ivan 'Boots' Irvin. Boots Irvin left Farmington while still a young man. He was living in the small town of Choteau, Wyoming in 1928, based on an address he gave while attending his sister Elsie's funeral in Farmington that year. It was only through such notices that I was able to track him at all. I also discovered that he had resided in Hollister, Twin Falls, Idaho, based on his draft registration card. Further research in archived newspapers from Idaho provided evidence that Boots had married and had at least one child, a daughter, and was still in Idaho as late as 1946.[227]. There are no further news articles in Idaho after that date, in which he is mentioned. Where did he go?

The next location I found for Boots Irvin was mentioned in his older brother NH Irvin's 1955 obituary. Boots is listed as a surviving brother, residing in Washington state. However, I found no mention of Boots Irvin in any online Washington state newspapers from that time period. Casting a wider net, I discovered a brief obituary in the February 1, 1963 edition of the *Billings Gazette*, a Montana newspaper. It reported that a T. Boots Irvin, who had previously resided in Montana, had died in a Seattle, Washington hospital. His birthdate was given as about 1903 and his spouse listed as Effie Foix. I was unable to locate an obituary notice from a Seattle newspaper near that date, but not all old newspapers are available online yet. Boots was not mentioned as a survivor in his sister Daisy's 1969 obituary, so this *Billings Gazette* listing was almost certainly Nat's youngest son, Ivan 'Boots' Irvin, where the I (for Ivan) was mistaken for a T. The clincher was the correct name of his spouse, Effie.

The death of Nat and Levina's last child was almost one-hundred and two years after the birth of their first child. Musically talented Agnes Irvin Bell died in Joliet, Montana on Sept. 23, 1981. As was the case with her other sisters who had moved out of state, the Farmington newspapers carried no story of her death.

None of Agnes's brothers had lived past the age of sixty-five. At almost ninety years of age, she outlived all of her siblings, including her youngest brother, Boots. Maybe that says something important about music and its effect on those who make it.

My last contact with any of Nat and Levina's family was with my first cousin, Midge Brink Smith. Except for her early childhood in Farmington, a couple of wartime years in California, and a few years in Texas when her husband Jimmy's work required moving there, Midge lived in and around Bloomfield, New Mexico for most of her life. Her widowed and aging mother, Ruth Brink Young, lived nearby in a small home until her death in 1975. Midge's husband, Jimmy Smith, died in 1994. He was a quiet and gentle man who sometimes struggled with alcoholism. He won that struggle and then began to help others in Alcoholics Anonymous a few years before his death.

Midge with husband Jimmy Smith, Bloomfield, NM, 1978

After she was widowed, Midge continued to live in Bloomfield in the same home that her and Jimmy had lived in for so many years. It was an older model, medium-sized mobile home, just off a dirt road less than half a mile north of the San Juan River, just a few blocks west of the Bloomfield to Albuquerque highway. That same road and bridge had once connected our camp with Bloomfield.

Her modest home was usually filled with cats and dogs and caged birds and children and sometimes grandchildren. There was always a pot of hot coffee. In spite of serious health and mobility problems, my cousin Midge was always taking care of one or more of her children or grandchildren. She was always in high spirits, in spite of her own infirmities. When she laughed, which was often, it was spontaneous and spirited and always contagious. She was one of the warmest people I've ever known.

My wife Rosemarie and I visited Midge several times shortly before I began working on this book. During each of those visits, we always took the time to drive up onto the mesa south of the San Juan river and search for remnants of our beloved camp. On each consecutive visit, we had to search for a longer period of time before we could discover some artifact or feature that identified the location. The twin ruts that marked the old road were mostly gone. On our last visit to the mesa, we searched for hours through sage and pinon pines and dry arroyos but found nothing. The wind and rains had finally erased all traces of the small cluster of homes that Tom Irvin and Nick Brink had built for their families so many years ago. The writer, Thomas Wolfe, had it right. *You can't go home again.*

A few years after that last visit to the mesa, Midge's health failed significantly and she moved in with her oldest daughter, Corrine McCoy. Corrine's husband, Bob, owned a small ranch on the south side of the San Juan River, just a few miles east of the road from Bloomfield to Albuquerque. It was there that she died, on May 3, 2009, surrounded by family and friends, no more than a few hours walk north of the 'camp' where she'd grown from a young girl to a young woman.

*Author with last surviving Irvin of his generation,
first cousin, Iris 'Midge' Brink Smith, 2003*

Midge was my last close link to my New Mexico relatives. Like me, she was one of Nat Irvin's many great-grandchildren. Now, there are only a very few of our generation still alive. Those that are, I've never met. However, there are younger generations of great-great grandchildren and beyond, too numerous to locate and keep track of. Each one descended from Nathanial Irvin, an only child and first-generation Texan, and his young Georgia-born wife, Levina Ricketson.

Nat and Levina were the children of pioneering Irvins and Ricketsons who had left their homes in Georgia and the Carolinas and headed westward in the pursuit of a better life. The Southwest at that time was often a difficult and dangerous place, but it offered high adventure and great opportunity. Nat and Levina continued that quest, moving even farther west, surviving Apache raids, cattle rustlers, droughts, floods and epidemics. They made a life together, raising all ten of their children to adulthood.

Their story is not unique. There must be many thousands of ordinary people, your ancestors as well as mine, who led exciting and adventurous lives while just trying to survive. You might be surprised and fascinated if you took the time to look into their past. There were times while I was researching and writing this book when I felt more like I was living in their world than in my own. It has been quite a trip.

Epilogue

There are gaps in my family history which may never be filled. There are still so many unanswered questions. They go back to the very beginning of the story you have just finished reading.

Just when did the Irvins first arrive in America? Did they arrive in New England and then migrate south, as the Ricketsons had done? I've been unable to find any records that might answer these questions.

How did my great-great-great grandfather Absalom Irvin meet his wife, Sarah Hunt Greer? Marrying into her family certainly played a major role in his migrating to Texas. Would he have ever done so if he hadn't met Sarah's brother, Nathanial Greer?

How did Absalom Irvin's son Powhatan (PB) meet his wife Mary Williamson? Were they neighbors? Did they meet in school? They were both just children when their families arrived in Texas before it had become a state. I was unable to find any land or school records from that far back.

When did PB and Mary and their only child Nathanial leave Bee County, Texas and drive their herd north to Llano County, Texas? It's possible that they were in Llano County for a number of years and Nathanial and Levina might have met in school. I could find no land or school records. Many of the records from that county were destroyed in a fire in Oxford, the county seat.

Just when and where did PB Irvin's younger brother Absalom Jr. join up with him again? Was it in Llano County, shortly before they left for New Mexico Territory? I assumed that was the case, given their history in Lake Valley, NM., even though they settled originally in different counties in New Mexico. And why did Absalom decide to migrate westward to Arizona at the time that his brother chose to move back to Texas? And did those two brothers make a really substantial profit from their silver mines? I could find no record of the sale of their mines but it's likely that they did. Otherwise, wouldn't they have moved their herd to Kingston and continued their prospecting for silver? The answer to these questions is complicated by Nat Irvin's arrest for cattle rustling with the Kinney gang. The outcome of that arrest was never clear.

How did my grandfather Tom Irvin meet his wife, Mary Irene Bulloch? Might they have met in college at nearby Simmons College in Abilene, Texas? Tom was still listed as in school at age 20, and Irene's father was a well-known newspaper editor who likely would have sent her to college. I never thought to ask them when I was a child living with them. None of my relatives ever volunteered that information, if they even knew. I still find it remarkable that I never knew until long after she died, that my mother and her siblings were all born in Texas. I had always assumed they were born in Farmington, New Mexico, where they all started and finished school.

Shortly after Tom Irvin arrived in Farmington, he purchased a sizeable plot of land between Farmington and Bloomfield. Was at least part of that for his own livestock? Did he build a home there? Is that where his brother PB was ranching when he married young Georgia Salmon? Whatever became of that ranch? I couldn't find any land records online that showed ownership during those years.

Why did Nat's son NH never marry? His closest older brother PB married twice. And why did he and PB lead such troubled lives? Were they spoiled by six older sisters? Was their oldest brother Tom too many years older to be a role model? Did they feel that their father being well-off and well-known gave them license to misbehave? Maybe all of the above. I'll never know.

And, it looks like I'll never know what my great grandfather Nathanial Irvin looked like. During all my researching and with all the contacts I've had with my New Mexico relatives, I never came across a single photograph of him. Not from anyone who knew him and not from any newspaper article that mentioned him. My only picture of him is the verbal one that I've put together in this book.

Maybe that's enough.

Tom Irvin's Ancestral Family Tree

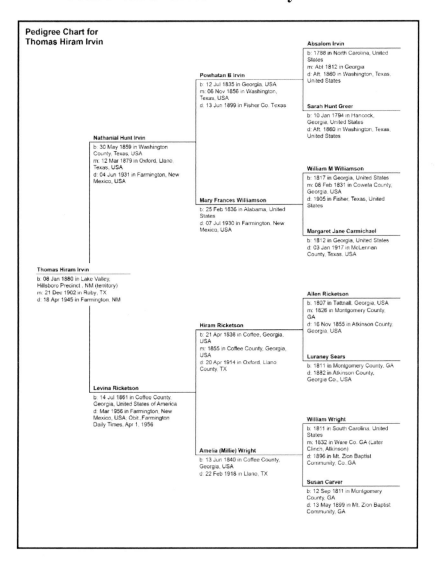

**Pedigree Chart for
Thomas Hiram Irvin**

Absalom Irvin
b: 1788 in North Carolina, United States
m: Abt 1812 in Georgia
d: Aft 1860 in Washington, Texas, United States

Powhatan B Irvin
b: 12 Jul 1835 in Georgia, USA
m: 06 Nov 1856 in Washington, Texas, USA
d: 13 Jun 1899 in Fisher Co. Texas

Sarah Hunt Greer
b: 10 Jan 1794 in Hancock, Georgia, United States
d: Aft 1860 in Washington, Texas, United States

Nathanial Hunt Irvin
b: 30 May 1859 in Washington County, Texas, USA
m: 12 Mar 1879 in Oxford, Llano, Texas, USA
d: 04 Jun 1931 in Farmington, New Mexico, USA

William M Williamson
b: 1817 in Georgia, United States
m: 08 Feb 1831 in Coweta County, Georgia, USA
d: 1905 in Fisher, Texas, United States

Mary Frances Williamson
b: 25 Feb 1836 in Alabama, United States
d: 07 Jul 1930 in Farmington, New Mexico, USA

Margaret Jane Carmichael
b: 1812 in Georgia, United States
d: 03 Jan 1917 in McLennan County, Texas, USA

Thomas Hiram Irvin
b: 08 Jan 1880 in Lake Valley, Hillsboro Precinct , NM (territory)
m: 21 Dec 1902 in Roby, TX
d: 18 Apr 1945 in Farmington, NM

Allen Ricketson
b: 1807 in Tattnall, Georgia, USA
m: 1826 in Montgomery County, GA
d: 16 Nov 1855 in Atkinson County, Georgia, USA

Hiram Ricketson
b: 21 Apr 1836 in Coffee, Georgia, USA
m: 1855 in Coffee County, Georgia, USA
d: 20 Apr 1914 in Oxford, Llano County, TX

Luraney Sears
b: 1811 in Montgomery County, GA
d: 1882 in Atkinson County, Georgia Co., USA

Levina Ricketson
b: 14 Jul 1861 in Coffee County, Georgia, United States of America
d: Mar 1956 in Farmington, New Mexico, USA. Obit ,Farmington Daily Times, Apr 1, 1956

William Wright
b: 1811 in South Carolina, United States
m: 1832 in Ware Co. GA (Later Clinch, Atkinson)
d: 1896 in Mt. Zion Baptist Community, Co. GA

Amelia (Millie) Wright
b: 13 Jun 1840 in Coffee County, Georgia, USA
d: 22 Feb 1918 in Llano, TX

Susan Carver
b: 12 Sep 1811 in Montgomery County, GA
d: 13 May 1899 in Mt. Zion Baptist Community, GA

Nathanial and Levina Irvin's Family

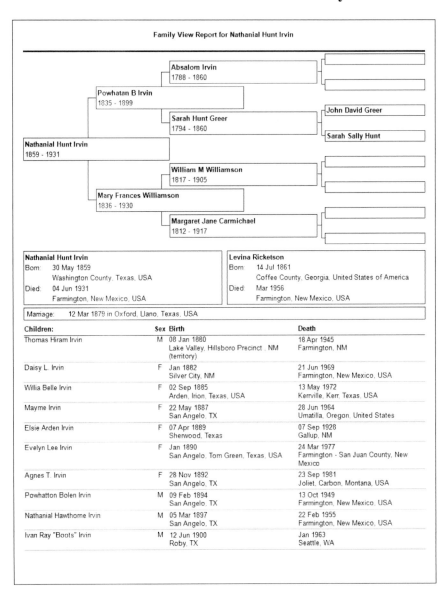

Family View Report for Nathanial Hunt Irvin

	Absalom Irvin 1788 - 1860	
Powhatan B Irvin 1835 - 1899		
	Sarah Hunt Greer 1794 - 1860	John David Greer
		Sarah Sally Hunt
Nathanial Hunt Irvin 1859 - 1931		
	William M Williamson 1817 - 1905	
Mary Frances Williamson 1836 - 1930		
	Margaret Jane Carmichael 1812 - 1917	

Nathanial Hunt Irvin		Levina Ricketson	
Born:	30 May 1859	Born:	14 Jul 1861
	Washington County, Texas, USA		Coffee County, Georgia, United States of America
Died:	04 Jun 1931	Died:	Mar 1956
	Farmington, New Mexico, USA		Farmington, New Mexico, USA

Marriage: 12 Mar 1879 in Oxford, Llano, Texas, USA

Children:	Sex	Birth	Death
Thomas Hiram Irvin	M	08 Jan 1880 Lake Valley, Hillsboro Precinct , NM (territory)	18 Apr 1945 Farmington, NM
Daisy L. Irvin	F	Jan 1882 Silver City, NM	21 Jun 1969 Farmington, New Mexico, USA
Willia Belle Irvin	F	02 Sep 1885 Arden, Irion, Texas, USA	13 May 1972 Kerrville, Kerr, Texas, USA
Mayme Irvin	F	22 May 1887 San Angelo, TX	28 Jun 1964 Umatilla, Oregon, United States
Elsie Arden Irvin	F	07 Apr 1889 Sherwood, Texas	07 Sep 1928 Gallup, NM
Evelyn Lee Irvin	F	Jan 1890 San Angelo, Tom Green, Texas, USA	24 Mar 1977 Farmington - San Juan County, New Mexico
Agnes T. Irvin	F	28 Nov 1892 San Angelo, TX	23 Sep 1981 Joliet, Carbon, Montana, USA
Powhatton Bolen Irvin	M	09 Feb 1894 San Angelo, TX	13 Oct 1949 Farmington, New Mexico, USA
Nathanial Hawthorne Irvin	M	05 Mar 1897 San Angelo, TX	22 Feb 1955 Farmington, New Mexico, USA
Ivan Ray "Boots" Irvin	M	12 Jun 1900 Roby, TX	Jan 1963 Seattle, WA

Working Map of Irvins' Travel Routes

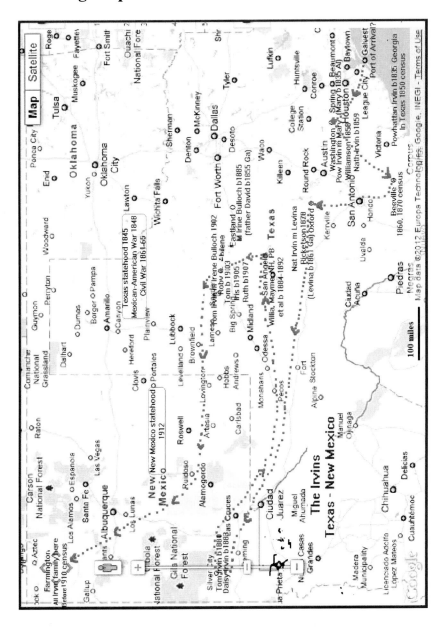

NOTES

Abbreviations used:
AIME American Institute of Mining Engineers
FDT *Farmington Daily Times* newspaper
FE *Farmington Enterprise* newspaper
FTH *Farmington Times Herald* newspaper
FR *Farmington Republican* newspaper
(mm-dd-yyyy date format used with Farmington newspapers)
SJCHS San Juan County Historical Society
    TSHA Texas State Historical Society

---

[1] Greer, W. (2010, June 15) Greer, Nathaniel Hunt. *The Handbook of Texas Online*. Retrieved from https://tshaonline.org/handbook/online/articles/fgr45

[2] Texas State Historical Association. Ibid.

[3] Handbook of Texas Online, Grace Bauer, "BEEVILLE, TX," accessed October 25, 2019, http://www.tshaonline.org/handbook/online/articles/heb04.

[4] Handbook of Texas Online, Hobart Huson, "EIGHTH TEXAS INFANTRY," accessed October 25, 2019, http://www.tshaonline.org/handbook/online/articles/qke03.

[5] Various. (2017, December 8). Cattle Drives in the United States. *Wikipedia.com*. Retrieved from https://en.wikipedia.org/wiki/Cattle_drives_in_the_United_States

[6] Handbook of Texas Online, James L. Haley, "RED RIVER WAR," accessed October 25, 2019, http://www.tshaonline.org/handbook/online/articles/qdr02.

[7] Handbook of Texas Online, James B. Heckert-Greene, "OXFORD, TX," accessed October 25, 2019, http://www.tshaonline.org/handbook/online/articles/hno24.

[8] Flora, S. (2007). The Covered Wagon. Horses-Mules-Oxen. Retrieved from http://www.oregonpioneers.com/ortrail.htm

[9] Hillsboro Historical Society, 2011, *Around Hillsboro.* Charleston, SC, Arcadia p. 9

[10] AIME Publication 1. 1908. p. 3

[11] Pettengill, Jim (2017, April). Ghost Town: Lake Valley, New Mexico. Retrieved from

https://www.historynet.com/ghost-town-lake-valley-new-mexico.htm

[12] 1879, September 27. Indian Troubles. *Phoenix Herald*. p. 2

[13] Gibson, S.A., February 2016, Sara Gibson's Story, *Guajalotes, Zopilotes, y Paisanos*, Hillsboro Historical Society, 9,1 pp. 4-6

[14] *Desert Exposure*, Sept 2012, "Hillsboro's Other 9/11's"

[15] 1879, September 20. The New Mexico Indian Raid. *The New York Times* p.1

[16] Silva, L. (2006, December). Warm Springs Apache Leader Nana: The 80-Year-Old Warrior Turned the Tables. *Wild West*. Retrieved from https://www.historynet.com/warm-springs-apache-leader-nana-the-80-year-old-warrior-turned-the-tables.htm

[17] River Gold (2017, April) Carson, Thelma, "Notes on Carson Family History". Retrieved from https://rivergold.net/notes_2017-4%20thelmacarsonsnotes.html

[18] Hillsboro Historical Society. 2011. *Around Hillsboro*. Charleston, SC, Arcadia, p. 11

[19] Boardman, M. (2017, Sept 21). A Cochise-led Apache Ambush. *TrueWest*. Retrieved from https://truewestmagazine.com/cochise-led-apache-ambush/

[20] Editor. (1882, June 14). *Rio Grande Republican*. p. 2

[21] Koogler, J. (1882, Oct. 1). Lake Valley. Who Are There, and What They Are Doing. *Las Vegas Daily Gazette*. p. 3

[22] Koogler, J. (1882, Oct. 4). Lake Valley. Her Mines and Future Prospects. *Las Vegas Daily Gazette*. p. 4

[23] Beckett, V. (1883, Feb 2) New Mexico News. *The Black Range*, p. 3

[24] Becket, V. (1883, Jan 19). News and Comments. *The Black Range*. p. 1

[25] Becket, V. (1883, May 25) *The Black Range*, p. 2

[26] Becket, V. (1883, May 25) *The Black Range*, p. 2

[27] Weiser, K. (2014 January). Lake Valley – Silver Mining Heydays. *legendsofamerica.com*. Retrieved from https://www.legendsofamerica.com/nm-lakevalley/

[28] (Jones, F. (1904) *New Mexico Mines and Minerals*. p 89. Note: Fayette Jones served twice as the President of the New

Mexico School of Mines in Socorro, NM and spent most of his career as a mining engineer in the southwestern United States

[29] Murray, J. (1882, Oct 14). KINGSTON. The New Metropolis of the Percha District— Fifty Houses Commenced in One Day. *Albuquerque Morning Journal*, p. 4

[30] Editor. (1883, Feb 17). *Rio Grande Republican*, p. 3

[31] *The Black Range,* March 30, 1883 p. 2

[32] Cool, P. (2014, April). The Capture of New Mexico's Rustler King. *Wild West Magazine*, p. 40-41.

[33] Ibid p. 41

[34] Beckett, V. 1883, April 27)'To the Pen. *The Black Range*, p. 2

[35] Bell, B. (2014, Jan. 6). The Fountain Murders: A.J. Fountain vs Oliver Lee's Gang. *True West*. Retrieved from https://truewestmagazine.com/the-fountain-murders/

[36] McFie, J. (1884, May 4) Notice. U.S. Land Office. Las Cruces, NM. *Rio Grande Republican,* p. 4

[37] Weiser, K. (2014, January) Lake Valley-Silver Mining Heydays. *Legends of America* Retrieved from https://www.legendsofamerica.com/nm-lakevalley/2/

[38] Noelke, V. (2011) *Early San Angelo.* Charleston, S.C. Arcadia Publ. p. 15

[39] ibid p. 75

[40] Crawford, L. (1966) *A History of Irion County Texas.* p. 5

[41] Hunt, W. & Leffler, J. (2019, Apr 10). Irion County. *Handbook of Texas Online.* Retrieved from https://tshaonline.org/handbook/online/articles/hci01

[42] Crawford, L. (1966) *A History of Irion County Texas.* pp. 22-23

[43] ibid. p. 13

[44] Mims, E. (1888) Arden. *Irion County Commemorative Edition*, locally published by the Irion County Sesquicentennial Committee and Irion County Historical Society, p. 26

[45] Noelke, V. (2011) Early San Angelo. Charleston, SC. Arcadia

[46] Matthews, J. (2005) *Fort Concho*. TSHA. pp. 54-55

[47] Matthews, J. op. cit. p. 60

[48] Noelke, V. op. cit. p. 29

[49] Railroad Celebration Edition. (1888, Sep. 17). *San Angelo Daily Standard*

[50] Ibid. p. 16

[51] Tom Green County Historical Preservation League. (2003). Clark, M. "Irion City School" *The Chronicles of Our Heritage, a history of Tom Green County*. Abilene, TX. H.V. Chapman & Sons.

[52] Crawford. L. (1966). *A History of Irion County Texas*. Mertzon, TX. pp. 20-21

[53] *Austin Weekly Statesman*, Aug 9, 1888. p. 12

[54] *Austin Weekly Statesman,* February 27, 1890. p. 12

[55] Handbook of Texas Online, William R. Hunt and John Leffler, "IRION COUNTY," accessed October 28, 2019, http://www.tshaonline.org/handbook/online/articles/hci01.

[56] Loomis. J. (1982) *Texas Ranchman: The Memoirs of John A. Loomis.* Chadron, NE. The Fur Press. p. 30

[57] XIT Ranch *Wikipedia*. Retrieved from https://en.wikipedia.org/wiki/XIT_Ranch

[58] Henry, T. (2011, Nov 29). A History of Drought and Extreme Weather in Texas. Retrieved from https://stateimpact.npr.org/texas/2011/11/29/a-history-of-drought-and-extreme-weather-in-texas/

[59] letter from Irene Irvin to Iris Scanlan, dated March 20, 1945

[60] 1907, Aug 15. Fisher County Mourns Death of Citizen. *Abilene Daily Reporter*. p. 3

[61] 1906, Oct 5. *Hamlin Herald.* p. 1

[62] 1907, June 21. *Farmington Enterprise.* p. 2

[63] FE 11-23-1906. p. 3

[64] Duke, R. (1999) *The Early Years.* Flora Vista, NM. SJCHS p. 4

[65] Brothers, M. (1952. Oct 25). "Frontier Days in New Mexico". *Farmington Daily Times* pp. 2, 5

[66] Sneed, D. (2017, Jan 11). Retrieved from http://wheelsthatwonthewest.blogspot.com/2017/01/george-yule-bain-wagon-company.html

[67] FE 11-23-1906 p. 3

[68] 1907, July 12. Land of Sunshine. *San Juan County Index.* p. 3

[69] Waybourn, M. (2001). *Homesteads to Boomtown*. Farmington, NM. p28

[70] Waybourn, M. & Mickey, V. (1984) *Meet Me at the Fair*. Farmington, NM. Pro Media. p. 12

[71] Waybourn, M. op. cit. p. 38 pic

[72] Waybourn, M. ibid. p. 39

[73] Duke, R. (1989). *San Juan County, the Early Years.* Farmington, NM. San Juan County Historical Society. p. 11

[74] Waybourn, M. op. cit. p. 19

[75] FTH 8-13-1926. Old Farmington' column. p. 7

[76] Dugan, T. & Arnold, E. (2002) *Gas.* Farmington, NM. Dugan Production Co. p. 1-2

[77] FE 1-13-1906. p. 3

[78] FTH Dec 8, 1921. History of Farmington Oil and Gas Company. p. 1

[79] Waybourn, M. op. cit. p38

[80] Brothers, M. (1952. Oct 25). "Frontier Days in New Mexico". *Farmington Daily Times* pp. 2, 5

[81] FE 4-5-1907. p. 3

[82] Waybourn, M. op. cit. p39

[83] FE 6-21-1907. p. 2

[84] FE 4-10-1908. p. 1

[85] FE 7-10-1908. p. 1

[86] FE 7-3-1908. p. 1

[87] FE 9-4-1908. p. 6

[88] FE 9-25-1908. p. 1

[89] FE 10-2-1908. p. 1

[90] FE 10-2-1908. p. 1

[91] FE 10-30-1908. p. 4

[92] FE 11-13-1908. p.1

[93] FE 11-27-1908. p. 1

[94] FE 5-7-1909. p. 1

[95] Duke, R (2000). *San Juan County Roars Into the '20s.* Farmington, NM. San Juan County Historical Society. p. 16

[96] FE 5-28-1909. p. 1

[97] FE 1-8-1909. p.2

[98] FE 6-25-1909. p. 6

[99] FE 9-17-1909. p. 6

[100] FE 11-26-1909. p. 12

[101] FE 2-4-1910. p. 6

[102] The Black Knight (1910, Dec 22). *Farmington Times Hustler.* p. 1

[103] FE 12-30-1910. p. 7

[104] FE 8-5-1910. p. 7

[105] Waybourn, M (2001) op. cit. p 50

[106] FE 10-6-1911. p. 2

[107] FTH 10-12-1911. p. 1)

[108] Waybourn, M (2001) op. cit. p59

[109] FTH 12-21-1911. p. 1

[110] Farmington. A few facts worthy of note. FTH. 8-17-1911. p. 5

[111] Waybourn, et al. (1984) *Meet Me at the Fair* op. cit. pp. 20-21

[112] FE 5 10-1912. p. 1

[113] FTH 5-16-1912. p. 1

[114] (1912, June 6). Decoration Day. *Farmington Times Hustler.* p. 1

[115] FE 8-9-1912. p. 2

[116] FTH 10-10-1912. p. 1

[117] FE 12-6-1912. p. 2

[118] FE 12-20-1912. p. 2

[119] FTH. 5-15-1913. p. 1

[120] FE 6-21-1912. p. 2

[121] FTH 4-17-1913. p. 1

[122] FE 4-18-1913. p. 2

[123] FE 10-24-1913. P. 1

[124] FE 4-18-1913. p. 2

[125] FE 6-18-1913. p.1

[126] FTH 10-16-1913. p. 6

[127] FTH 3-12-1914. p. 1

[128] FTH 1-8-1920. p. 1

[129] FTH 3-12-1914. p. 1

[130] FTH 7-9-1914. p. 1

[131] FTH 3-19-1914 p. 1

[132] FTH 5-21-1914 p. 1

[133] FTH 7-9-1914 p. 2

[134] Ibid. p. 2

[135] FTH 11-26-1914 p. 2

[136] FTH 7-13-1916 p. 6

[137] FTH 3-8-1917 p. 4

[138] FTH 4-12-1917 p. 4

[139] FTH 5-10-1917 p.1

[140] FTH 5-31-1917 p. 4

[141] FTH 7-12-1917 pp. 4-16

[142] FTH 6-27-1918 p.4

[143] FTH 8-18-1918 p. 1

[144] Maddox, M (2018, Feb 18) Retrieved from
https://www.facebook.com/SanJuanCountyHistoricalSociety

[145] FTH 2-6-1919 p. 4

[146] FTH 2-20-1919 p. 4

[147] FTH 2-27-1919 p. 4

[148] FTH 9-30-1920 p. 1

[149] FTH 2-5-1920 p. 4

[150] FTH 9-30-1920 p. 10

[151] FTH 12-30-1920 p. 4

[152] FTH 12-28-1922 p. 1

[153] FTH 5-4-1923 p. 1

[154] FTH 6-1-1923 p.1

[155] FTH 1-25-1924 p. 1

[156] FTH 4-4-1924 p. 2

[157] FTH 11-7-1924 p. 2

[158] FTH 10-10-1924 p. 4

[159] FTH 5-8-1925 p. 1

[160] FTH 7-31-1925 p. 1

[161] FTH 11-20-1925 p. 1

[162] FTH 6-18-1926 p. 5

[163] FTH 7-2-1926 p. 1

[164] FTH 11-19-1926 p. 8

[165] FTH 7-9-1926 p. 4

[166] FTH 8-13-1926 p. 5

[167] FTH 8-20-1926 p. 5

[168] FTH 10-1-1926 p. 2

[169] FTH 10-22-1926 p. 2

[170] FTH 6-3-1927 p. 2

[171] FTH 9-7-1928 p. 4

[172] FTH 9-14-1928 p. 4

[173] FR 9-25-1929 p. 5

[174] FTH 2-28-1930 pp. 1&8

[175] FTH 7-11-1930 p. 5

[176] FTH 5-4-1934 p. 4

[177] FTH 6-15-1934 p. 8

[178] FTH 1-12-1934 p. 1

[179] FTH 8-10-1934 p. 4

[180] FTH 9-7-1934 p. 3

[181] FTH 4-3-1936 p. 1

[182] FTH 4-3-1936 p. 1

[183] FTE 9-4-1936 p. 6

[184] FTH 7-9-1937 p. 7

[185] FTH 8-6-1937 p. 8

[186] FTH-9-17-1937 p. 3

[187] FTH 10-29-1937 p. 6

[188] FTH-10-21-1938 p. 1

[189] FTH 6-23-1939 p. 2

[190] FTH 3-1-1940 p. 17

[191] FTH 6-28-1940 p. 1

[192] FTH 4-18-1941 p. 1

[193] FTH 12-12-1941 p. 2

[194] FTH-2-6-1942 p. 4

[195] FTH 2-27-1942 p. 4

[196] FTH 3-23-1945 p. 1

[197] FTH 3-23-1945 p.2

[198] FTH 6-22-1945 p. 5

[199] FTH 7-13-1945 p. 6

[200] FTH 7-18-1947 p.17

[201] FTH 12-12-1941 p. 8

[202] FTH 11-1-1945 p. 1

[203] FTH 4-19-1946 p. 8

[204] FTH 2-4-1949 p. 1

[205] FTH 8-15-1947 p. 4

[206] FTH 8-27-1948 p. 8

[207] FTH 9-10-1948 p. 3

[208] FTH 2-25-1949 p. 4

[209] FTH 4-15-1949 p. 4

[210] FDT 10-21-1949 p. 8

[211] FDT 12-13-1949 p. 1

[212] FDT 10-14-1949 p. 8

[213] *Gallup Independent*-5-28-1951 p. 2 & Death Cert. Utah #51-100006

[214] FDT 9-7-1951 p. 2

[215] FDT 1-5-1952 p. 2

[216] FDT 11-21-1953 p. 2

[217] FDT 12-31-1953 p. 3

[218] FDT 11-15-1954 p. 1

[219] FDT 11-16-1954 p. 1

[220] FDT 11-17-1954 p.1
[221] FDT 11-18-1954 p. 4
[222] FDT 11-21-1954 p. 6
[223] FDT 2-22-1955 p. 1
[224] FDT 4-1-1956 p. 4
[225] FDT 6-22-1969 p.1
[226] FDT 3-24-1977 p. 14
[227] *Twin Falls News*, Sept 10, 1941. p. 3 & *The Times News*, December 12, 1946. p. 10

BIBLIOGRAPHY

Crawford, Leta. *A History of Irion County Texas*. Waco, Texas: Texian Press, 1966

Daniels, George D., Editor. *The Spanish West*. Alexandria, Virginia: Time-Life Books, 1976

Dugan, Tom & Arnold, Emory. *Gas: Adventures into the history of the world's largest gas fields-the San Juan Basin of New Mexico*. Farmington, New Mexico: Dugan Production Company, 2009

Duke, Robert W. *San Juan County: The Early Years (part 1 of 2)*. Flora Vista, New Mexico: San Juan County Historical Society, 2013

Duke, Robert W. *San Juan County Roars into the '20s*. Flora Vista, New Mexico: San Juan County Historical Society, 2000

Forbis, William H. *The Cowboys*. Alexandria, Virginia: Time-Life Books, 1973

Hillsboro Historical Society. *Around Hillsboro*. Charleston, South Carolina: Arcadia Publishing, 2011

Historical Society of New Mexico. *Sunshine and Shadows in New Mexico's Past*. Los Ranchos, New Mexico: Rio Grande Books, 2011

Hutton, Paul H. *The Apache Wars*. New York: Crown, 2016

Loomis, John A. *Texas Ranchman; The Memoirs of John A. Loomis*. Chadron, Nebraska: Fur Press, 1982

Mathews, James T. *Fort Concho*. Austin, Texas: Texas State Historical Association, 2005

McKenna, James A. *Black Range Tales*. Silver City, New Mexico: High-Lonesome Books, 2014

Nevin, David. *The Texans*. Alexandria, Virginia: Time-Life Books, 1975

Noelke, Virginia. *Early San Angelo*. Charleston, South Carolina: Arcadia Publishing Company, 2011

Texas State Historical Association. *Texas Almanac 2016-2017*. Austin, Texas: Texas State Historical Association, 2016

Wallace, Robert. *The Miners*. Alexandria, Virginia: Time-Life Books, 1976

Watt, Robert N. *'I Will Not Surrender the Hair of a Horse's Tail' The Victorio Campaign 1879*. West Midlands, England: Helion & Co., 2017

Watt, Robert N. *'Horses Worn to Mere Shadows' The Victorio Campaign 1880*. Warwick, England: Helion & Co., 2019

Watt, Robert N. *'With My Face to My Bitter Foes' The Victorio Campaign 1881*. Warwick, England: Helion & Co., 2019

Waybourn, Marilu. *Homesteads to Boomtown. A Pictorial History of Farmington, New Mexico, and Surrounding Area*. Virginia Beach, Virginia: Dunning Company Publishers, 2001

Waybourn, Marilu & Mickey, Vernetta. *Meet Me at the Fair*. Farmington, New Mexico: Pro Media, 1984

INDEX

Ancestry.com, 7
Animas River Bridge
  early investment and
    construction, 151
Apache
  1879 raid, 60
  activities in west Texas, 93
  other accounts of McEvers
    raid, 66
  raids continue until 1886,
    73
Apache chief Nana, 68
Apache chief Victorio, 66
Archaeological sites
  Aztec Ruins, Chaco Canyon,
    national recognition of,
    194
Arden
  as described by settlers'
    descendants, 97
  early settlement, 93
Battle of San Jacinto, 30
Battle of the Alamo, 29
Battle of Velasco, 29
Bee County, 36
Billy the Kid, 56
Bridal Chamber, 57
Brink, Iris 'Midge'
  author's first cousin, 16
  birth, 189
  her husband dies, 224
  living in Kermit, Texas, 215
  living in Rattlesnake, NM,
    217
  marries Jimmy Smith in
    Farmington, 211
Brink, Leonord P.

  Nick's father, important
    role educating Navajo,
    187
Brink, Nick, 186, 202
  dies from gas explosion,
    216
  driller with Tom Irvin, 201
  in Vallejo, CA as welder
    during WWII, 205
  marries Ruth Irvin, 188
Brink, Paul 'Buster', 206
  attends New Mexico
    School of Mines, 214
  author's very close first
    cousin, 17
  childhood adventures with,
    19
  crossing the San Juan River,
    20
  detailed obituary, 220
  joins Marines, 211
  killed in plane crash, 218
  marries Shirley Smith, 212
  working as driller in Utah,
    216
buffalo soldiers, 66
Bulloch, 129
  ancestry, 126
Bulloch, D.T.
  Irene Irvin's father, 127
Bulloch, Mary Irene
  birth, 215
Buster
  father killed in gas
    explosion, 215
Butch Cassidy, 56
camp, 14
cattle ranch

growth of Irvin ranch near
  Arden, TX, 109
growth of Irvin ranch near
  Roby, TX, 123
Irvin ranch in Fisher
  County, TX, 121
Irvin's ranch near Arden,
  TX, 107
sale of Irvin ranch near
  Arden, TX, 125
cattle ranching
  becoming difficult, 131
  big ranches buy out smaller
    ranches, 118
cattle rustling
  convictions, 89
  Nat Irvin's arrest, 87
chief Nana's raid, 74
Chisholm Trail, 39
Civil War
  Texas' involvement, 36
Comanche, 30, 32
  campaign to remove, 41
  continue to raid farms, 33
  raids during Civil War, 40
  raids on early colonists, 31
  Texas army's main concern,
    37
Concho River, 94
covered wagons, 49
Crossing the San Juan\, 22
Decoration Day
  predecessor to Memorial
    Day, 162
drilling
  early activity in
    Farmington, 142
  early failures, 143
  Paul English, Farmington
    drilling company, 216
  Tom Irvin and Nick Brink
    Kutz Canyon activity, 200

Tom Irvin's wildcatting with
  cable-tool, 188
drought
  plagued west Texas farms,
    ranches, 131
Family Tree Maker, 7
Farmington
  attraction for new settlers,
    135
  early history of, 140
  major fire of 1910, 159
  Oil and Gas Company, 132
Fisher County
  description of, 120
flood
  major flood of October
    1911, 158
floods
  San Juan Basin flood, 1927,
    188
Fort Concho
  closing of in 1889, 102
forty-niners, 34
Geronimo, 72
Gibson, Sarah
  her account of Apache raid,
    61
Greer, Nathanial, 28, 32
Greer, Nathanial Hunt
  Absalom Irvin's brother in
    law, 27
Greer, Sarah
  Nathanial Hunt Greer's
    sister, 27
Hamilton, Mike
  third generation rancher in
    Mertzon, TX, 96
Hillsboro, 46, 53
  author's visit to, 47
Hillsboro Historical Society,
  48, 66
Homestead

in Farmington area, 139
Irvins abandon Lake Valley,
    90
Homestead Act, 39
Irion County
    description, 94
Irvin, Absalom
    first Irvin family in Texas,
    31
    Nat Irvin's grandfather, 27
Irvin, Absalom D., 39, 71, 91
    death, 91
    in Confederate Army, 38
    Powhatan B. Irvin's
    brother, 71
Irvin, Agnes, 223
    active role as high school
    senior, 162
    attends teaching institute,
    163
    birth, 104
    death in Montana, 224
    living in Montana, 221
    now wife of Byron Bell, 187
    popular songtress, 168
    praise for role in Christmas
    play, 159
    role in high school play,
    155
    sings solo at eighth grade
    commencement, 148
Irvin, Daisy, 93, 157, 201
    attended college?, 124
    birth, 72
    death, 222
    elected officer of Eastern
    Star, 155
    Halloween party with John
    Graham, 144
    marries John Graham, 158
    memories of Farmington
    home, 25

Irvin, Elsie, 157, 164
    acting and musical talent,
    146
    birth, 104
    bridesmaid to sister Daisy,
    158
    closeness with sisters Daisy
    and Evelyn, 144
    death in Gallup, NM, 190
    elected Conductress in
    Eastern Star, 155
    living in Texas, 166
    surprise marriage in
    Albuquerque to Fred
    Carson, 161
    travel to Washington State,
    154
Irvin, Evelyn 'Eva'
    birth, 104
    death, 223
    Halloween party with
    Charlie Brothers, 144
    marries Charlie Brothers,
    tells parents afterwards,
    148
Irvin, Iris, 157, 205
    attends father's funeral in
    Farmington,NM, 208
    attends mother's funeral in
    New Mexico, 215
    birth in Roby, Texas, 129
    birth of children Patricia
    and Thomas, 192
    death at Bethesda Hospital,
    Maryland, 216
    gradurates at head of high
    school class, 182
    hired to teach in rural
    Largo, NM, 187
    marries Fred Scanlan in
    California, 190

pursues career in teaching, 185

Irvin, Ivan 'Boots'
also lived in Wyoming and Idaho, 223
birth, 124
in Montana, 202
living in Washington State, 221
married, at least one child, no death date, 223
registers for draft, 177

Irvin, Levina, 9, 43, 45, 48, 73, 90, 104, 157, 208, 211
accompanied by Nat's parents, 54
alive for fifth generation descendant's birth, 214
birth, 43
birth of second son, 110
death, 221
death of father, 168
executrix of husband's will, 201
four more daughters, 104
fourth son, final child, 124
her Ricketson ancestry, 43
her third child, Arden, Texas, 93
homekeeping as pioneer woman, 106
marriage, 42
memories of her Farmington home, 24
motivated to leave Lake Valley, NM, 91
pregnant during Apache raids, 67
relationship with chief Geronimo, 61
second pregnancy during raids, 72

settled in Lake Valley, NM, 52
the last of her children die, 223
third son, 122
widowed, 196

Irvin, Mayme, 112
birth, 104
death in Oregon, 222

Irvin, Nathanial, 27, 28, 36, 40, 58, 71, 91, 104, 107, 113, 116, 122, 128, 132, 141, 142, 153, 154, 155, 157, 158, 180, 184, 226
an only child, 9
arrested for rustling, 87
author's maternal great-grandfather, 6
cattle sales to Colorado, 172
dabbles in local politics, 147
death, 195
failed trip to California, 179
first listed in Farmington newspaper, 132
his first child marries, 126
his mother dies, 194
hunting trip, bear trophy, 150
inherits father's ranchland, 124
invests again in gas and oil, 166
invests in oil and gas exploration, 141
Irvin's picket home safe from Apaches, 64
Lake Valley census, 52
migrates back to Texas, 111
migrates to Farmington, NM, 132

migrates to Fisher County, TX, 117
migrates to Lake Valley, NM, 48
moves to Bee County, TX, 35
purchases first automobile, 173
sells his sheep, 164
speculates on land, 149
travels to Oregon, Washington state, 154
why pull up stakes?, 138
Irvin, NH Jr., 24, 135, 201
arrested for break-in, wine theft, 180
assault and battery, 186
death, 220
draft registration, 177
reprimand for under-age drinking, 175
Irvin, PB, 135, 154, 177, 201, 207
birth, 110
death, 214
high school performance, 154
is widowed, 181
jailed and fined for knife fight, 204
jailed at sixteen, 164
knife fight, Christmas Eve, 180
marries Georgia Salmon, 172
sentenced to state penitentiary, 184
son of Levina Irvin, 24
wins horse race at fair, 171
Irvin, Powhatan 'PB', 31, 33

among wealthiest cattlemen in Tom Green County, TX, *111*
began farming at sixteen, 33
death and burial, 123
earliest mention in San Angelo news, *111*
early success raising cattle, 40
enlists in Confederate Army, 37
in Lake Valley, New Mexico, 54
Irion County, TX commissioner, *114*
leaves New Mexico, 90
marries and begins ranching, 35
moves herd to Roby, Texas, 122
prominent cattleman in Tom Green County, TX, *107*
wagon team runs loose, *117*
Irvin, Ruth, 14, 157, 211
attends father's funeral in Farmington, 208
attends mother's funeral, 215
birth in Roby, TX, 129
elected officer of high school senior class, 185
in Vallejo, CA working in ammunition factory, 205
injured in car accident, 185
injured jumping from car, 183
living at camp, 16
living near daughter in Bloomfield, NM, 224

remarries after death of
husband, 216
son's funeral, 220
Irvin, Sarah, 35, 71
death, 91
Irvin, Tom, 46, 93, 110, 128,
157, 171, 175, 189, 192,
225
attending college?, 124
birth, 53
breaks out of jail, 164
buys new Dodge, 202
charged with assault and
battery, 165
draft registration, 177
drilling activities halted by
'fishing' job, 203
elected to research
committee of local
archeology chapter, 194
has three children, 130
home south of Bloomfield,
NM, 197
in Hamlin, Texas, 128
injured in drilling accident,
199
marriage to Mary Irene
Bulloch in Roby, TX, 126
moves family
toFarmington, NM, 157
news of death, 206
school age, 112
visits father in Farmington,
NM, 147
wildcat drilling near
Bloomfield, NM, 188
Irvin, Tom, Jr.
captured by Japanese in
Philippines, 205
death, 209
home from the Philippines,
209

member of senior class
Literary Society, 180
participates in high school
mock state convention,
180
rescued from Philippine
prison camp, 207
Irvin, Willia, 104, 201
birth, 93
death in Texas, 222
known as 'Willie', 112
King of the Rustlers
John Kinney, 87
Lake Valley
cattle-rustling, 86
decline and fall, 91
description of mines, 80
detailed description of
town, 77
first account of Irvins in
area, 48
how it originated, 57
now a ghost town, 91
silver production, 84
LDS, 7
Llano, 42, 44
now a ghost town, 45
longhorn
crossbreeding with
shorthorn, 95
during 1870's, Concho
River area, 101
in Bee County, TX, 36
in Irion County, TX, 94
proliferation during Civil
War, 38
size of horns, 115
Major Fountain, 86
his murder, 90
Mammy, 24
McEver's ranch, 61
Mexican-American war, 33

mules vs. horses, 51
Nana's raid, 68
Navajo country, 14
New Mexico Statehood, 161
newspaperarchives.com, 8
newspapers.com, 8
pioneer women
    homemaking activities, 106
Pocahontas, 33
Powhatan, Indian chief, 33
Red River War, 41
Ricketson, 9, 43
    Levina Ricketson's
        ancestry, 43
Roby
    brief description of Roby,
        TX, 121
    loses out to northern town
        of Hamlin, TX, 129
San Angelo
    as hub of Tom Green
        County, TX, 102
    origin of, 100
San Juan County
    physical and economic
        description, 135–38
Sardis Cemetery
    burial site of Powhatan
        Irvin 1899, 123
school
    early school in Irion
        County, TX, 105
Shaw, Harley, 46, 61
Silver City, 56
silver mines
    A. D. Irvin & Brother's Lake
        Valley mines, 76

arrival of miners in Lake
    Valley, 59
major producer in 1882, 83
Spanish flu
    illness and deaths in
        Farmington, 178
temperance
    Farmington votes to
        remain 'dry', 166
    last saloon shut down, 153
    political party in
        Farmington, 148
Texas Army scout, 38
Texas Confederate Army
    Irvins enlistment, 37
Texas Rangers, 31
*The San Angelo Daily
Standard*
    articles describing Irvin
        activities, 110
Treaties of Velasco, 30
Treaty of Guadalupe Hidalgo,
    34
Velasco, 28
wagon
    Irvin's Bain wagon, 134
wagon travel, 50
Washington-on-the-Brazos,
    32
Williamson, Mary, 37, 59,
    157
    birth, 194
    death, 194
    lifelong Baptist, 123
    moves with son to Lake
        Valley, NM, 48
    Powhatan marries, 35